THE CCD Camera Cookbook

How to Build Your Own CCD Camera

by

Richard Berry,
Veikko Kanto and John Munger

Willmann-Bell, Inc.

Publishers and Booksellers Serving Astronomers Worldwide Since 1973

P.O. Box 35025 • Richmond, Virginia 23235 • United States of America • ☎ (804) 320-7016

First published 1994.

Printed in the United States of America. 99 98 97   9 8 7 6 5 4 3

Also by Richard Berry:
      Build Your Own Telescope
      Discover the Stars
      Telescope Optics: Evaluation and Design (editor)
      Introduction to Astronomical Image Processing (includes AIP software)
      Choosing and Using a CCD Camera (includes QwikPIX software)

Library of Congress Cataloging-in-Publication Data

Berry, Richard, 1946-
      The CCD camera cookbook / Richard Berry, Veikko Kanto, John
Munger.
          p.   cm.
      Includes bibliographical references and index.
      ISBN 0-943396-41-7
      1. Astronomical photography--Instruments. 2. CCD cameras-
-Handbooks, manuals, etc. 3. Astronomy--Amateur's manuals.
I. Kanto, Veikko. II. Munger, John. III. Title.
QB121.5.B45 1993
621.36'7--dc20   93-6378

Acknowledgements

The authors wish to thank the following individuals who helped make *The CCD Camera Cookbook* possible:

Jack Judson, Product Systems Development Engineer at Texas Instruments, for technical help with respect to the CCD sensors, especially in explaining binning sequences and in supplying many reference documents and data sheets.

Betsy Kanto, for building the first Cookbook 211 camera from the rough draft of the instructions and suggesting improvements in the CARD and PREAMP computer-aided test programs.

John Cooley at CED Circuit Engineering (602) 294-1221, for his invaluable help in producing prototype circuit cards.

Phil R. Bright, for building and testing the Cookbook 211 and 245 cameras, software testing, and commercial power supply suggestions.

Brian Manning, one of the first to build the TM#46 CCD camera, for supplying images and photographs of his camera.

David Groski, another early builder of the TM#46 CCD camera, for his many insights and suggestions on cooling the TC211 CCD chip.

Dave Otto and Dan Joyce, for the use of their 20-inch reflector at the 1993 AstroFest Convention to test the Cookbook 245.

For their suggestions and technical assistance: Dr. William Gensler, Eric Kanto, Glenn Seplak, Jay Givens, Wes Stewart (N7WS), Charles Schien, and Robert Schmidt.

Dick Suiter, Dennis di Cicco, David Bruning, David Groski, Diane Lucas and Laurence Marschall, who kindly read and commented on the manuscript. Their help has made this a much better book. Of course any errors or omissions that remain are the responsibility of the authors and their publisher.

Contents

Yes! You *Can* Build a CCD Camera

Just as they swept professional astronomy a decade ago, CCDs (Charge Coupled Devices) are now sweeping amateur astronomy. The benefits of CCD imaging are many. CCDs provide linearity, broad spectral response, and extremely high sensitivity to faint light: exactly the characteristics needed for high-performance astronomical imaging. And just as it revolutionized professional astronomy, CCD imaging promises to revolutionize amateur astronomy, bestowing upon amateur astronomy capabilities only dreamed of a few short years ago.

Until very recently, CCD cameras appeared to be fantastic gadgets for the favored few. This book proves otherwise. Indeed, our message is that CCD cameras are *easy* to build. Amateur astronomers with the drive and desire to do so can reap the benefits of CCD imaging by building their own CCD cameras.

As the authors of this book, we take pride in bringing the potential of CCD imaging within the reach of all amateur astronomers. As we have written this text and tested the Cookbook designs, we have been amazed at the power our home-built cameras possess. If you, the reader, wish to share the coming age of CCD imaging in amateur astronomy, we invite you to join us.

Our goal in writing *The CCD Camera Cookbook* is to provide detailed instructions and sufficient theory so that anyone can successfully build a CCD camera. We and our friends have built over a dozen of these cameras and every camera has worked. No special skills and no special tools are required to build a CCD camera. As the images shown in this book demonstrate, the CCD cameras described in this book work remarkably well.

The "Cookbook cameras" are based on two CCD chips from Texas Instruments, the TC211 and the TC245, hence the names "Cookbook 211" and "Cookbook 245." These chips offer proven performance at low cost, and they are readily available throughout the world. Incorporated into a home-built CCD camera, these chips capture outstanding planetary, lunar, or deep-sky images that can be used for photometry, astrometry, or imaging studies, or the simple enjoyment of capturing images that one decade ago were only dreamed of in amateur astronomy.

Before you begin work on your own CCD camera, we want to warn you that building a CCD camera is a empowering experience. As you work your way through *The CCD Camera Cookbook*, you will learn a great deal about CCDs. The first time you read a given chapter, it may seem complicated and full of terms that you do not understand. This will pass. You will master the terms we use and the techniques we explain in this book, and you will feel a swell of pride and confidence. And when your camera first works, your excitement will know no bounds.

The CCD Camera Cookbook is organized to make building your CCD camera systematic and logical. The first chapter introduces you to the Cookbook 211 and Cookbook 245 CCD cameras. This will help you select the camera that best matches your needs and allow you to assess the materials and workspace that you will need to build a camera. On the basis of this chapter, you may decide to work alone or to team up with friends who have electronics, machine shop, or computer skills that complement your own.

For those who are new to electronic imaging, Chapter 2 summarizes what a CCD chip is and how a CCD camera operates. This chapter explains what each of the components of a cameras does and how those components work together to produce a digital image.

You will learn more about the theory behind the operation of the Cookbook cameras in Chapter 3. Each of the major systems—chips, electronics, software, and cooling—is covered in turn. Although you may initially skip this chapter, you will eventually find yourself drawn to learn more about the seeming "magic" that your Cookbook camera performs.

Chapter 4 serves as a road map for the rest of the book. Here you encounter the practical side of building the Cookbook cameras: what to do first, what components to order, what order to follow, and our best estimate, based on our experience building a dozen prototype Cookbook cameras, of how long it will take you to complete your own camera.

Your next stop is Chapter 5. Here you will find instructions for building the camera's power supply. We

This image of M42 was taken with a Cookbook 245 on a 6-inch f/5 Newtonian in a 60-second integration.

designed this power pack to supply the needs of the camera's electronics and cooling system. If your electronics skills are rusty, building the power supply gives you an opportunity to become familiar with electronic circuits and to exercise your soldering skills.

With the power supply completed, you'll next turn your attention to the interface circuit card and the preamplifier circuit card described in Chapter 6. These two circuit boards carry signals from your computer to the CCD chip and return images from the CCD chip to your computer. With the aid of two computer-based test programs provided with this book, you are virtually guaranteed success. It's easy even if you've never soldered before. And to make things even easier, we've arranged for University Optics to sell a kit containing the circuit boards and the electronic parts that are sometimes hard to find.

Chapter 7 details the most exacting task in building your camera: making the camera head. The camera head is machined from aluminum using a lathe and milling machine. The machining is simple, but if you don't want to make the parts yourself, you can purchase a kit of machined aluminum castings from University Optics, or you can find a friend willing to machine the parts for you. (Here's where taking a team approach to building a CCD

really pays dividends.) After you have scrubbed the mechanical parts clean, you follow detailed step-by-step instructions for installing the CCD in the camera head.

The last major subsystem to build for your camera is the fluid cooling system, described in Chapter 8. The cooling system is the simplest part of building your camera. When you complete it, all that remains is to put everything together as detailed in Chapter 10—but first you must read all about the software that runs your Cookbook camera in Chapter 9. (That's right—*The CCD Camera Cookbook* includes complete ready-to-run image acquisition software for your camera! We've worked hard to make this software both easy to use and powerful.)

With your camera fully operational, you'll want to review Chapter 11 for tips and hints on making outstanding CCD images. As we've tested the Cookbook 211 and the Cookbook 245, we've learned a lot that you'll find helpful as you point your camera toward the heavens. Finally, gaze into a crystal ball with us as we try to predict the impact that CCD cameras will have on the next two decades of amateur astronomy.

To round out the book, five appendices provide everything from a reminder to take electrical safety seriously to an accessory that converts your Cookbook camera into a sensitive and accurate autoguider.

In writing *The CCD Camera Cookbook*, we hope that we have continued the tradition established by Porter, Ingalls, and Texereau. We have tried to provide enough detail to make the book a source of ideas for experimenters while at the same time meeting the practical needs of those who want to build a working camera. For a more theoretical approach to building a CCD camera, we recommend Christian Buil's *CCD Astronomy*, an important work that has been a continuing source of inspiration to us.

We hope that in writing this cookbook, we have succeeded in furnishing a recipe that any amateur astronomer, regardless of technical background, can follow with success. Although we sought to design a camera that is sensitive, easy to use, and affordable, we sought above all else to make a buildable camera. Resist the temptation to "improve" on the design. As you read this book, remember our motto: *"If you build it as we have described it in this book, your camera will work!"*

Richard Berry
Cedar Grove, WI

Veikko Kanto
John Munger
Tucson, AZ

Chapter 1. Introduction to CCD Cameras

This book describes two extremely sensitive CCD cameras that you can build in your own home. These cameras are comparable in performance to the best commercial products made for the amateur astronomy market. They are suitable for both deep-sky imaging and planetary astronomy. These CCD cameras are called the Cookbook 211 and the Cookbook 245.

The Cookbook 211 is based on the Texas Instruments TC211 CCD chip. This is the chip used in the Lynxx-PC, the SBIG ST-4, and the Electrim EDC-1000. The image from this chip is 192 pixels wide by 165 pixels deep, a pixel count entirely adequate to capture diffraction-limited images of the moon and planets, to search for supernovas in distant galaxies, or to perform precise photometry on stars.

The Cookbook 245 is based on the TC245 CCD chip, also made by Texas Instruments. The chip itself is 755 pixels wide by 242 pixels deep, and you have your choice of reading out an image 378 pixels wide by 242 pixels deep or 252 pixels wide by 242 pixels deep. Although the Cookbook 245 excels as a deep-sky machine, it is a versatile camera and can be used for planetary and lunar imaging, too.

Building a Cookbook 211 camera will cost you about $200 in materials. Building a Cookbook 245 costs about $350 in materials, assuming that you have a reasonably good scrap box. The skills needed to assemble the camera are roughly equal to the skills needed to construct a model airplane or to build a telescope. You can combine your skills with those of friends by teaming up to build a CCD for your astronomical society or alternatively, to build a CCD camera for each member of the CCD team.

1.1 What You Are Building

Perhaps the best way to get a sense of the Cookbook cameras is to examine the pictures in this book. You will see what the Cookbook cameras look like and you will also see what kind of images you can expect to make with a Cookbook camera.

Look at the pictures. You will see that the camera head plugs into the eyepiece tube of your telescope, and that wires lead from the camera to a nearby computer. To take pictures, you press keys on the computer keyboard. Each time you take a picture, the computer transfers image data from the camera and displays the picture you have taken on the computer monitor.

You may notice a small metal box (called the interface box) near the camera as well as wires and tubes leading to a power supply box and a plastic tub. The interface box, power supply and plastic tub are essential parts of the camera. The interface box converts image data from the camera to a form that your computer can read, and the box on the ground provides power to run the camera's internal electronics. The tub contains water that absorbs waste heat from the camera's Peltier module cooling system.

The camera head is smaller and lighter than some of today's high-performance eyepieces. Most telescopes will have no trouble carrying it. Inside the camera head is the CCD itself. The CCD is the light sensor in the camera; like most electronic components today, it is a silicon integrated circuit chip. When an image of a celestial object falls on the CCD, the light is converted into an electrical signal. (The term "CCD" stands for "charge-coupled device," describing how the signal is "read out" from the CCD.) The entire CCD in the Cookbook 211 is barely three-eights of an inch square, while the CCD in the Cookbook 245 is smaller than a postage stamp.

To work well for astronomy, the CCD must be cooled to a temperature of −30° Celsius. To accomplish this, inside the camera the CCD is mounted on a thermoelectric cooler, which acts as a pump, extracting heat from the CCD. In the Cookbook cameras, a water cooling system removes the excess heat. The plastic tub and tubing are part of the CCD's cooling system.

The computer plays two vital roles in operating the Cookbook cameras: it sends commands to the CCD chip and displays the images you shoot. Virtually any IBM-clone PC can operate the camera, from a laptop to a full-size desk machine. The only requirements are that the computer have a parallel port (the plug normally used for the printer) and also that it have a VGA graphics display card. (While CGA and EGA displays *do* work, we think

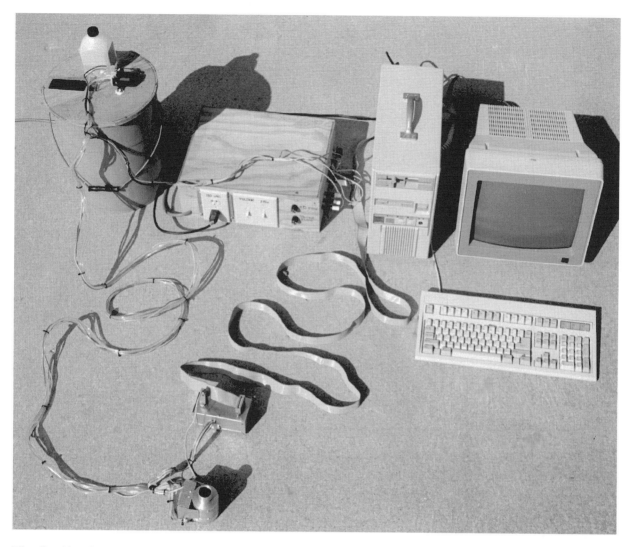

The Cookbook cameras consist of a camera head, interface box, power supply, cooling system, wires and tubes connecting the components, and a computer. The Cookbook cameras can be used on any telescope.

you'll be happier with a VGA display.)

In theory the cables that connect the computer and the camera head should be no more than 15 feet long, but in practice cables 35 feet long work just as well. This means that for wintertime observing you can keep the computer indoors or in a heated enclosure.

Although a Cookbook camera could in theory be run on battery power, it is far more practical to run it from 120-volt house current. The camera itself draws about 100 watts of power, and you will also need to supply power for your computer and monitor, typically another 150 to 200 watts.

One myth that has sprung up is that you need a big telescope to use CCD cameras. The fact is that CCD cameras are really fantastic with small telescopes. With an ordinary 6-inch f/5 Newtonian or a quality 4-inch

refractor such as the TeleVue Genesis, you can take great deep-sky photos. Your telescope mounting must be solid, of course, and because most deep-sky CCD exposures lie between 60 seconds and 10 minutes, the drives on good-quality telescopes are adequate to the task although guiding may be needed for exposures longer than a few minutes.

The Cookbook cameras are easy to use. The software supplied with this book has commands that allow you to focus the camera, efficiently locate objects—including deep-sky objects—using the computer monitor as a real-time finder, and to make exposures up to 15 minutes long. After you have captured an image in the computer, you can view it and save it to the computer's hard drive. You can copy images onto floppy disks and give them to your friends, send images across the country via modem,

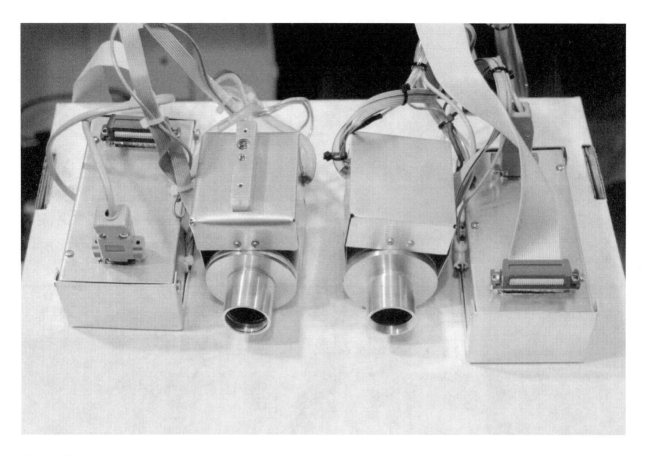

Externally, the Cookbook 211 and Cookbook 245 are identical. Inside, however, the Cookbook 211 Texas Instruments TC211is 2.5 mm square. The Cookbook 245 uses the TC245 measuring 8mm corner-to-corner.

and you can optimize the images using software such as *Astronomical Image Processing for Windows (WINAIP)*.

When you first consider building a CCD camera, you may think that you are just constructing another accessory for your telescope. Although that is true, there's a lot more: you will soon discover an entirely new way of observing. You'll observe deep-sky objects in "real time" using the cameras' finder mode. Objects barely visible to the eye through *any* size telescope will stand out clearly in 60-second exposures. The moon and planets will reveal unprecedented detail. And the images you'll capture potentially have real scientific value.

Perhaps the most important gain is something you can't see in the pictures, and that's the gain in observing satisfaction. If you've been active in amateur astronomy for more than a few years, you've already seen and done a lot of the things that you as an amateur can do. CCD imaging could open for you a whole new realm of amateur astronomy, and make observing a richer and more rewarding experience than ever before.

1.2 What You Will Need

If you think that building a CCD camera is beyond your ability, think again. Certain skills are required, but they are skills that you'll learn on the job as you build your camera. Furthermore, persistence and a can do attitude will see you over almost any obstacle.

The most obvious stumbling blocks for most potential builders are soldering the circuit boards and machining the metal parts for the camera body. Once you learn the basic techniques, soldering is surprisingly easy, and the step-by-step test software included with this book makes the work simple and straightforward. If you've never used a lathe or milling machine, you probably know someone who would be happy to machine the housing for you in return for looking through your telescope and seeing the camera in operation.

Alternatively, you may opt to team up with a group of fellow amateur astronomers to construct several cameras. By sharing the work with a small group, you're almost guaranteed access to the skills required.

To help you get a better grasp of the project, here is a list of critical knowledge, skills, and equipment that you will need to build your CCD camera:

Basic 120VAC (house wiring) experience. To construct the power supply, you will need to wire circuits that use 120-volt house current. Because house current is

Cookbook Camera Specifications

	Amplifier Gain	Sensitivity, electrons per ADU	Maximum Storage Electrons (1)	Typical Storage Electrons (2)	Readout, ADC Range
Cookbook 211	10±10%	61.0	220,000	150,000	500-4095
Cookbook 245 (3)	17.7±10%	34.4	106,000	80,000	1000-4095
Cookbook 245 (4)	5.9±10%	137.7	320,000	240,000	750-3071

Note 1: Ability to achieve this level depends on the individual chip well capacity.
Note 2: Typical well capacity according to Texas Instruments.
Note 3: 252 wide by 242 line format with internal binning.
Note 4: 252 wide by 242 line format with external pixel binning.

Achievable Readout Noise:		Cookbook 211	~100 electrons rms		
		Cookbook 245	~40 electrons rms		

Physical Attributes:		Camera Head:	Size:	3" long, 3.75" tall, 2.75" wide	
			Weight:	17 ounces	
		Interface box:	Size:	5.5" long, 4" tall (w/ plugs), 3" wide	
			Weight:	9 ounces	
		Power Cable:	Useful length:	12 feet	
			Weight:	1 ounce per foot	
		Ribbon Cable:	Length:	15 feet (optionally, 35 feet)	
			Weight:	½ ounce per foot	
		Power Supply:	Size:	17" long, 5.5" tall, 13" wide	
			Weight:	12 pounds	
			Power Required:	1A @ 120VAC	

potentially lethal, familiarity with basic electrical circuits is absolutely necessary. We recommend that if you are not comfortable with 120-volt wiring practice that you seek the help of a person who is.

Basic electronic measurements. The only test equipment you will need to construct the camera is a digital volt-ohm meter. You should understand how to measure resistances, AC and DC voltages, and check for circuit continuity. The test software that comes with the book guides you through the required measurements.

Soldering. To construct the printed circuit boards, you will need to solder components to a printed circuit board. Even if you have never soldered anything before, you'll soon realize that soldering with a 15-watt soldering iron and 0.030-inch rosin-core solder is easy. It takes just a few seconds to make each connection. Basic soldering techniques are covered in Appendix B.

Wood construction. The power supply for the Cookbook cameras is housed in a plywood box. Building the box requires basic woodworking hand tools. The box can be as crude or as elegant as you want.

Basic home-shop metal work. To cut and shape heat sinks and other small parts for the power supply, and to make the aluminum covers for the interface box and camera head, you should be able to drill and cut thin metal parts. No more than basic skills are required.

Lathe and milling machine operation. The parts for the CCD camera head are simple shapes and therefore easy for an *experienced* machinist to make. If you have never machined anything before, you will probably need help from someone with machine-shop experience. Safety is an important part of working with lathes and mills; do not attempt to use a lathe or mill without the guidance of someone familiar with good shop practice. Remember too that many home machinists are always looking for projects to do, and would be happy to make the parts for you.

1.3 How to Find Parts

You may regard finding parts for your CCD camera as a painful and aggravating trial or as an enjoyable "game" that you play with a high-quality CCD camera as the prize. Either way, you must round up a collection of specialized electronic and mechanical components and blend them to make your camera. (And are not great cooks always looking for specialized ingredients to use in their next creation?)

For most people, electronic components will be the most difficult parts to find. Of those parts, the CCD chip, the analog-to-digital converter chip, and the Peltier cooling device are the most difficult to locate. Large electronics supply houses such as Hall-Mark Electronics usually carry the required components, but when specialty items

Your Cookbook camera can take deep-sky images with short exposures. This picture of the Lagoon Nebula was taken with a 4-inch f/5.5 TeleVue Genesis refractor and a 60-second exposure. Image by Richard Berry.

such as CCD chips are out of stock, you may have to wait several months before they are again available from the manufacturer.

We have included a list of electronics suppliers willing to deal with small orders from electronics hobbyists and amateur astronomers in the back of this book to provide you with a starting point. You'll find even more suppliers listed in *The ARRL Handbook* (see the bibliography for more information on this valuable reference.)

You can in theory obtain aluminum stock for the camera body from local suppliers, but you may face minimum order requirements. Most firms want to help amateur and hobbyist machinists, so ask if you can purchase odd lengths or cutoffs. The stores are often willing to help a customer with an interesting or different project. Show them this book so that they understand what you're trying to do, and be willing to return a favor with an evening of stargazing through your telescope.

Alternatively, ask your local machine shop if they have suitable cutoffs of scrap pieces that you can pur-

chase, or look in scrap yards for machine-shop scrap that meets your needs. Again, you'll often find that shops love customers with odd and interesting jobs. Even if the first couple of places you ask cannot help you, the people there may know of another shop that can. Be nice about asking, and keep asking.

Another place to look is your local high school. Many high schools offer evening courses in machine shop or take small jobs on a cash basis. Check the situation in your area; you may be pleasantly surprised.

As a member of an astronomy club, you may have access to the scrap bins and scrounging instincts of dozens or even hundreds of other amateur astronomers and telescope makers. You may find that you have lots of willing folks interested in helping you make your CCD camera.

If you decide not to machine the parts yourself and don't happen to know hobbyist machinists willing to make the parts for you, obtain quotes from local machine shops. The plans provided in this book give a machinist enough information to make the parts. Commercial shops are not cheap, and if the shop has lots of work you'll probably pay a premium price for a one-off job. On the other hand, you might be lucky enough to ask during a slack time and get a good quote.

Willmann-Bell and University Optics offer a set of printed circuit boards. Furthermore, a kit containing machined parts for the camera body will be available from University Optics.

Outside the specialty electronic and metal components, you should be able to find everything you need in local hardware stores, auto-parts stores, and consumer electronics stores. The power supply, for example, is designed around parts you can obtain at most Radio Shack stores. Copper tubing is available at well-stocked hardware stores and the brass fittings you'll need can be obtained from a plumbing outlet. The water pump we used is a replacement auto windshield-washer pump.

The spirit of scrounging parts and using things for other than their intended purposes runs deep in amateur astronomy. If you cannot find some odd part you need, think about its purpose and function, and ask yourself how else you could accomplish the same goal. In the Cookbook camera, you don't have to follow every part of the recipe exactly. Always remember that the housing for Veikko's first CCD camera looked like an old soup can!

1.4 Prepare a Work Area

As you pore over this book, you will realize that you need to dedicate a work space to this project for about two months. Ideally, you would like a small room or a corner of the basement that you can leave from one day to the next knowing with certainty that children, pets, or a helpful spouse will leave everything strictly alone. Short of the ideal, you need a place where you can spread out parts, tools, and materials for several uninterrupted hours, and where you can easily store parts while various paints and epoxies dry or cure.

After good lighting and several convenient electric outlets, the primary consideration for your work area is static electricity, or ESD (electrostatic discharge) as it's known in the electronics trade. Even in humid weather, when you cannot feel them, electric potentials of hundreds of volts build up on rugs, plastic surfaces, and synthetic fibers. You must completely avoid these materials in your CCD work area because they can damage your ICs.

The floor of your work area should be bare wood, concrete, or linoleum tile. These materials do not allow electrical charges to build up. Your work table should be unpainted wood or metal. Sit on a wood or metal chair and wear clothing made of cotton that has been washed with an "anti-cling" detergent. Wear a 1MΩ grounded wrist-strap to safely dissipate the build-up of charges. Avoid crepe or rubber-soled shoes. For more on ESD safety, see Appendix A.

If you have a home shop or have a lathe and mill in the garage or basement, machining the parts for the camera body is a perfectly straightforward turning and milling job. If you don't have a home shop but know machining, you can make the parts in any shop. Alternatively, you may be able to persuade a friend to make the parts for you or purchase the metal components in kit form from University Optics.

1.5 Work Safely!

As you build your camera, keep safety uppermost in your mind. Machines, solvents, and electrical power are dangerous when they are used improperly. If you are uncertain of the proper techniques for running a lathe, cleaning with solvents, or wiring a circuit, don't take chances. Learn safe techniques before proceeding.

In quick summary, around machinery, do not wear loose clothing, jewelry, or anything else that could get caught in a moving part of the machine. Run the machines at speeds recommended in standard manuals for machinists, never push the work, and never make adjustments without stopping the machine and letting all moving parts come to a complete stop.

When you use solvents such as alcohol and acetone, or solvent-bearing materials such as adhesives and paints, work in a well-ventilated area. Never allow potentially explosive or harmful vapors to build up, and remember to store materials where children and pets cannot reach them. Purchase solvents in small quantities and dispose of leftover solvents in an ecologically sound way as mandated by local and state laws.

With all electrical circuitry, but especially with the 120-volt house current in the power supply, work only with the power off and the unit unplugged. Use one hand for measurements so that current never flows through your body. Remember that even low-voltage components such as capacitors can store a considerable amount of electrical energy. Allow time for them to discharge before you begin to work on a circuit.

Building a CCD camera should pose no danger providing you use tools and materials in a proper manner. We have provided two appendices at the end of this book to remind you of basic safety techniques and to teach you basic electronics skills. You may also wish to check references such as *The ARRL Handbook* listed in the bibliography section of this book.

If you have any doubts about safe techniques, procedures, or methods of handling or using machines, materials, electronics, or electricity, seek competent advice. We want you to be healthy and happy when the camera is completed and you're making images of the night sky with it. That way you'll have the double satisfaction of a job well done and a whole new world of astronomical observing opening before you.

Chapter 2. What a CCD Camera Does

Because of their high sensitivity and versatility, among amateur astronomers CCD imaging has acquired something of a mystique. "CCDs can do anything," people say wistfully. They are wrong. Making images with a CCD is simply astrophotography with a more powerful camera. As does any instrument, CCD cameras have limitations and strong points. Successful CCD imaging lies in avoiding the weaknesses and exploiting the strengths.

2.1 What a CCD Camera Is

The Cookbook 211, the Cookbook 245, and other CCD cameras are electronic light sensors. When a CCD camera is placed so that an image of the sky falls on a silicon chip inside the camera, an image accumulates in the silicon chip. After an exposure that may last from a few seconds to many minutes, the image in the silicon chip is electronically converted into numbers and transferred to a computer. Once the image is stored inside the computer as numbers, it can be manipulated and displayed on the computer screen.

If CCDs have created a sensation in the world of amateur astronomy, it is largely because the image that the camera has captured is digitized, or stored as numbers. The computer can display with equal ease an image that occupies the full range of numerical values in the image or a very tiny range of values. The ability to display a very narrow range of pixel values gives CCD cameras their apparent high photographic speed.

For example, with a modest telescope you can obtain an excellent image of a galaxy with an exposure of 200 seconds. The range of numerical values in the image of the galaxy might span a range from 0 to 1,000, with 0 representing the black of the background sky and 1,000 the brightness of the nucleus. However, you can capture a recognizable image of the same galaxy with a 2-second exposure. How so? The numbers representing the image of the galaxy now span a much smaller range—from 0 to 10—with 0 the black of the background sky and 10 representing the nucleus. Although the quality of a 2-second image cannot equal that of a 200-second image, it is entirely adequate for finding deep-sky objects.

So—what is a CCD camera? Basically, it's a gadget that you place at the focus of your telescope, where the eyepiece would normally go. Wires and tubes connect this camera head to some auxiliary gadgets and to your computer. You operate the camera from your computer. The ribbon cable connecting your computer to the camera head should be less than 35 feet long. When you take an exposure with the CCD camera, the image you have taken appears on the computer monitor. The image is digital and can be stored in your computer.

Consider the practical implications.

With 35 feet between them, you can put the telescope out under the stars and keep your computer in a warm, dry place. You'll need house current. And, with the telescope and the computer in difference places, you may do a lot of running back and forth between the telescope and the computer, or decide that two observers are better than one.

The CCD, of course, simply records the image from your telescope. It follows therefore that the quality of the images you make with a CCD camera depends entirely on the quality of the image that your telescope creates. If your telescope creates sharp images, tracks well, and focuses nicely then you'll get sharp, well tracked, and in-focus images.

Your skill in managing the multiple demands of operating a telescope is also crucial. Before you can even start imaging, there's a lot of equipment to set up. You'll need to string wires and tubes hither and thither. You'll need to align your telescope for tracking, cope with any computer problems that may arise, and monitor the camera's performance.

So—once again—what is a CCD camera? Clearly, *a CCD camera is a gadget that changes the way you observe*. It will change what you *can* observe, it will change what you *do* observe, and it will change *how* you observe. We want you to be aware of these impending changes and to be prepared to take full advantage of them. We also want to remind you that even after you've built a CCD camera you can still spend quiet nights under the stars—simply looking.

The Cookbook camera attaches to the focus tube of your telescope, where the eyepiece normally would go. Imaging with CCD cameras is much like astrophotography—except that the image is captured on a computer.

2.2 What Each Part of the Camera Does

The Cookbook cameras consist of five major systems. These are: (1) the camera head, (2) the camera electronics, (3) the power supply, (4) the cooling system, and (5) a computer running image acquisition software.

The Camera Head. Mounted in the focuser, the camera head replaces an eyepiece. Instead of passing through the eyepiece and going into your eye, light from the objective lens or mirror falls directly on the CCD chip inside the camera head. The purpose of the camera head is to create a safe and suitable environment for the CCD chip.

The ideal environment for a CCD chip is a place that is cold and dry. It must protect the CCD from light and stray electrical fields while allowing the image from your telescope and the electrical signals from your computer to reach the CCD.

The camera head is simply an airtight metal cylinder with a window in the front to admit light from your telescope, an electrical feedthrough to admit signals from your computer, and a water-cooled base to remove the heat generated when the CCD is cooled.

Inside the camera head, the CCD rests on a metal support called a cold finger. Fine wires connect the pins on the sides of the CCD to the electrical feedthrough in the side of the camera head. Between the base of the cold finger and the bottom of the camera head is a thin sandwich of special alloys called a Peltier cooler.

When an electrical current flows through the Peltier cooler, it pumps heat from the cold finger to the water-cooled base of the camera head, taking the CCD chip to temperatures far below freezing. Inside its cold, dry shelter, the image from your telescope enters, and the CCD records the subtle light of galaxies.

The Camera Electronics. Although the CCD and your computer are both electronic devices, they do not speak the same language. The voltages, currents, and speeds of operation that suit computers and CCDs are sometimes far apart. The camera electronics bridge this

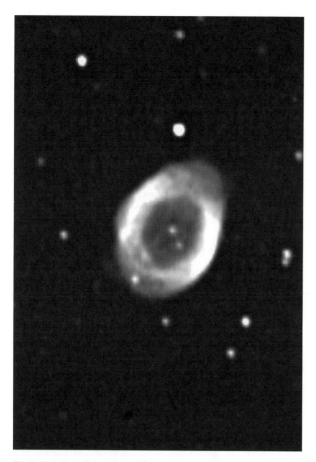

Phil Bright shot the Ring Nebula from his Tucson home using a 10-inch SCT and a Cookbook 245.

supplies that the Cookbook cameras need. One supply powers the digital and analog components in the electronics subsystem, the second powers the Peltier cooler in the camera head, and the third powers the pump that circulates the water that removes heat extracted from the CCD.

The Cooling System. It is necessary to remove unwanted heat that the Peltier cooler removes from the CCD chip, and that is the function of the cooling system. The cooling system consists of the water-filled base of the camera head, plastic tubing to carry water to and from the camera's base, a coil of copper in a bucket of water to soak up the excess heat, and a small water pump to circulate the coolant water.

The Computer. To operate the camera and store images from it requires a computer running the image acquisition software included with this book. The computer sends control signals to the CCD and receives images via the parallel port normally used by the printer. The computer must be an IBM-PC compatible to run the software and a VGA display card works best to display the images.

When the software runs in the computer, it tells the computer how to control the CCD. The software tells the camera how to take each image and how to return the image data to the computer. In addition, once the image has been returned to the computer, the software can display the image on the screen or save the image data to a hard disk or floppy.

2.3 What CCD Images Look Like

Some people like CCD images and some people don't. Those who like CCD images see images full of faint stars and dim galaxies, images with extraordinary dynamic range capable of revealing sights heretofore barred from amateur astronomers. Those who do not like CCD images see grainy images with gross pixelation, narrow fields of view, and muddy tonal values. It depends on your point of view. The fact is that CCD images can be all (or none) of the above.

The best way to view CCD images is on a computer with a powerful image-processing program such as *Astronomical Image Processing for Windows* at your fingertips. You then become fully aware of the dynamic qualities of an image that you can lighten, darken, blur, or sharpen in a few seconds. You realize that you can accurately measure the brightness of every star you see, combine images to reduce noise, enlarge the field of view, or make color. You realize that with enough effort you can extract every scrap of information present in that image. You realize that the raw image is just the beginning.

2.4 How You Will Use Your CCD Camera

We cannot predict what you will observe with your Cookbook camera, but if you will gaze into our crystal ball, you can imagine a night you might experience a year after you have completed your Cookbook camera.

electronic chasm, converting signals from the computer to signals that control the CCD, and converting the varying voltage from the CCD into the digital signals your computer comprehends.

The electronic subsystem of the Cookbook cameras consists of two printed circuit boards. One, mounted piggyback on the camera head, is called the preamplifier card. The second, located roughly 12 inches distant, is called the interface card. The two cards split the tasks involved in controlling the CCD and transmitting its images to the computer.

Metal housings protect both cards. This means that the camera head has a square box on one side, and attached to it by three cables is another box that houses the interface card. The same printed circuit boards serve for both the Cookbook 211 and the Cookbook 245, though a different set of electronic components must be installed for the two cameras. It is possible to convert a Cookbook 211 to a Cookbook 245 by changing and retesting the electronics and changing the CCD.

The Power Supply. The power supply is housed in a wooden box that holds the three separate power

When an unexpected astronomical event happens, you can swing into action with your CCD camera. Phil Bright captured this image of supernova 1993J in M81 using a 60-second exposure with his Cookbook 245 camera.

The mist clears and you see yourself sitting in a small observatory—yes, we know you don't have an observatory now, but you will. It's in your backyard too, because you've discovered that your CCD is less bothered by light pollution and moonlight than your eyes are. You can observe on any clear night.

In your observatory, you see your telescope on a new mounting—an equatorial that's a lot heftier than your telescope's present mounting. Just a few feet away is a built-in hutch with a portable computer in it. (The hutch keeps the computer warm and dry.) Neatly tied cables run from the CCD on the telescope to the power supply and cooling system. You're sitting on a low stool, positioned so that you can comfortably reach telescope controls and the computer keyboard.

You touch a few keys. Every few seconds a new image appears on the screen. Your fingers move over the keyboard and the image brightens, so the image is filled with faint stars.

You reach over to the telescope and slew it to a new place on the sky. Stars trail across the computer screen as the telescope moves. With one eye on a digital readout,

you zero in on your chosen coordinates. Then a galaxy appears on the screen. You touch the slow-motion buttons on the telescope's hand paddle. The galaxy moves to the center of the screen. Although it's a crude image, the galaxy's spiral arms are clearly visible.

You touch a key to check focus. The galaxy doubles in size. You inspect the star images, then, satisfied with what you see, touch more keys to start an exposure. Sixty seconds pass. The computer beeps and a detailed image of the galaxy flows onto the screen.

You lean close to inspect the image, then touch a few keys. The image brightens. Look at the grin on your face! The supernova is still shining—and though you were not the one to discover it, you follow it every clear night. With a few more keystrokes the image is saved to disk. Later you will measure the brightness of the star and report the resulting measurement to the AAVSO.

The picture fades. As you watch your future self in our crystal ball, though, you sense new energy and new vitality. Observing projects that today seem like the wildest of daydreams could well be the nightly realities in the not-too-distant future.

Chapter 3. How a CCD Camera Works

You need not understand the technical details of CCD cameras to build and use one. However, we suspect that everyone who builds or uses a Cookbook camera will eventually want to learn how the camera works.

This chapter describes the operation of the CCDs themselves, how the supporting electronics cards transfer timing signals to the CCD and images back into the computer, and how the computer runs the whole system. An additional section covers the theory and operation of the cooling system.

3.1 How a CCD Chip Works

CCDs take advantage of certain electrical properties of the shiny, crystalline element silicon. When light strikes a piece of silicon, electrons are freed from their positions in the crystal lattice, and move around, or migrate, within the silicon. If you attach wires to the silicon and apply a voltage to them, a current of electrons will flow in proportion to the intensity of the light falling on the silicon.

CCDs are fabricated on thin slices of very pure silicon. The basic strategy is to divide the surface of the silicon into a checkerboard of tiny light-sensitive areas. Each sensing area is called a photosite. To make a CCD, the chip designer must immobilize electrons in their photosites during an exposure and then selectively move the electrons through the silicon to an amplifier so that the number of electrons liberated in each photosite during an exposure can be measured.

To form a checkerboard pattern on the silicon, chip manufacturers lay down narrow strips of dopants—atoms that alter the electrical properties of pure silicon. Electrons that have been freed cannot cross these strips of dopant called channel stops. These define the columns of photosites on the CCD.

Free electrons in silicon can be controlled by nearby electrical charges. (The words "charge coupled" in "charge coupled device" refer to this.) If the surface of the silicon is coated with silicon dioxide, an insulating material, so that the electrons do not escape to strips of conducting material coated on top of the insulator, when you apply a positive voltage to the strips, "potential wells" are generated in the silicon. The potential wells trap the free electrons, that is, the wells prevent the electrons from moving away from their place of origin. This means that when light falls on the CCD, an image made of electrons builds up in the silicon.

However, if you want to move the electrons, it is only necessary to raise and lower the voltages on the strips in a regular fashion—(a process called "clocking")— and the electrons are pushed into an adjacent well after each clock. The charge packets dutifully march down the silicon toward the amplifier.

Because these strips, or image area gates, extend across the full width of the array of photosites, each time the image-area voltages are clocked, all of the rows of electrons move down the chip, marching in parallel.

To bring all of the electrons to the amplifier, however, it is necessary to move electrons across the checkerboard as well as down. At the bottom end of the CCD, the designers construct a special row of potential wells called a serial register. Here the conducting strips are perpendicular to the strips on the face of the checkerboard; they are called serial register gates. After each row of electrons is marched into the serial register, it is then marched down the serial register to the amplifier.

Thus you can move packets of electrons from every photosite on the CCD to the amplifier. Because the signal is a packet of electrons, the amplifier is designed to convert the electrical charge represented by the packet of electrons into an output voltage. Because of its function, the amplifier is also called a "charge detection node."

The amplifier consists of an output gate, a reverse-biased diode, connected to the gate of a field-effect transistor. This structure acts like a capacitor, so that when that the electron packet is placed in it, its voltage changes in proportion. Sensing the change in voltage, the field-effect transistor generates an output voltage proportional to the charge on its gate. This is the output signal.

Also attached to the output diode is a second field-effect transistor called the reset transistor. The electron packet is first admitted to the output diode when the reset transistor is turned off, that is, nonconducting. After the output transistor has measured the charge, the reset tran-

The TC211 and TC245 chips are the basis for the Cookbooks 211 and 245. The TC211 has 192 rows by 165 lines of pixels and costs around $32; the larger TC245 has 755 rows by 242 lines and costs under $150.

sistor turns on and restores the charge on the output diode to its original value. Unfortunately, when the output gate is reset, the charge it puts on the output gate varies by a small amount, due to the random motion of the electrons. This random variation is termed reset noise.

Reading an image from a CCD consists of three nested operations: reading the output gate, reading each charge in a line, and reading each line from the array. Reading the output gate consists of two steps: reading the voltage induced by the packet of electrons followed by resetting the output gate to its original value. Reading a line consists of moving individual charge packets to the output gate by clocking the serial register gates. Finally, moving lines to the serial gate consists of clocking the image area gates.

3.1.1 CCD Chip Operation Theory

Although all CCDs work according to the same set of principles, the architecture of each CCD is different. CCDs may be tailored for scientific imaging, image scanning, video imaging, or any of the many other uses. The most obvious differences involve the large-scale organization of the chip.

The simplest way to organize a CCD is as a full-frame device. The generic CCD described above is a full-frame device because the entire image is read out at once. However, there is a problem associated with the full-frame device: light continues to fall on the chip as it is read out. This lowers image contrast and smears the image. The TC211 CCD is a full-frame device.

To avoid this, chip designers sometimes opt to cover the lower half of the image array with an opaque mask. By rapidly clocking the top half of the image array to the covered bottom half of the image array, smearing is eliminated. The TC245 is a frame-transfer device.

For video cameras and other imagers that must operate at high speed, CCD designers may opt to build an interline transfer device. In this design, alternate rows of photosites are covered with an opaque mask, and special gates extend across the CCD from top to bottom. To read out an image, all the charge packets in the image area are moved over one row to the covered photosites, then read

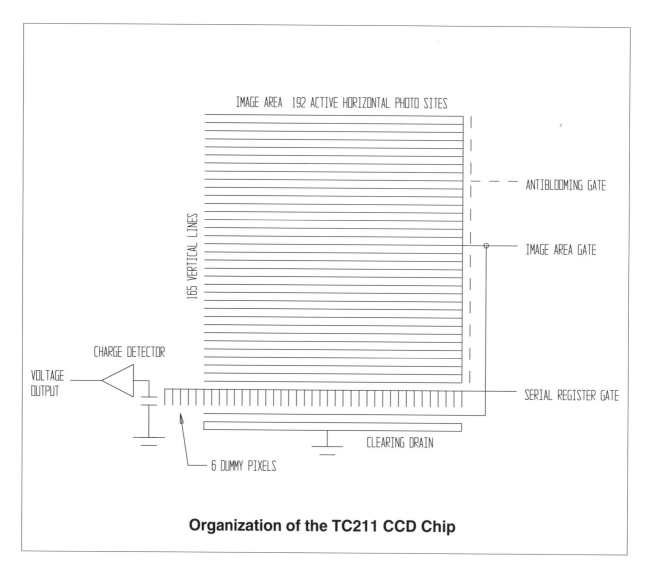

IMAGE AREA 192 ACTIVE HORIZONTAL PHOTO SITES

165 VERTICAL LINES

ANTIBLOOMING GATE

IMAGE AREA GATE

CHARGE DETECTOR

VOLTAGE OUTPUT

SERIAL REGISTER GATE

CLEARING DRAIN

6 DUMMY PIXELS

Organization of the TC211 CCD Chip

out like a full-frame array.

Finally, many CCDs are designed for color imaging. In color CCDs, adjacent rows of photosites are covered with red, green, and blue color filters. To speed reading of the array, these three groups of rows may be moved to three separate serial registers and three output amplifiers. The TC244 is just such a color imager, and the TC245 is the same chip *but without the color filters*. In the Cookbook 245, we have ganged the adjacent rows of pixels together for extremely high sensitivity to light.

3.1.1.1 The Organization of the TC211

The TC211 is a full-frame imaging device organized as 192 horizontal photosites by 165 vertical photosites. A single photosite measures 13.75μm horizontally by 16μm vertically. Multiplying the horizontal or vertical photosite count by its size reveals the image area is 2640μm (or about 0.104 inches) square. This CCD has an area which is about $1/140$ that of a 35mm film frame and

the angle of coverage is reduced to $1/10$ that of a 35mm film frame. Because of the small size of the TC211, an 8-inch telescope with a 2000mm focal length has a field of view less than 5 arc minutes on a side.

In the TC211, the charge packets that form the image move down one line after each clock pulse on the image area gate (IAG). When the IAG clock goes from a low voltage state to a high voltage state, charge is pushed into a holding area in front of it. After the IAG clock returns to the low voltage state, the charge drops from the holding area into the next line.

The last line in the image area of the TC211 is attached to a special line that shifts sideways instead of down. This is called the serial register. The last line in the image area serves as a holding area with the serial register gate (SRG) under it. By pushing the charge packets first with the IAG then with the SRG, each line of the image gets dumped into the serial register. Below the serial register is another line gate which is connected to the IAG

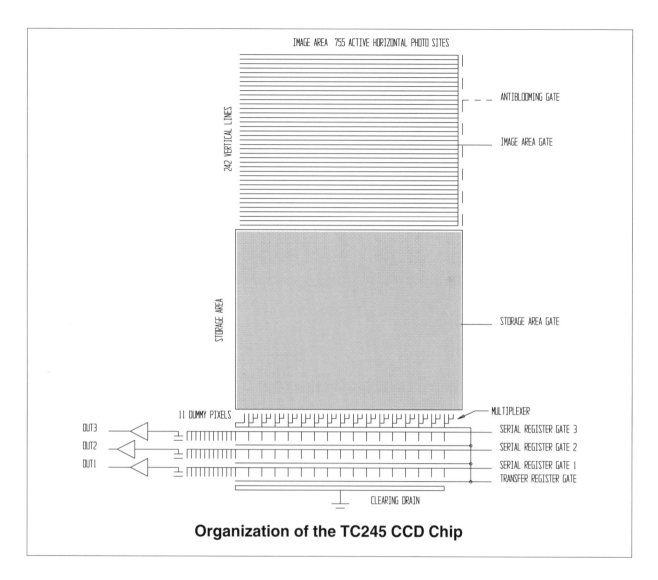

Organization of the TC245 CCD Chip

clock input. This allows the serial gate charge to move one more step down where it is removed from the TC211. The serial gate is therefore cleared of charge each time the IAG clock is pulsed.

In the TC211, each line of charge moves from right to left in the serial register by clocking the SRG input. Thus, the image area charge is shifted out of the chip by first shifting the image area down one line, transferring the line to the serial register, then shifting the line out horizontally. Reading the entire image from the TC211 requires 198 serial shifts for each line times 165 image area shifts. (The extra serial shifts are required because the serial data must travel through dummy photosites before the charge reaches the charge to voltage conversion circuitry.)

Acquiring an image in the TC211 chip is performed in three operations. The first is clearing all charge out of the image area by shifting the lines into the clearing gate below the serial register. Next comes integrating an image by letting light fall on the chip for some length of time.

During this time, the image area gate is set to a low voltage level. The image is then shifted line by line into the serial register and each line is shifted serially to the amplifier.

In the Cookbook 211 camera, the light sensitive area of the TC211 chip is always exposed to light. As the image is shifted during readout, more charge gets added to the lines as they are shifted down. Smearing is not a problem with faint astronomical objects because the read-out time is generally considerably faster than the integration time.

3.1.1.2 The TC245 CCD Chip

The TC245 chip is a frame-transfer device. To prevent image smear, the exposed frame is rapidly shifted to a temporary storage area which is protected from light by an opaque aluminum mask. In the Cookbook 245, the image is shifted at a rate of 40µs per line, so it takes about 10 milliseconds to shift the image into the storage area.

Although the TC245 is a monochrome imager, its first cousin, the TC244, has a color mask coated on top of

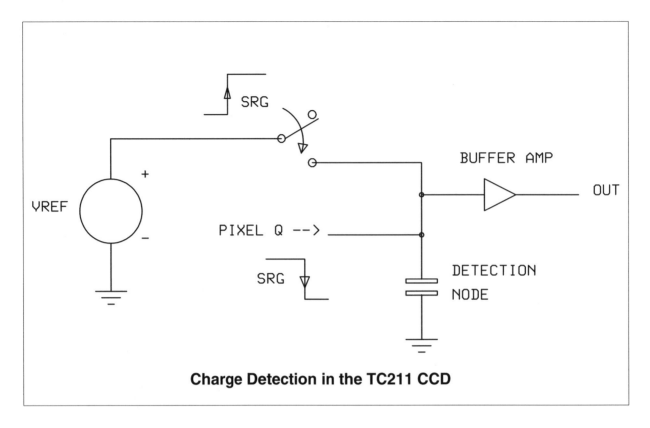

Charge Detection in the TC211 CCD

the silicon CCD structure. The TC245 has no mask. However, because the underlying chip was designed with color as an option, the photosites are grouped horizontally into threes, with rows of photosites for the primary colors.

The useful image area on the chip is 755 photosites horizontally by 242 photosites vertically. Each photosite measures 8.5μm horizontally by 19.7μm vertically—tall, skinny photosites.

For TV imaging, it makes sense to have an image with different resolutions in the horizontal and vertical axes because the vertical resolution can be increased by interlacing, but it does not make sense for astronomy.

By combining adjacent photosites into twos, we can make nearly square photosites that measure 17μm wide by 19.7μm high. However, depending on how the image is read out, the three rows of photosites may pass through amplifiers whose properties are not precisely matched, leading to stripes in the final image. The Cookbook 245 produces a stripe-free image 378 pixels wide because the entire image has been read out through a single amplifier. For the highest image resolution, use this mode.

For normal operation of the Cookbook 245, however, we prefer to bin adjacent photosites in groups of three. This yields 252 horizontal by 242 vertical photosites. In our design, each 25.5μm-wide by 19.7μm-high "superpixel" passes through the same amplifier. Images in the 252 by 242 format fit the width of a standard 320 × 200 VGA card. However, because the height of the image

exceeds that of the standard display, we resample the image and display a 252-by-193-pixel image on the screen. This is used for display only; the full 252-by-242-pixel data is stored in the computer's memory.

As we noted above, the TC245 is a frame-transfer device. Since it requires only 10 milliseconds to transfer the image to the storage area, image smearing during readout is reduced to a minimum. However, because light continues to strike the image area during readout, if an object is extremely bright, excess charge may bleed into the storage area to produce blooming.

To shift a TC245 image to the storage area, the charge present in the image area and the storage area must be shifted down simultaneously. This is accomplished by raising the Image Area Gate (IAG) to a high level, then raising the Storage Area Gate (SAG) to a high level. The IAG is then returned to a low level followed by returning the SAG clock to a low level. To prevent it from piling up at the end of the storage gate, clocked-out charge must be read serially or shifted into a clearing gate.

For maximum flexibility, the image acquisition software can read out an image four different ways. These are binning adjacent photosites internally (that is, on the chip), binning externally (that is, in the computer), binning internally as well sampling the reference voltage, and binning externally to produce a 378-pixel-wide image.

3.1.2 CCD Charge Detection Amplifiers

When the charge packets from the array of pho-

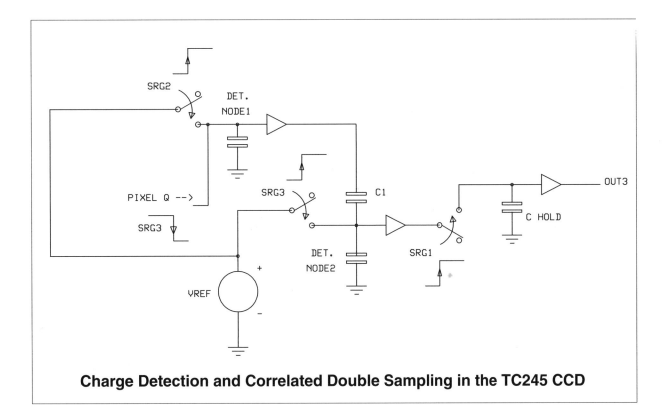

Charge Detection and Correlated Double Sampling in the TC245 CCD

tosites on the CCD reach the end of the serial register, the electrons must be converted into a signal. This is accomplished in a structure called the charge detection node, which is basically an on-chip amplifier. The amplifiers on the TC211 and TC245 differ considerably in noise level and sophistication.

3.1.2.1 Charge Detection in the TC211

The TC211 CCD chip dumps the charge from the end of the serial gate into the amplifier, a capacitive charge detection node, that converts the charge into a voltage. The device is specified to have a conversion coefficient of 4μV per electron. From the capacitance equation, $Q = C \times V$, and knowing that the charge on a single electron is 1.602×10^{-19} coulombs, we deduce that capacitance of the detection node is only 0.04pF. The detection node connects to a high impedance amplifier that prevents external circuitry from loading the detection node.

At the beginning of each readout cycle, the node, acting like a capacitor, is charged to a level called the reset voltage. (To accomplish this, a transistor switch connects the node to a reference voltage when the SRG clock signal is high.) When the SRG clock goes low, the transistor switch opens, disconnecting the reference voltage and simultaneously shifting the charge packet from the serial register into the charge detection node. The charge packet changes the voltage on the node. The voltage difference is proportional to the image intensity.

The purpose of resetting the charge detection node

is to place it at exactly the same voltage before reading each charge packet. Unfortunately, resetting creates its own source of noise. Even if no charge were transferred to the detection node, clocking the SRG line from a high to low state adds a random variation of 72 electrons to the measurement of the charge packet. Reset noise therefore limits the faintest signal that the TC211 can detect.

3.1.2.2 Charge Detection in the TC245

Charge detection in the TC245 differs significantly from charge detection in the TC211. Of course, the TC245 has three charge-sensitive amplifiers, one for each of the three color channels built into the chip. More importantly for the Cookbook 245, however, reset noise is eliminated. The chip has built-in correlated double sampling circuitry. As a result, the TC245 can detect light as much as four times fainter than the TC211.

Correlated double sampling is performed on the TC245 by a switched capacitor circuit. Recall how the charge packet is normally measured: the node, acting as a capacitor, is charged to the reset voltage, the charge packet is admitted, and the voltage on the node is taken as the signal. The problem is that the reset voltage varies randomly from reset to reset.

To do correlated double sampling, the normal readout sequence must be altered. The node is charged to the reset voltage. The reset voltage is measured and stored. The charge packet is then admitted and the node charges. The voltage is measured again. The circuit then subtracts

This TC211 closeup shows the image area and along the chip's edges, the detection node circuitry.

the stored reset voltage from the sum of the reset voltage and the voltage induced by the charge packet. The difference is the output signal.

The beauty of this scheme is that even though the reset voltage varies, we measure it before the charge packet is introduced and again after the charge packet is introduced. The difference between the two measurements is due solely to the charge packet.

Here's how it works in detail. The detection circuit has three transistor switches each controlled by one of three SRG clocks. When its associated SRG clock is at a high level each switch is closed, and when the SRG clock is at a low level, it is opened. The clocks are called SRG1, SRG2, and SRG3.

When SRG2 is at a high level, detection node1 is connected to a voltage reference, V_{ref}. Switching SRG2 to the low state places a reset voltage on detection node1 so its voltage becomes $V_{ref} + V_{reset}$. Then the SRG3 clock is set to a high state, and a capacitor, C1, has V_{ref} on one side and the voltage from detection node1 on the other. Thus, the voltage across capacitor C1 is $-V_{reset}$. Capacitor C1 thus serves to store the initial value of the reset voltage.

SRG3 is then clocked to the low state and detection node, node2, is disconnected from V_{ref} so the end of C1 floats open. Then a charge from the serial register, Q, is dumped into detection node1 by the SRG3 high to low transition. Detection node1 now has a potential which is $V_{ref} + V_{reset} - Q/C$.

The voltage drop across C1 is V_{reset} so the voltage on the floating end of the capacitor is $Vref - Q/C$. This is now the value we want to keep. To prevent C1 from

discharging, a buffer amplifier is connected to the node. When SRG1 is clocked to a high state, the voltage is transferred to a holding capacitor, C_{hold}. This voltage remains on the output even when SRG1 returns to a low state, and does not change until SRG1 is clocked high.

Although it sounds complex, the TC245 takes care of the tricky part for us. Our job is to feed the right control signals to SRG1, SRG2, and SRG3. We benefit amply from the added complexity because correlated double sampling makes the TC245 considerably more sensitive than it would otherwise be.

3.1.3 Acquiring an Image from the CCD Chip

Image acquisition from the CCD chip can be accomplished with a variety of techniques. Because the Cookbook cameras use your computer to control every operation of the CCD, you can very easily try these methods. Each method has certain advantages and disadvantages. As you become familiar with your Cookbook camera, you will come to prefer one of the methods.

3.1.3.1 Normal Image Acquisition

The simplest form of image acquisition is shifting each line down then serially shifting out the charge packet from each photosite. In this method, the total intensity is acquired. In the Cookbook 211 camera, the photosite intensity contains the dark current, the reset step, the reference voltage and the image charge. When you subtract a dark reference frame from raw image data, you are left with the image charge (converted to a voltage) plus random noise from various sources.

Operation of the TC245 is similar except the reset noise is removed by the internal double-correlated sampling circuit. However, we do not read the TC245 in the normal way because the rectangular photosites would produce a badly stretched image. Instead, we "bin" the signal in two- or three-photosite groups.

3.1.3.2 Internal Binning

By combining (or binning) adjacent photosites and adjacent lines together on the CCD chip, you can improve the signal-to-noise ratio and light sensitivity of your camera. However, for this gain you must trade off resolution and dynamic range of the chip. Increased sensitivity turns out to be extremely useful for locating objects prior to making an exposure.

Vertical binning is easy with the TC211 and TC245. When lines of data are shifted to the end of the image register, the electrons pile up unless they are shifted to the serial register. To bin two lines on the TC211 or the TC245 chip, you simply line shift twice to combine them and then transfer the combined line to the serial gate.

Horizontal binning is not possible with the TC211, and in the TC245, horizontal binning is limited to combining the three columns. Further binning of horizontal photosites can only be accomplished by adding the acquired data in your computer.

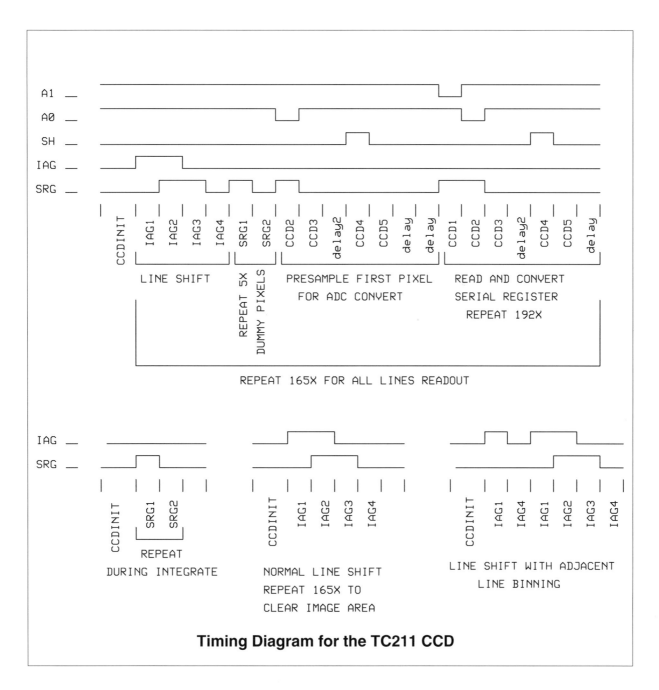

Timing Diagram for the TC211 CCD

Although internally binned images can be read out very quickly, multiple packets of charge are combined into a single charge packet that may saturate, overflowing the charge well and blooming. This objection notwithstanding, we have selected internal binning as the default method of reading the TC245.

3.1.3.3 External Binning

External binning, that is, binning data in software as an image is read, gives greater dynamic range than internal binning. This occurs because the unbinned serial registers do not saturate as quickly. However, because of saturation, the maximum useful exposure time with inter-

nal binning on the Cookbook 245 is about 5 minutes—but with external binning the Cookbook 245 can take exposures up to about 15 minutes.

External binning is normally accomplished by shifting a line consisting of photosite numbers 1, 4, 7, 10,... into the serial register, and then by reading out this line of 252 charge packets. After this line is read, the next column is shifted into the serial register and we read photosite numbers 2, 5, 8, 11,.... Finally the last column of photosites—numbers 3, 6, 9, 12, etc.—are shifted into the serial register and read out. This information is then sorted and combined externally, in the computer, to write

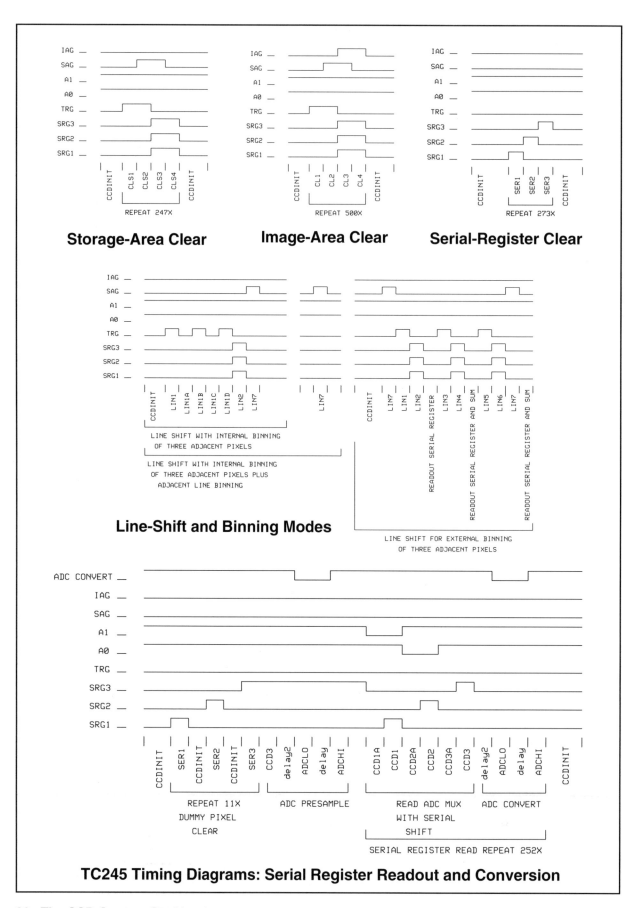

Storage-Area Clear

Image-Area Clear

Serial-Register Clear

Line-Shift and Binning Modes

TC245 Timing Diagrams: Serial Register Readout and Conversion

each pixel value into the proper place in the 252×242-pixel image array.

However, the line of photosites can also be binned into 378 pairs of pixels, producing a 378×242-pixel image with somewhat higher horizontal resolution than the standard format. Readout proceeds just as it does for normal external binning, but the information is sorted and combined differently in the computer to produce the 378-wide image.

The principal disadvantage of external binning is that is takes longer to read image data from the chip. However, because the readout time for external binning is only a matter of seconds, external binning is preferable to internal binning for faint deep-sky objects.

3.1.3.4 Combination Binning

Internal and external binning are combined in the Cookbook cameras to produce quarter-frame images for the finding mode. These binned images are *extremely* useful for finding objects; you can readily detect most deep-sky objects with finder-mode exposures a few seconds long.

Quarter-frame images from the Cookbook 211 contain the combined signal from four photosites. The image is 96 pixels wide by 82 pixels high. Quarter-frame images from the Cookbook 245 contain the combined signal from twelve photosites, for an image 126 pixels wide by 121 pixels high.

3.1.3.5 Double Sampling

A powerful method of reducing noise during readout is double sampling. Although the double sampling technique that we use in the Cookbook cameras does not remove reset noise in the TC211, it does remove many types of low-frequency noise. Noise is removed by subtracting the voltage reference signal from the photosite signal. Over the $20\mu s$ interval between sampling the signal and sampling the reference voltage, low-frequency noise sources remain constant. This mode allows you to operate the Cookbook cameras under adverse conditions, and under favorable conditions, to eliminate bias drift.

The Cookbook 211 and 245 designs both have double-sampling readout modes in their software. The Cookbook 211 has a "low noise" mode in which the reference voltage is read once, the charge packet is read twice, and the reference voltage is read again, for a total of four reads. In addition, the Cookbook 211 software supports correlated double sampling, a special readout mode that eliminates reset noise in the TC211 chip. Taking advantage of the correlated double sampling readout mode, however, requires changing components installed on the printed circuit cards.

3.1.3.6 Pseudo-Shuttering

The TC211 does not have a storage area. When you read out images of bright objects such as planets, you may

therefore see smearing of detail during the readout. However, it is possible to use the lower half of the TC211 to store an image. To do this, the image area is clocked very rapidly down by half a frame, and then read out slowly.

Because the storage area does not have a mask on it, sky background adds more signal to the planetary image, but usually too little to matter. To prevent blooming with bright planetary images, you may also need to use a filter to reduce the brightness of the planet.

In a variation on pseudo-shuttering, it is possible to clock out just part of the image. Such partial readouts can be used for focusing, where speed is important. It is faster to read and display only one fourth of the chip. Excess lines are shifted into the clearing register and the excess columns are shifted from the serial register without measuring the electron packets.

3.2 How the Support Electronics Work

Two circuit boards, the interface card and the pre-amplifier card, support the operation of the CCD chip. These cards have four primary functions: (1) passing timing signals from your computer to the CCD, (2) supplying necessary voltages to the CCD, (3) inverting and digitizing the analog signal from the CCD, and (4) passing the digitized signal to the computer. These functions are shared by the two cards. In this section you will see how the cards accomplish these functions.

3.2.1 Passing Timing Signals to the CCD

The computer commands the CCD through its parallel, or printer, port. The printer port operates at very high speed and thus can convey every operation that the CCD carries out. Text is normally sent to the printer using transistor-transistor logic (TTL) signals. Each byte of data that goes to the printer is sent simultaneously on eight wires of the printer cable.

The software uses each of the eight bits to control a single function, for example to clock the image area gate or the serial register gate. This is accomplished by setting the logic level on a particular output bit. To control the TC211, the IAG and SRG clocks previously mentioned are needed, plus three more signals to start the analog-to-digital converter chip and handle the return flow of data.

Because it is a more complex chip, the TC245 requires nine control lines: all eight data bits plus an additional device control line. The image area gate (IAG) and storage area gate (SAG) require two lines, and the serial register gates (SRGs) and transfer register gates (TRG) require four more. Two more lines are need to handle the return flow of data, and a ninth line is needed to start the analog-to-digital converter chip.

On the interface card, these signals go to a 74LS14 logic chip with Schmidt-triggered input gates. The 74LS14 inverts the signals, making "on" signals into "off" and *vice versa*. The signals from the 74LS14 chip travel through a short cable to the preamplifier card, where they

```
Clear image area of charge.
Set clock levels for integration.
    FOR line = 1 TO number_of_lines.
        Shift image down one line.
        Shift out dummy photosites.
        FOR serial = 1 TO number_of_columns
            Shift charge to detection node
            Digitize analog output.
            Transmit digital data to computer
            Store digital value.
        NEXT serial.
    NEXT line.
Display image on the computer monitor.
```

Here are the operations that the acquisition software carries out to obtain an image with the TC211 chip.

are used as inputs to logic chips on the preamplifier card. The clock driver chips on the preamplifier card again invert the data input, so that a logic low from the printer port reaches the CCD as a low-voltage state of the clock for the CCD chip.

3.2.2 Supplying Voltages for the CCD

Five voltage regulators on the interface card convert the ±15 volts from the power supply into the precisely regulated power that the CCD requires. These supply +12VDC and −12VDC, +5VDC, and −9.5VDC and +2.3VDC.

The +5VDC drives the logic chips and the analog-to-digital converter chip. The +12VDC supplies voltage references needed on both boards, and −12VDC supplies the A-to-D converter. The −9.5VDC and +2.3VDC are switched by logic chips on the preamplifier board to drive the IAG, SAG, and SRG gates.

3.2.3 Inverting and Digitizing the Image

When the CCD is in total darkness, the output signal from the chip is at roughly 4 volts and drops as more light falls on the CCD. As soon as the signal enters the preamplifier board, it goes to a transistor operating as a unity-gain voltage follower. This transistor exactly reproduces whatever voltage is supplied to it and places minimal load on the CCD's output amplifier.

The analog-to-digital converter chip, however, needs signals that become more positive for higher levels. The output from the transistor is passed to an operational amplifier that subtracts the 4-volt offset from the signal. You set the amount of the offset with the 15-turn potentiometer on the preamplifier card.

The operational amplifier is set up to work with a negative gain, that is, it inverts the sign of the voltage and multiplies it by the gain. Because the full-scale output range of the TC211 is roughly 1 volt and the full-scale output range of the TC245 is roughly 0.4 volts, the amplifier has a gain of −10 in the Cookbook 211 and −18 in the Cookbook 245. The analog output fed to the analog-to-digital converter therefore varies from 0 to +10VDC.

When presented with a signal between 0 to +10 volts, the AD1674JN returns a 12-bit number between 0 and 4,095, or 0000 0000 0000 and 1111 1111 1111 binary. The conversion takes about 10µs; that is, 10µs elapse before the proper binary logic level signals appear on the twelve output pins of the analog-to-digital converter.

3.2.4 Returning the Image to the Computer

Once the signal is digitized, it must be sent to your computer. Unfortunately, the printer adapter can receive only four bits at a time. On the interface card, a multiplexer circuit breaks the data into three 4-bit nibbles, and then each nibble is returned to the computer using pins 10 through 13 of the parallel cable to transmit the bits.

Under control of two input bits, each multiplexing chip on the interface card selects data from one of two inputs and sends the selected data to its output. The image acquisition program in your computer controls which bits are sent, and, therefore, which bits the multiplexer returns to the computer. As soon as the three nibbles have been received, the image acquisition program combines these bits into an integer between 0 and 4,095. Thus the computer receives a digitized output from one photosite on your CCD.

3.3 How Software Controls the Camera

The video applications for which the TC211 and TC245 CCD chips were designed require special circuits to generate high-speed clock signals. However, for the relatively slow readouts we use in the Cookbook 211 and Cookbook 245, a standard PC computer is capable of generating all of the clock signals and passing them to the CCD camera through a standard parallel printer port. Generating the clock signals is performed using a combination of assembly language and QuickBasic. The software included with the book is ready to run on virtually any IBM-compatible PC.

3.3.1 Controlling the Cookbook 211

To read an image from a CCD, the computer must generate appropriate signals for the different clocks. To drive the TC211, the computer must drive SRG and IAG clock input signals, the A0 and A1 digital data conversion

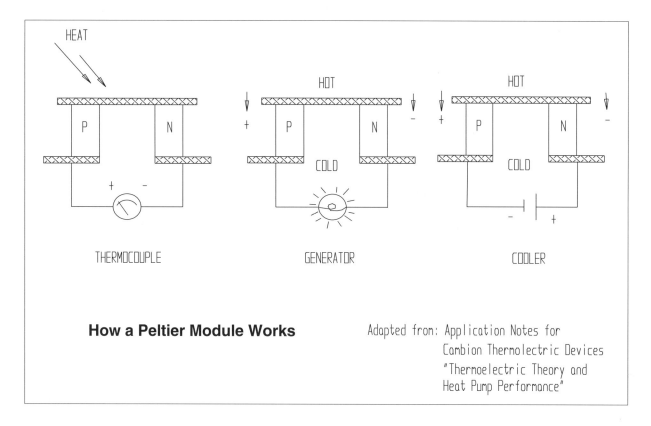

How a Peltier Module Works

Adapted from: Application Notes for
Cambion Thermolectric Devices
"Thermoelectric Theory and
Heat Pump Performance"

controls, and the SH line to start an A-to-D conversion.

To describe the complex sequence of events, electrical engineers use charts called timing diagrams. The timing diagram for the TC211 shows the state of the SRG, IAG, A0, A1, and SH lines at each instant in the readout sequence. In the software, each timing sequence has a software routine associated with it. Constants such as CCDINIT are defined in the assembly language driver. A lower-case constant such as delay2 represents a timing delay required before the next clock sequence can occur.

The TC211 chip requires only the IAG and SRG clock signals for readout, so the clocking for this device is relatively simple. The basic operation required for reading out and clearing the image area is a single line shift operation from the image area to the serial register. Clearing the entire image area takes 165 line shifts.

Once the image area has been cleared of charge, the IAG clock is left in a low state during the period of integration. Although the SRG clock can be left in a low state during integration, if the SRG clock is toggled during integration, you can reduce the electroluminescence from the amplifier. On the timing diagram, you will see that the SRG continues to toggle during the integration.

After the integration interval, the IAG line shift is used prior to readout of each line. For internal line binning, the IAG line can be toggled once more for each additional line binned. A normal line shift follows the line binning. After a line is shifted into the serial register, it must be shifted with six SRG clocks before the first charge

packet reaches the detection node.

In the control software, the readout loop must allow the amplifier time to settle and the analog-to-digital converter time to complete its conversion. Because today's computers are *so* speedy, the image acquisition program allows you to define the number of loops necessary to create the desired 10μs delay.

The software contains many other routines that make using the Cookbook cameras convenient and easy. See Chapter 9 to learn about operating the software.

3.3.2 Controlling the Cookbook 245

Operation of the TC245 chip is similar to operation of the TC211, except that both the image area and the storage area must be cleared before readout and the photosites must be binned during readout. The timing diagrams show these differences.

The image area is cleared by shifting the image down through the storage area into the clearing drain below the three serial registers. All of the CCD clock lines are left in a low state during image integration. Just prior to readout of the image area, the storage register is cleared of charge for good measure.

The image is shifted out of the storage area one line at a time and the serial register is read out much as the TC211 is read. The major difference is binning. To bin the three photosites internally, the TRG gate is clocked three times and this combines the photosites.

For external binning, three lines must be read out

and summed in the computer. Because the sum of the values from external binning can be three times the range of a single photosite, the sum is divided before storage in the computer's data array.

3.4 How the Cooling System Works

Cooling a CCD reduces the effects of thermally induced signal, or dark current. When the CCD is shielded from light, charge accumulates in the photosite and the photosite will become saturated, or filled with charge, after a period of time. The colder the CCD is, the longer it takes for thermally induced charge to fill the well.

The number of electrons that flow in the dark current varies randomly, so that even after you have calibrated the image by subtracting a dark frame, the random variation, called noise, remains. The greater the dark current, the higher the noise level, and the greater the variation in the pixel values.

Reducing the temperature of the CCD lowers the dark current significantly. This means that you can take longer exposures because it will take longer for dark current to saturate the CCD. To a good approximation, the dark current decreases by half for every 7° Celsius (12.6° Fahrenheit) drop in temperature. The table below shows the effect of cooling on the dark current relative to room temperature.

The Effect of Cooling a CCD Chip	
Temperature (°Celsius)	Dark Current*
+25°	1.0
+20°	0.60
+15°	0.37
+10°	0.23
+5°	0.14
0°	0.084
–5°	0.051
–10°	0.031
–15°	0.020
–20°	0.012
–25°	0.0071
–30°	0.0043
–35°	0.0026
* relative to room temperature (25° Celsius)	

Thermal noise is proportional to the square root of the dark current level. The dark current level depends on the temperature and the exposure time. Long exposures with low noise (and their corresponding low dark-current levels) can only be easily obtained by cooling the CCD to very low temperatures.

The table that follows shows how the theoretical noise varies for different levels of dark current. You can see that even though the r.m.s. noise level expressed in pixel values rises, the signal-to-noise ratio improves with increasing exposure. Doubling the exposure time improves the signal to noise ratio by the square root of two, or a factor of 1.4. Why is this? When we double the dark current in doubling the exposure time, we also increase the noise. It is a factor of square root 2, or 1.4 times greater. However, the ratio of the signal to the noise is increased by 2/1.4, or 1.4 times.

Noise versus Dark Current in the TC211		
Percent Saturation	RMS Noise (PV)	Noise Ratio*
10	2.6	1.0
20	3.7	1.4
30	4.5	1.7
40	5.2	2.0
50	5.8	2.2
60	6.3	2.4
70	6.9	2.7
80	7.3	2.8
90	7.8	3.0
* r.m.s. noise normalized to 10% saturation		

Noise reduction is also possible by averaging more than one image frame. The noise level is reduced by the square root of the number of frames which are averaged. Averaging two frames is equivalent to taking an exposure of twice the length or by reducing the temperature of the CCD by 7°C. (In actual practice, averaging multiple frames is somewhat less effective in reducing noise than making longer exposures because each readout contributes reset noise and amplifier noise as well as thermal noise.)

As a side note, the same principle applies to binning photosites. By binning three pixels in the Cookbook 245 camera, we obtain a square-root-3 better signal-to-noise ratio, or a factor of 1.7, compared to the same chip unbinned.

The bottom line is clear: cooling a CCD is essential to get the performance needed for astronomical imaging. However, we must be judicious in the application of cooling. Cooling too fast or cooling too cold can cause failure in the CCD due to differential thermal expansion of its materials. Our goal is not to see how cold we can make the CCD, but to cool it enough that sky fog rather than thermal signal becomes the limiting factor in setting our exposures.

3.4.1 Methods of Cooling

Several methods of cooling the CCD chip are available. These include mechanical refrigeration, liquefied gas or dry ice cooling, and TEC, or thermoelectric cooling. We selected thermoelectric cooling for the Cookbook cameras because cooling with a Peltier module is compact and economical.

3.4.2 How the Peltier Module Works

Heat is the result of particle motions within a substance. In a metal, heat is carried by electrons which can

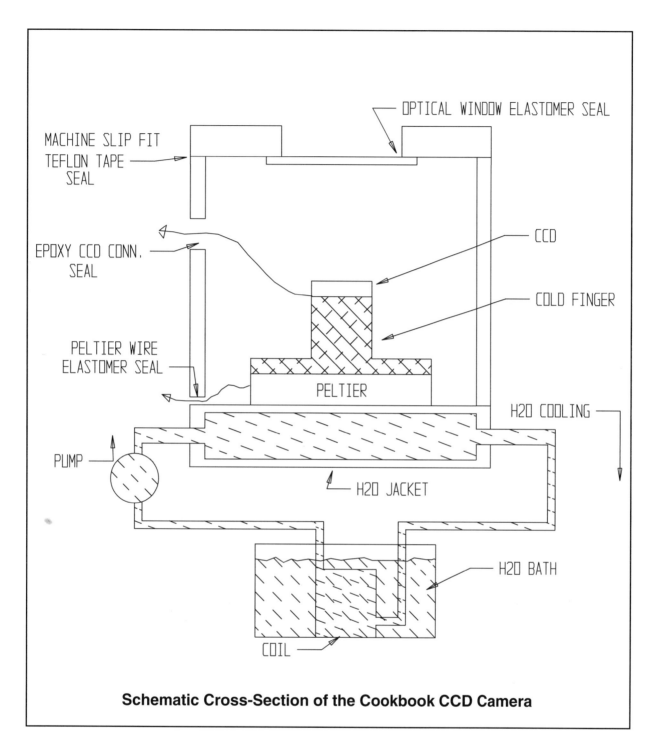

Schematic Cross-Section of the Cookbook CCD Camera

freely move about the metallic lattice. In a metal, heat is effectively caused by the motion of electrons.

Electrons are charged particles. If an uneven distribution of electrons is created in a metal, a voltage results due to the concentration of charge. One way to alter the concentration of electrons is by heating. If one part of a metal slab is heated, then the electrons at the hot end, having more thermal energy (that is, they're bouncing around more), move to the cold parts. Heat flows rapidly from the hot parts to the cold parts of the slab. However, before the slab comes to equilibrium, the charge imbalance produces a voltage difference between the hot and cold regions.

The energy of the electrons in different metals has a different average value. If two different metals are placed in contact, the electrons in the metal with the higher average electron energy move into the metal containing the lower energy electrons. As a result of the

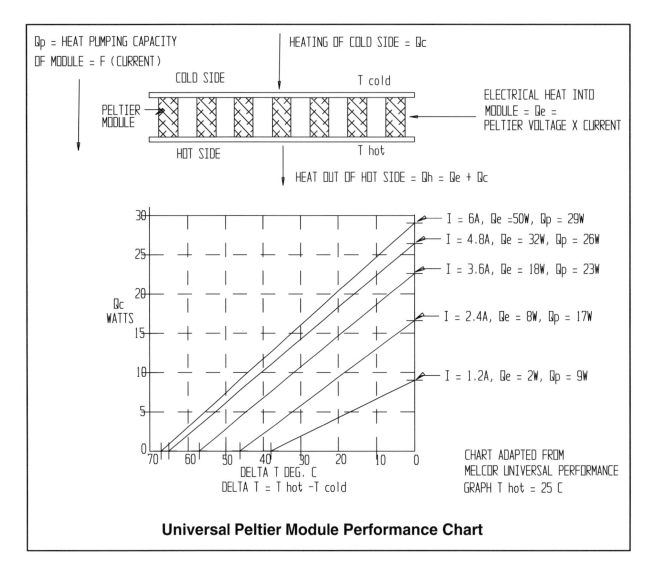

Universal Peltier Module Performance Chart

preferential motion of the electrons, a charge imbalance is created and a voltage appears between the metals. The motion of the electrons continues until the two metals come to equilibrium and the voltage caused by the charge imbalance balances the tendency of the electrons to diffuse into the higher electron energy metal.

In this balanced condition, a junction voltage exists and electrons continue to move back and forth between the metals in equal numbers in both directions.

If an electron goes from the low-energy metal to the higher, the junction voltage is in the direction that acts to speed the electron up. The faster electron bumps into electrons on the other side and transfers its energy to them. Similarly, if an electron goes from the high-energy side to the low, the junction voltage slows it down. It bumps into electrons which transfer their energy to it, and a net cooling occurs on the low-energy side of the junction because this lowers the average speed (or temperature) of the electrons on this side.

However, the system does not remain in equilib-

rium if an external voltage is applied to the two metals. When the external voltage is in the direction that causes electrons to move from the higher energy metal to the lower, a net cooling results. Similarly, a net heating effect is produced as the electrons transfer their motion to electrons on the other side of the junction. If the voltage is reversed, the net cooling and heating effects are reversed.

Commercial Peltier devices utilize semiconductor compounds such as bismuth tellurium compounds that enhance the effects. These are either N- or P-type semiconductors, depending on the manufacturer. In N-type, electrons transfer charge and heat. In P-type, holes (that is, places where an electron is missing from the crystal lattice) do the work.

The P- and N-type materials are connected in series. If one side of the junction is heated, a voltage appears across the device, and the device acts as a thermocouple generating a voltage proportional to the temperature difference. If the circuit is completed, with a load in series and the temperature difference maintained, a current

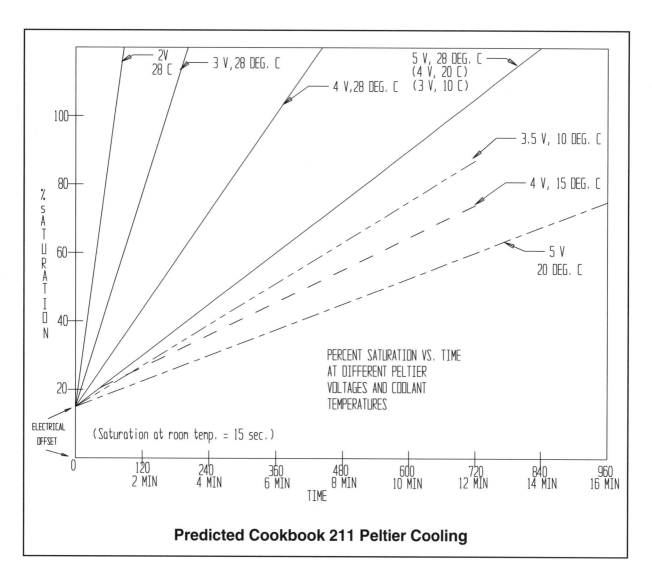

Predicted Cookbook 211 Peltier Cooling

flows and the device generates power.

When a battery is connected to provide an external voltage, one side of the device heats and the other cools. If the polarity of the battery is changed, the heat flow changes directions. In the Cookbook cameras, a Peltier device makes the CCD cold.

3.4.3 How the Cooling System Works

The Peltier device is extremely effective for cooling a CCD chip because it is compact and simple. When power is applied to the module, heat flow occurs. The heat pumping capability is related to the current applied to the module. For the Cookbook camera, we selected the Melcor CP1.4-71-06L thermoelectric cooling (TEC) module. In this Peltier module, current is approximately the supply voltage divided by 1.65Ω.

To maintain the desired temperature differential across the Peltier module, the heat input on the cold side must be less than the heat pumping capability of the module. Furthermore, the maximum temperature differ-

ential across the module can be no greater than about 67°C, even when there is no heat input on the cold side.

To make an effective cooler for a CCD, you must create a heat budget for the cooling system. The heat that flows to the hot side of the module equals the sum of the heat flow from the cold side plus Joule heating due to the power dissipated in the module. Joule heating increases as the square of the current flow.

In the Cookbook cameras, Joule heating amounts to several tens of watts. If this waste heat cannot be removed from the hot side of the module, the cold side of the Peltier will fail to cool the CCD because the temperature of the cold side is the temperature of the hot side minus the temperature differential of the module. In other words, to achieve low temperatures on the cold side of the Peltier, the hot side temperature must also be kept low.

We took the minimum storage temperature for the TC245 as specified by Texas Instruments of −30°C for our basic guideline. Dark current and thermal noise at this

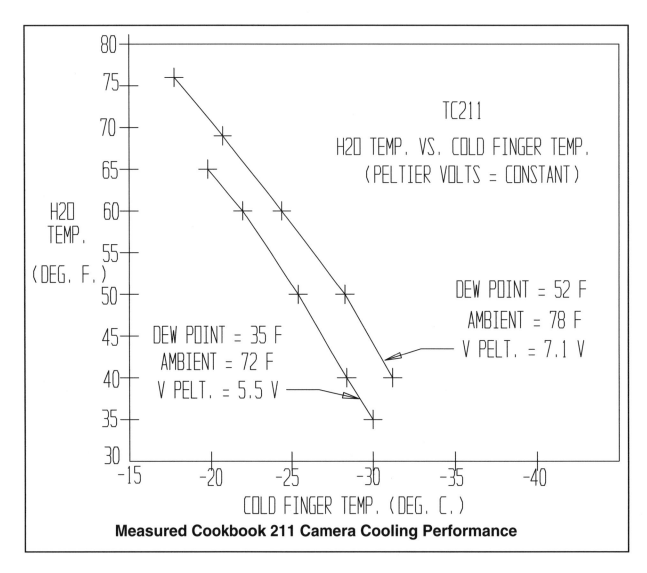

Measured Cookbook 211 Camera Cooling Performance

temperature are low enough for good astronomical performance but not so low that the CCD might fail. At this temperature, and under most skies, your exposure times will be sky-fog limited.

The Cookbook cameras employ a single Peltier module to cool the CCD to a temperature of −30°C under favorable conditions. After reviewing the alternatives—including convecting air and a forced draft of air—we selected circulating water to remove waste heat from the hot side of the Peltier. Water's capacity to absorb heat is far greater than that of air. To increase the temperature of one cubic centimeter of water by one degree Celsius takes one watt of power 4.2 seconds. Thus, a moderate flow of water can remove the heat generated in cooling the CCD and maintain a high degree of thermal stability.

Although it is possible to use an open circulation system, we opted for a closed-loop system. The circulating water contains about 30% isopropyl alcohol to control algae and bacteria. Heat from the Peltier cooling module

is passed to the water through an aluminum heat exchanger. To circulate the water, we found that a windshield-washer pump operated at a low voltage would suffice. Windshield washer pumps are readily available at discount auto parts stores. However, any small pump will work.

Heat is removed from the water by immersing a radiator in a water bath. The radiator is simply a coil of $\frac{1}{4}$-inch copper tubing. The coil is placed in a two- to five-gallon bucket filled with water. Although this much water heats very slowly, you can keep it constant, if you wish, by adding ice to the water at regular intervals.

The Cookbook cooling system is a "brute force" approach that works. The amount of heat generated by the module itself is a significant part of the total heat load. The cold finger and CCD chip contribute a thermal load of about 7W and the Peltier module contributes between 19W and 40W of heat, depending on the operating point of the module. In other words, to remove just a few watts of thermal loading from the CCD, we must remove three times as many watts from the cooling system. However, the system is simple, dependable, and easy to build.

Because of the large power dissipation in the Peltier module, it is important that you operate the system only when water is circulating. You can safely test the camera without water circulation providing the voltage on the Peltier does not exceed 1.5 volts. At higher voltages, the low-temperature solder in the Peltier module could melt and ruin the module.

Even with coolant circulating, the Peltier module has limitations which you should not exceed. The operating voltage must not exceed 8.6 volts and the module current must remain below 6 amperes at all times.

Because the entire camera housing is cooled by the heat exchanger, the temperature of the camera is regulated by the temperature of the circulating water. If the water is below the dew point, moisture may condense on the window at the front of the camera body. You can prevent condensation by keeping the coolant temperature above the dew point.

Condensation on the CCD itself may present a problem for some CCD cameras, but not for the Cookbook cameras. We determined that we could prevent frost from forming on the CCD by using a cold finger large enough to freeze most of the moisture in the air in the chamber. Because the camera body is airtight, once the moisture condenses on the cold finger, the CCD chip remains dry. Providing the housing remains airtight, no frost will ever form on the CCD.

Three charts presented in this chapter will help you understand how our system for cooling the Cookbook cameras works. Refer first to the table of Peltier Voltage *versus* Current, immediately below. Select a Peltier current from the table or divide the supply voltage you plan to use by 1.65Ω:

Peltier Voltage *versus* Current	
Peltier Supply Voltage	Current Flow through Peltier
2.0 volts	1.2 amperes
4.0 volts	2.4 amperes
5.9 volts	3.6 amperes
7.9 volts	4.8 amperes

Once you know the current, refer to the Peltier Universal Performance Chart. Construct a horizontal line representing the total thermal load, Q_c, which is 7W for the Cookbook 211. Where this line intersects the operating current you have selected, drop a vertical line and read

off the temperature difference, ΔT, that the module can maintain at that thermal load and current. For the TC211, this temperature difference is about 50°C.

The temperature of the cold finger is the water bath temperature minus ΔT. With a coolant temperature of +20°C, you can expect to achieve a CCD temperature of about −30°C.

The Predicted Cookbook 211 Cooling graph shows the percentage of saturation due to the CCD's thermal signal *versus* time for a variety of operating voltages and coolant temperatures. It is evident from this graph that you will be able to make your longest exposures on dry, cold nights when you can run the Peltier near its maximum operating voltage. Once again, please note that if you make the coolant colder than the dew point, moisture will form on the outside of your camera.

How cold can you make the CCD? Because the efficiency of the Peltier decreases as the hot-side temperature falls, you cannot easily "supercool" the CCD by pumping ice-cold water through the cooling loop. For each 1°C drop in the cooling water temperature, you will gain only about 0.4°C at the CCD. On a dry night that is well below freezing, you might reach −45°C.

If you want to measure the temperature of the cold finger directly, glue a thermistor such as Radio Shack's #271-110, with 10kΩ resistance at 25°C, to the cold finger. A calibration curve is supplied with the thermistor.

We tested one of the prototype Cookbook 211 cameras this way; the result of our testing is shown in the graph Measured Cookbook 211 Cooling Performance. The graph shows measurements for two Peltier voltages and a range of water-bath temperatures.

It is also possible to deduce the temperature of the CCD indirectly by monitoring the thermally generated dark current at various operating points. For example, if you know the dark current at room temperature, then from the fact that the dark current drops by a factor of two for every 7°C drop in the temperature of the CCD, you can estimate the CCD temperature from its dark current. This function is tabulated earlier in this chapter, in the Effect of Cooling on a CCD table.

For builders who wish to experiment with different cooling schemes, we advise first building the Cookbook camera with water cooling, and then carrying out cooling experiments on a second camera. Our experience has been that dissipating the heat from a Peltier module using convection or forced air cooling is far more difficult to achieve than effective cooling with water.

Chapter 4. Starting Your CCD Camera

First things first! Sage advice—assuming that you know what comes first. The purpose of this chapter is to help you sort through the tasks involved in building your Cookbook camera, and to help you get started.

Because the specific recommendations in this chapter may not apply to your situation, you are of course free to build your camera any way you want to. However, we ask that you take the time to read this chapter. Our goal is to help you build a working CCD camera, and the logic in this chapter reflects that goal.

4.1 Order Electronic Components First

To set the wheels of progress in motion, order the electronic components for the camera. Although most of the electronic components are common and readily available from a variety of electronics suppliers, a few are hard to find and sometimes have long delivery times. Before you can start, you need all of the parts. The lack of one key component could delay your camera for weeks or even months.

The toughest (and most expensive) parts to get are the Texas Instruments TC211-M (about $40) and TC245-40 (about $140) CCD chips, the Analog Devices AD1674JN Analog-to-Digital converter (around $25), and the Melcor CP 1.4-71-06L Peltier modules ($18 direct from Melcor, subject to $10 surcharge for orders under $100). The rest of the components are not only easier to find, but they are also less expensive.

Of course, the easiest way to obtain the parts is to order a kit. The publisher of this book, Willmann-Bell, has arranged for University Optics (see the supplier list in the back of this book) to offer a mechanical parts kit for the camera head. University Optics also plans to offer electronic parts kits and Willmann-Bell offers the circuit boards to buyers of this book.

If you wish to order the components yourself, we have provided a list of electronics supply houses in the back of this book. Because of possible delays , we suggest that you order the electronics early. Once these have arrived, you can proceed to build everything else for the camera secure in the knowledge that you've got everything you need on hand.

4.2 The Best Order for Building Parts

Once you have the electronic components on order, what comes next? For most builders, we suggest the following as the most efficient order:

Obtain parts for the power supply. Parts for the power supply are relatively easy to come by. For example, your local Radio Shack store should have everything that you need. If a few parts are out of stock, at least you have gotten the process under way.

Assess your computer. To acquire images with a Cookbook camera, you need a minimum of an XT-class PC-compatible with a standard VGA card and a monochrome VGA display. You will need about 30 megabytes of storage to hold a night's observing. Depending on where and how you plan to observe with your Cookbook camera, you may wish to obtain an old XT or AT for exclusive use in your observatory. If you have a notebook PC portable, be sure the display supports 64 shades of gray. For image processing, you will be happiest with a fast 386DX with a math coprocessor or a 486DX2.

Obtain metal for the camera head. Depending on where you live, getting aluminum may be easy or difficult. A trip to the scrapyard or a few calls to friends may suffice, but after a frustrating and fruitless search, you may decide to order a kit of finished mechanical parts from University Optics. If getting parts for the camera head is going to be a problem, you want to learn this early so that you have time to find or order the parts you need.

Construct the power supply. To assemble and test the electronics assembly, you'll need a working power supply. The power supply goes together quickly, and if you're new to electronics, it'll get you in practice for building and testing the camera electronics.

Purchase all remaining hardware. Here's where—as you search for tiny screws, brass fittings, and windshield-wiper pumps—you'll learn the whereabouts of things in your local hardware, plumbing, and auto-supply stores. Having all the parts on hand will save lots of individual trips later on.

Machine the camera head parts. Evenings in your neighbor's garage bent over a lathe, a weekend visit

Soldering circuit boards, electronics, machine-shop work–perhaps skills new to you. Approach them with a positive attitude and you'll be amazed by how much you learn and how easy they'll seem when you try them.

to a friend who owns a drill press, and watching intently as the milling machine skims the last 0.005 inches off the side of your camera's cold finger characterize this phase.

Assemble the interface and preamp boards. Everything is in place now to assemble your camera from a pile of parts. Assembling and testing the interface and preamplifier circuit boards takes close concentration, and because you test the boards as you build them, you always know that everything is on track.

Assemble the camera body. The project gains momentum as each night you complete a few more steps on the camera body. While epoxies cure in the kitchen oven, you can wind the coil for the cooling system, but your focus should remain on completing the camera head.

Build the cooling system. Finishing the cooling system may take as little as one evening's work. You'll need the cooling system operational for the upcoming bench tests and field tests of your camera.

Integrate the parts into a working camera. The time has arrived to clean up all the loose ends, collecting all of your previous work into a working package. You bundle loose tubes and wires into a cable harness, solder neatly labeled plugs to the ends of wires, and it's done.

Bench-test the camera. Although your camera is now ready to operate, it's best to learn the camera software and take your first images indoors where you can control everything that happens. You verify the camera's operation by imaging a target such as your wristwatch.

Begin observations with the camera. As the camera goes from "developmental" to "operational status," you become an amateur astronomer again. You discover first-hand that in a 1-second exposure your camera sees fainter stars through your telescope than you do. You realize that for you, amateur astronomy will never be quite the same.

Throughout the process of constructing your Cookbook camera, as you work on each step, you should be gathering the parts and materials for the steps that follow. That way, by the time you are ready to begin a new phase of construction, you'll have the things you need on hand. In the long run, working this way greatly reduces the potential frustrations in carrying out a complex project.

4.3 How Long Will It Take to Build?

Plan on spending roughly three months from the time you order parts for your camera until the time you

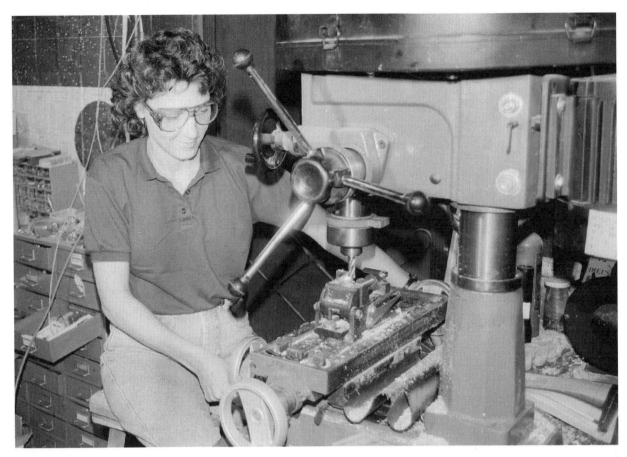

Betsy Kanto built one of the first Cookbook 211 cameras so we could take pictures and test the accuracy of this book's directions. In the process, Betsy added machining and electronics to her repertoire of craft skills.

make your first telescopic images. Some of that time will be consumed in waiting for parts to arrive and some in waiting for adhesives to cure and paints to dry. Some will be lost waiting for Saturday to arrive for taking the first excursion to the scrap metal yard, and perhaps some days will be lost before you have time to drive downtown to replace a missing 3-cent resistor.

If everything were to go perfectly, your total work-time on the camera would total about 50 hours. Of that time, about 15 hours would be machine shop work, 10 hours circuit construction, 5 hours building the power supply, 10 hours assembling the camera head, 5 hours making the cooling system, and 5 hours checking out the camera's performance.

Actual times required can easily be twice to three times these "straight shot" estimates. In the normal course of events, big stuff goes smoothly and *little* things eat up time. For example, suppose that as you build the printed circuit card, you accidentally solder a 220Ω resistor where a 22Ω resistor is supposed to go. No big deal!—except that when you remove the 220Ω resistor, you overheat the copper trace on the printed circuit card and it lifts a little.

After inspecting it carefully and putting in a phone call to a buddy who knows more about printed circuits than you do, you conclude that the lifted trace is not fatal and install the 22Ω resistor. You run the test sequence and everything checks out perfectly. Total loss: three hours of your time. Total gain: another job completed.

In planning your work on the Cookbook camera, don't forget that your spouse, your children, your parents, and your friends may value your company more than you realize. Even though you're working on a CCD camera, you should still talk to other people, go for walks, mow the grass, and generally act civilized.

The bottom line is simple: don't push too hard. Work carefully, work safely, and don't railroad yourself, your materials, or the people around you to complete your camera. (After all, it is a hobby!) Stay calm, take things as they come, and you'll move steadily toward your goal. Remember that you are working in an environment ruled by Murphy's Law, and most of the things that *can* go wrong *will* go wrong. Expect a few problems and solve them as they happen. Remember that—provided you are willing to pay with either time or money—almost anything that goes wrong can be fixed.

At the 1993 Midwest Astrofest, a prototype Cookbook 245 rode at the focus of Dave Otto and Dan Joyce's 20-inch f/4.5 Newtonian and made this 30-second exposure of the Omega Nebula. Image by Richard Berry.

4.4 How Much Will It Cost?

Your out-of-pocket cost for materials should be close to $200 for the Cookbook 211 and $350 for Cookbook 245, assuming that you have a reasonably good scrap box and friends who will lend or give you the odd bits and pieces you don't happen to have. If you have to buy absolutely every little thing plus a set of tools, budget another $200. If you buy a kit containing printed circuit boards and electronic parts, allow a decent profit for the merchant who saved you the time and aggravation of finding all the materials by yourself.

If you already have a small shop and a good scrap box, you'll spend less out-of-pocket because you won't need to buy many of the small tools. Should you count the cost of a pair of wire cutters and a crimping tool you'll have for the rest of your life? It's your call.

Pooling skills and resources with other amateur astronomers is perhaps the best way to keep the cost of a CCD camera under control. If you team up with two or three friends you can share the machining, soldering, testing, and have a wonderful time fretting and rejoicing over every setback and triumph. And you'll have access to the goodies in other people's scrap boxes providing, of course, that you're willing to share the resources of your own.

Will you succeed? Will your camera work? Is the money well spent? There is no way to guarantee it with absolute certainty, but as you work on your camera remember this: the Cookbook cameras were designed to be built with ordinary tools by people like you. Mechanical and electronic tolerances are loose and components are run well within design specifications. By testing every step of the way, you'll catch errors before they cause trouble. This book contains pictures taken with Cookbook cameras, so the design clearly works and each of the 12 prototypes that we built have worked.

Chapter 5. Building the Power Supply

The power supply provides power for all components of your Cookbook 211 or Cookbook 245 CCD camera. The power supply consists of three separate power supplies: power for the precision electronics, power for the Peltier cooler in the camera head, and power for the cooling pump. In addition, an outlet on the power supply box provides 120-volt power to operate a computer and telescope drive. This means that your entire CCD imaging operation can be (and for grounding purposes, *should* be) run with a single grounded power cable.

All components of the power supply can be housed in a wooden box that is 16 inches wide, 12 inches deep, and 6 inches high. Jacks on the sides of the power supply carry power to the various components of your Cookbook camera. An internal fan cools the heat-generating components inside the power supply.

5.1 What the Power Supply Does

For the precision electronics in the camera head and interface box, the power supply generates filtered +15 volts and −15 volts relative to the common, or ground, reference voltage. This power is regulated to the voltages that the CCD and the components on the interface card require and supplied to the preamplifier card in the camera head via a ribbon cable.

For the Peltier cooler, a regulated power supply provides up to 5 amperes current at a voltage that you can adjust. Increasing the voltage increases the amount of cooling that the Peltier cooler provides. In normal operation of the camera, you will slowly raise the voltage to a desired operating point. This prevents thermal shock to the Peltier module and the CCD chip.

To run the coolant pump, the power supply generates half-wave rectified and filtered DC power. As protection against running the Peltier coolers without coolant circulation, whenever the Peltier cooler switch is turned on, power is supplied to the pump.

The 120-volt outlet on the power supply should be used for all power needs on and around the telescope. This insures that all circuits share a common ground and guards against ground loops and other sources of noise.

5.2 How the Power Supply Works

If you are familiar with electronic circuits, the power supply will hold no mysteries for you. However, for those who are relatively new to electronic circuitry, this section explains how the power supply operates and should help you in constructing your Cookbook camera.

The power supply actually consists of three power supplies that make different "grades" of power for different purposes. In all three cases, a power transformer reduces the incoming 120-volt alternating current to 12.6 or 25.2 volts of alternating current. This current is then rectified to produce a DC voltage and filtered to remove most of the remaining "ripple" voltage.

(Throughout this chapter and this book, we will refer to alternating-current voltages as "VAC", i.e., 120VAC and 25.2VAC. Similarly, we will call direct-current voltages "VDC", as in 15VDC.)

Coolant Pump Power: The power supply for the coolant pump has the simplest circuit because the requirements are the least demanding. Because the pump can run perfectly well with "rough" direct current, alternating current from the center tap of one of the 12.6-volt 3-ampere power transformers (which also supplies the Peltier cooler) is passed through a diode. The diode, a 1N4001, blocks current flow in one direction while freely passing up to 1 ampere of current in the other direction. A 1000 microfarad electrolytic capacitor smooths most of the remaining voltage ripple; the result is a satisfactory approximation of direct current to power the pump.

(The units of current flow are amperes. We will refer to 3 amperes as "3 amps" or "3A." Thousandths and millionths of an ampere are shorted to milliamperes (mA) and microamperes (μA). The unit of electrical capacitance is the farad (F). Because the farad is a large unit, most electronic components are rated in units of 10^{-6} farad, or microfarads (μF); 10^{-9} farad, or nanofarads (nF); and 10^{-12} farad, or picofarads (pF).)

Peltier Cooler Power: The cooler power is the most sophisticated circuit in the power supply unit because it must provide a regulated and adjustable voltage. Two 12.6-volt 3-ampere transformers are needed to run

The power supply is a tidy box that provides all of the voltages that your Cookbook camera requires for its operation. You should even plug your computer and monitor into it, so that they share the camera's ground.

this low-voltage, high current device. (A single 6-ampere transformer could have been used, but the 3-ampere transformers are widely available standard parts.) Two 5-ampere bridge rectifiers provide ample power-handling capacity to convert the sine-wave alternating current from the transformers into full-wave rectified direct current output, and two 4700µF electrolytic filter capacitors then smooth away most of the ripple in the output voltage. The bridge rectifiers produce considerable waste heat, so for cooler operation they are attached to a large heat sink.

The regulator section uses an LM317T adjustable voltage regulator to produce an accurate reference voltage on the base of the large 2N3055 power transistor. The power transistor operates as an emitter follower to boost the current capability of the regulator. When regulating the filtered DC from the transformers, the transistor dissipates a great deal of heat and it must be attached to a large heat sink. The size of the heat sink necessary was reduced by dissipating some of the heat in two 1-ohm 10-watt dropping resistors. A 6-ampere fuse protects the power supply against accidental short circuits.

(The unit of electrical resistance is the ohm, abbreviated Ω. We will thus refer to a 10-ohm resistor as 10Ω,

to a 10,000-ohm resistor as 10 kilohms, or 10kΩ, and a 10,000,000-ohm resistor as 10 megohms or 10MΩ. If you want to sound as if you know something about electronics, in speech call them 10 "kay" and 10 "meg" resistors.)

Card Power: To operate the electronics on the interface card and preamplifier card, the third power supply produces filtered but unregulated +15 and −15 volts DC. Precision regulation to the voltages required by the camera driver circuitry is carried out on the circuit boards themselves, rather than in the power supply unit.

This supply is based on a 26.2-volt 450-milliampere center-tapped transformer readily available at Radio Shack stores. However, a 450mA transformer may not provide enough voltage for the Cookbook 245. You may either substitute a 1-amp transformer or add a second 450mA transformer and 1.5A diode bridge in parallel.

To add a second transformer, wire the primary side of the second transformer in parallel with the first transformer. On the secondary side, wire the center tap to the ground and the secondary outputs to the AC inputs on the new bridge. Connect the plus output of the second bridge rectifier to the plus output of the first bridge, and the minus to the minus. Unless you know how to phase transformers,

Building the Power Supply: Tools Required

For the case: Saber saw, drill and bits in sizes 0.109", 0.156", 0.203", $5/16$", and $1/2$" sizes, screwdrivers, hammer, staple gun, hole saw with 2" diameter blade (alternatively, you can use a saber saw), tin snips, and a table saw (which is nice but not strictly necessary).

For the electronics: Volt/ohm-meter, diagonal cutters, wire strippers, crimping tool, soldering iron, rosin core solder, #4-40 tap, drill and bits in sizes 0.078" (for the #4-40 tap), 0.109", 0.156", hacksaw, screwdrivers, mill file, sand paper, small adjustable wrench, needle-nose pliers.

Power Supply Parts List

For the wooden housing:

Plywood sheet 2 ft. by 4 ft. by $1/4$ in. thick

Plywood sheet 12" by 16" by $3/4$" thick

Four plywood strips $3/4$" by $3/4$" by 16"
    ripped lengthwise along grain

Hardware cloth, $1/8$" mesh

Box of $3/8$" staples

White glue or carpenter's glue

25 1" panel nails

25 #8 by $5/8$" pan-head sheet-metal screws

6 #8 by $3/4$" wood screws

2 $1\frac{1}{2}$" sheet rock screws

For the electronics:

2 12.6VAC 3A center-tapped transformers

1 25.2VAC 450mA center-tapped transformer

2 5A 50V bridge rectifiers

1 1.5A 50V bridge rectifier

1 1N4001 1A 50V diode

4 4700µF 35V electrolytic capacitors

1 1000µF 35V electrolytic capacitor

2 0.1µF ceramic capacitors (for the regulator)

1 0.1µF 50V film capacitor (for pump supply)

1 1500Ω resistor

1 100Ω resistor

1 LM317T regulator

1 red indicator LED

1 10kΩ resistor

1 0-to-1 mA DC meter w/10kΩ series resistor
    or 10VDC panel voltmeter

1 1kΩ potentiometer

2 1Ω 10W power resistors

6 Nylon binding posts

5 Five-terminal strips

3 Panel-mount fuse holders

1 Fast-blow fuse 6A 250VAC

3 Slow blow fuses, 250V: $3/4$ A, $1/8$A, and 1.5A

1 In line fuse holder

1 Muffin fan, 3.5" 120VAC

1 3" by 6" heat sink with TO-3 mounting holes

1 TO-220 heat sink for LM317T

1 Double-gang $1/2$" raised socket cover

2 115 VAC wall switches

1 Two-switch wall cover

1 AC outlet cover

1 6-foot length of 3-wire AC power cord

1 3-wire plug for AC power cord

1 Dual-outlet 115 VAC 3-prong socket.

12 $3/8$" nylon clamps

18 Solderless crimp terminals for 18-gauge wire
    Package of heat-shrink tubing
    #6-32 and #4-40 machine screws and nuts
    Ten feet each stranded and insulated wire:
        18-gauge white
        18-gauge black
        18-gauge green
        22-gauge red

you must use a second 1.5-amp bridge rectifier to provide isolation.

In these circuits, the bridge rectifiers convert the output of the secondary windings in the transformer to a full-wave rectified output. Because the center tap of the transformer is connected to ground, two full-wave outputs, one plus and one minus with respect to ground, are present. The internal resistance of the transformer is used with 4700µF filter capacitors to reduce the ripple on the plus and minus outputs to an acceptably smooth level for the voltage regulator chips in the camera circuit.

5.3 How to Build the Power Supply

You can think of building the power supply as consisting of four basic steps: constructing a wooden case for the power supply, installing the large components in the housing, wiring the AC power components, and installing the DC components. As you complete each construction step, you must test the power supply to insure that it is working properly.

5.3.1 Construct the Wooden Case

The enclosure for the power supply consists of a $3/4$-inch plywood base and $1/4$-inch plywood sides and top. The front of the case is the AC power panel; it has openings for two ordinary 120-volt switches that turn on the power supplies and a 120-volt wall outlet. The right side is the DC power panel; mounted on it are banana jacks that provide DC power. The left side is the fan panel, with an opening for a cooling fan. The vent panel is the rear side of the box; it has vents that allow warm air to exit.

You will cut openings for plugs, switches, or cool-

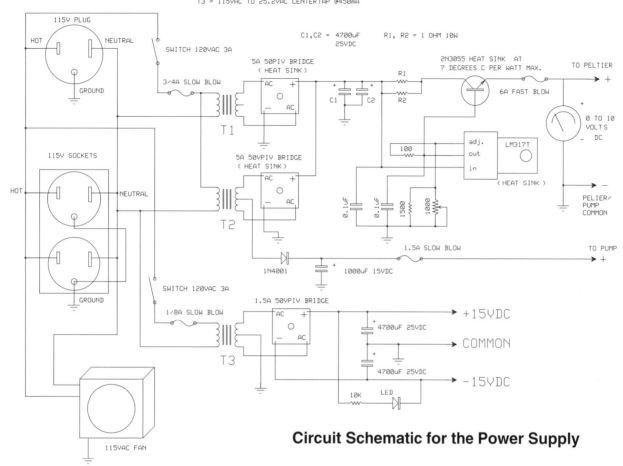

Circuit Schematic for the Power Supply

ing in all four side panels of the box. The top and bottom of the box have no openings. Most of the components are screwed to the bottom of the box. Thin strips of $\frac{3}{4}$-inch plywood along the tops of the side panels serve to strengthen the box and anchor the removable top- and rear-panel cover.

Begin construction by cutting the base and plywood strips from a sheet of $\frac{3}{4}$-inch plywood at least 16 inches wide by at least 15.5 inches long in the grain direction. Cut the bottom of the power supply to 12 inches by 15.5 inches, and rip four $\frac{3}{4}$-inch square strips from the remaining stock. The surface grain of the wood should run along the length of these strips. Cut two of these strips to 14-inch lengths and cut the other two 12 inches long.

Cut the side panels next. From a 2-foot by 4-foot sheet of $\frac{1}{4}$-inch plywood, rip one strip 12 inches wide and rip two strips 5.5 inches wide. Each of these strips will be 4 feet long. From the 12-inch-wide strip, cut one 15.5-inch length to be the top of the box. From one of the 5.5-inch strips, cut two 16-inch lengths to become the front and rear of the box. From the other 5.5-inch strip, cut two 12-inch lengths to become the sides of the box.

AC Power Panel: This panel carries two switches and one 120-volt power outlet, and it is the front of the power supply box. On the plywood, mark the centers for drill holes as shown in the plan drawing and also mark the positions of the holes for the plug and switches. Drill a $\frac{5}{16}$-inch hole for the power cord hole, $\frac{1}{2}$-inch holes for the two fuse holders, and starter holes for the plug and switch covers. Using a saber saw, cut the openings for the plugs and switches. Place the gang covers in the holes, mark the positions for screws, drill 0.109-inch holes for the screws, and attach the gang covers to the panel with $\frac{5}{8}$-inch #8 sheet-metal screws.

Using one of the $\frac{1}{4}$-inch plywood sheets as a guide for placement, mark a line $\frac{1}{4}$ inch down from the top of the panel on the inside surface. Mark another line 1 inch from the end of the panel. At the position indicated by the lines, glue and nail one of the $\frac{3}{4}$-inch by 14-inch-long strips with 1-inch panelboard nails. Apply the glue to the edge with the exposed ply. Set the AC power panel aside until the glue has fully set.

Vent Panel: The vent panel contains four screened holes that exhaust the cooling air the fan has blown in.

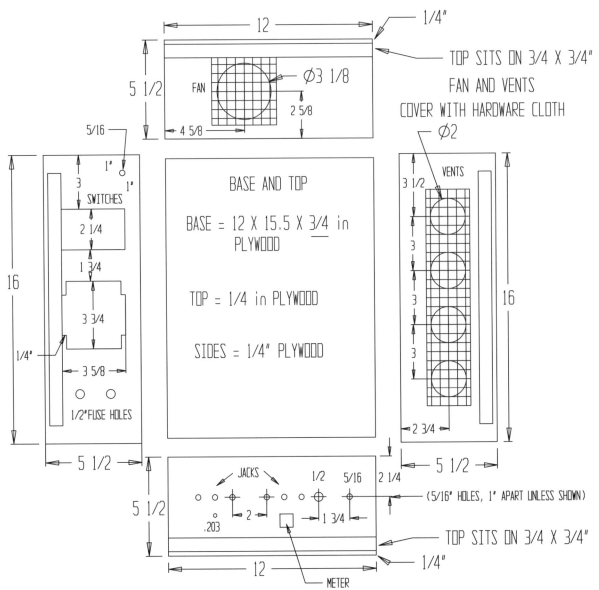

Power Supply Housing

Prepare this panel by marking a center line down the length of board. Starting 3.5 inches from one end of the panel, mark centers 3 inches apart, and then using a 2-inch hole saw, drill a hole at each location. Sand smooth the inside of each hole.

With tin snips, cut a 3-inch by 13-inch piece of $\frac{1}{8}$-inch mesh metal hardware cloth. Staple this material to the inside surface of the panel using $\frac{3}{8}$-inch staples. Hammer over the protruding ends of staples.

Complete the panel by marking a line $\frac{1}{4}$ inch down from the top of the panel on the inside surface, and mark another line 1 inch from the end of the panel. Glue and nail one of the $\frac{3}{4}$-inch by 14-inch-long strips with 1-inch

panelboard nails. Set aside the vent panel until the glue has fully set.

DC Power Panel: Jacks for DC power are mounted on this panel. From the plan drawing, mark the locations of each of the holes. You will probably need to adjust the dimensions shown on the drawings to accommodate your particular meter and potentiometer, and if your potentiometer has a short mounting shaft, to thin the panel around the potentiometer. If the potentiometer has a locking pin (this pin prevents rotation), drill a small hole off-center for the pin. Finally, attach the second $\frac{3}{4}$-inch by 12-inch long strip $\frac{1}{4}$ inch down from top and flush with the ends using glue and 1-inch panelboard nails, and set

Here you see the power supply interior with the first few components in place. Notice that the output jacks are clearly labeled on the inside of the box so that as you work you will clearly see where wires should go.

aside the panel until the glue has fully set.

Fan Panel: This panel holds a 3-inch muffin fan that exhausts warm air from the power supply. Refer to the plan drawing, and mark the hole for the fan. Drill starter holes, and using a saber saw, cut the opening for the fan. Cut a 3.5-inch square of $\frac{1}{8}$-inch hardware cloth and staple it to the inside of the fan opening. Position the fan over the center of the opening and mark the positions of the fastener. Drill holes 0.156 inch diameter for the screws that will hold the fan in place.

Complete the panel by marking a line $\frac{1}{4}$ inch down from the top of the panel on the inside surface. Glue and nail the second of the $\frac{3}{4}$-inch by 12-inch-long strips with 1-inch panelboard nails. Set the panel aside until the glue has fully set.

Assembling the parts: The completed box consists of two glued assemblies: the bottom with two sides and a front, and the cover and rear vent panel. This particular construction makes assembling the power supply reasonably convenient.

Glue and nail the fan panel and the DC power panel to the 12-inch-wide ends of the $\frac{3}{4}$-inch plywood base.

Attach the AC power panel to the front side of the base. Be sure to apply glue to the edges of the panels before you nail them to the base. Hold the upper end of the AC power panel to the two side panels by driving nails into the ends of the $\frac{3}{4}$-inch square plywood top supports.

Assemble the cover of the power supply box by nailing and gluing the top plywood panel to the vent panel. Center the 15.5-inch-dimension of the top on the 16-inch-dimension of the front panel. Set aside the cover until the glue is dry.

To hold the cover in place, drill pilot holes through the $\frac{1}{4}$-inch plywood top into the $\frac{3}{4}$-inch supports around the box, and through the vent panel into the $\frac{3}{4}$-inch base. Countersink these holes so that the heads of wood screws will be slightly below the surface of the panel.

You may wish to paint or stain the wooden box at this time, to improve its water resistance if you live in a damp climate, or simply to improve its appearance. Use a penetrating primer/sealer, and sand the surface lightly between coats of paint. Always allow paint to dry fully before applying the next coat.

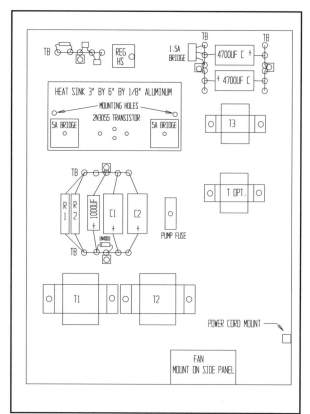

Here is the layout we suggest for power supply components, seen from above. Terminal boards are labeled TB. Jacks are at top; switches on the right.

5.3.2 Place the Large Components

Begin the assembly of the electronic circuitry by installing the plugs, fuses, switches, and meter in the front and side panels of the box. In waterproof marker, label each plug, switch, or fuse clearly on the *inside* of the box. You should also prepare neatly lettered labels for the outside of the power supply. If you have access to professional label equipment, the appearance of your power supply will benefit from the effort of making nice labels.

Examine the layout diagram and photographs that show the interior of the power supply. Placement of the components is not crucial, but you should place them to insure a good air flow. Drill pilot holes with a 0.109-inch drill and then fasten the three power transformers and two heat sinks to the bottom using the #8 sheet metal screws.

The fan and meter require #6-32 bolts and nuts to fasten the fan to the fan panel. If the fan has a metal case, use a #6-32 machine screw to connect a ground terminal. (If the fan has a plastic housing, this is not necessary.)

A commercial heat sink extrusion or a 3-inch by 6-inch sheet of ⅛-inch-thick aluminum work equally well as the heat sink for the large power transistors in the power supply. Support the heat sink with two spacers cut from ¾-inch-thick plywood, or with two right-angle brackets. Because the heat sink will have 12 volts DC on it, but sure to place it so that it will not come into contact with components other than the transistor and rectifiers you will mount on it.

Drill 0.156-inch clearance holes for the leads of the 2N3055 power transistor, and drill a pair of holes for mounting the transistor with #6-32 machine screws. Also drill two body holes in the heat sink and tap them with a #4-40 tap. Use #4-40 machine screws to mount the two 5-ampere bridge rectifiers. If you are using aluminum stock for your heat sink, sand flat the surfaces where the transistors and rectifiers will contact the heat sink.

Spread heat sink compound between the transistor and the heat sink. Fasten this transistor to the bottom side of the heat sink with #6-32 machine screws.

Spread heat sink compound on the bridge rectifiers. Thread #4-40x¾ machine screws from the reverse side of the heat sink, slip the rectifier over the threads, and then secure each with a washer and two nuts jammed together. Screw the heat sink to the bottom of the housing using two plywood spacers and two sheet-rock screws.

Mount the LM317T regulator on a small aluminum heat sink cut from ½-inch aluminum channel stock. Screw the heat sink to the bottom with a sheet-rock screw and bolt the regulator to the heat sink with a #4-40 machine screw. The heat sink is also at a DC potential, so it must remain electrically isolated from other parts.

5.3.3 Wiring the AC Components

The electronic components in the power supply convert 120-volt household current to the relatively low voltage direct current that your CCD camera requires. Because contact with household current is potentially lethal, exercise care in wiring and testing the power supply, and in using the power supply when it is completed.

For maximum safety, insulate exposed wires wherever possible. One of the most convenient insulators is heat-shrink tubing; to use this, slip a 1-inch length of tubing over the wire before you make the connection. After you have made and tested the connection, apply heat with a match or heat gun to make the tubing shrink tightly over the wiring. The key to success with heat-shrink tubing is to slip it over the wire *before* you make the connection.

5.3.3.1 AC Wiring Rules

It is crucial that you understand the rules that govern AC household wiring before you wire the power supply. The rules that follow apply to 120-volt AC power wiring codes in the United States. If you live outside the United States, or suspect that your household may not be wired to meet current electrical codes, seek competent advice before proceeding.

Carry out all wiring with the power supply unplugged. Remember: not only is the voltage on household

In point-to-point wiring, components jump from one lug to another. As you build the circuit, check off each wire in the circuit against its counterpart on the circuit diagram. What matters is making the right connections.

wiring sufficiently high to cause potentially lethal electrical shock, but the current available is sufficient to vaporize wiring in an improperly wired circuit. Work slowly and carefully, and at each step check your work.

The ground line: The ground line is intended to short hazardous voltages to the earth. Use green wiring for ground. On plugs and outlets, the half-round terminal is the ground pin. In all wiring that meets standards, ground terminals are marked green. Use your power supply only with grounded electrical outlets and grounded (three-wire) cords.

The neutral line: The neutral line is intended as a power return for AC current. Although neutral wires generally have no potential, the neutral line is *NOT* ground. High currents can cause a voltage to appear on neutral. Use white wires for neutral lines. On plugs, the neutral terminal is the wide blade, or if both blades are the same size, the silver-colored blade. Screw terminals for neutral use a silver-colored screw.

The "hot" line: The "hot" line is at a 120-volt potential. This voltage is present in the power supply box; correct wiring is important to ensure that this lethal potential does not appear on any of the low-voltage DC power

supply terminals. Use black wires for hot. On plugs, the hot terminal is the small blade or the brass-colored blade. The screw terminal for hot is the brass-colored screw.

Wiring to transformers: Transformers are generally marked "Primary 120VAC" on the AC power-input side. The AC power side generally has two black wires. One wire connects to the hot line through a fuse rated for the transformer's rating and the other connects to neutral.

It is essential to connect the 120-volt supply correctly to the primary winding of the transformer because if you connect the secondary winding to 120 volts, an extremely high voltage may appear on the primary windings. The secondary windings are usually marked, and among the wires exiting the secondary side you will see two wires of the same color. If the transformer has a third wire, it is the center tap of the secondary winding.

5.3.3.2 AC Wiring for the Power Supply

Use 18-gauge stranded wire for AC power connections. Connect wires to the outlet and switches with crimp lugs. Solder wires directly to the fuse holders, fan, and transformers.

Begin by wiring the power cord plug. (If you have

a cord with a molded plug, this step is not necessary.) Strip each of the wires in the 3-wire cord and connect it to the appropriate terminal in the AC plug. Pull on each wire to test that it is fastened well. Before reassembling the plug, inspect it to insure that you have wired the plug correctly according to color code.

Insert the free end of the cord through the power plug hole. Strip the cord back about 3 inches to expose the internal wires, and strip $1/4$ inch of insulation from the end of each wire. Twist the strands together. Insert the wire in the solderless connector and, using a crimping tool, crimp the terminal by crushing the metal end near the lug. After making the crimp, tug on the lug to ensure that you have made a sound crimp.

Feed the cord through the front panel until 6 inches of the cord remain inside the box. Clamp the cord to the bottom of the box with two plastic clamps. The clamps provide stress relief for the cord. Wire the cord to the wall socket that is in the box. On all wires that attach to the outlet and switch terminals, use crimp lugs.

Wire the AC lines one at a time according to the circuit diagram. Do not shrink-wrap or tape any soldered wires until the AC wiring is completed.

Begin with ground lines. Wire all of the ground connections, including the DC common points and the fan housing, to the ground connection on the plug. Use green 18-gauge stranded wire for the ground wiring. Test each of the ground wire connections to the plug with an ohm-meter or multimeter set to read resistance.

Next wire the neutral lines. Use white 18-gauge stranded wire for the neutral lines. Run a wire from the neutral terminal on the outlet to one of the primary leads coming from each of the three transformers. Run another wire from the fan to the neutral outlet. Use a crimp lug to attach each wire to the terminals on the outlet.

Wire the hot lines last, using black 18-gauge stranded wire. Hot-line power to the three transformers should be wired through the switches and fuses. From the circuit diagram, you will see that one switch controls power to the small 450 mA transformer and the other switch controls power to the two 3-ampere transformers. The second fan lead is wired directly to the hot line; the fan will run whenever the power supply is plugged in.

When the AC wiring is done, check your work. Place the AC fuses in their holders and measure the resistance of the circuits using an ohmmeter or multimeter. Between any two hot wires you should measure a short circuit (i.e., zero or very low resistance) except in that part of each circuit between the switch and transformer. When you turn on the switches, your meter should read a short circuit between any two points in the hot wiring.

Next, check for an open circuit (very high or infinite resistance) between the hot wiring and the ground and between the neutral wiring and the ground.

Between hot and neutral plug terminals, with both switches off, you should measure a resistance of around 200 ohms due to the resistance of the windings in the fan. With the 15-volt power switch on, the resistance should drop to a value that is typically between 12 ohms and 70 ohms. When you turn on the Peltier power switch the resistance should drop again, to a value typically between 4Ω and 10Ω.

If your wiring passes its resistance tests, insulate every exposed AC hot line and neutral line. If you have placed heat-shrink tubing over your wires, slip it over the exposed wiring and heat it. If not, wrap electrical tape over all soldered AC wiring. Although insulation is not possible on the switches and the AC outlet, cover the connections on the fuses. Covering the connections could prevent a nasty shock when you are working on the supply.

Tie all wiring neatly together and attach it to the bottom of the box with plastic cable clamps. This prevents wires from breaking due to flexure. It also prevents possible damage to the AC wire insulation from rubbing against exposed sharp surfaces.

Before you apply power to the AC circuitry, tape the secondary transformer windings securely to the bottom of the box. Make sure the wires do not touch and make sure the tape is strong enough to hold the wires in place.

Plug the AC plug into a grounded wall outlet. The fan should come on; it runs whenever the power supply is plugged in. Set the meter to the 200 volts AC (VAC) range. Measure the voltage between the hot and neutral holes of the outlet. As you handle the meter probes, take care that your fingers do not contact the metal probe tips. You should see a voltage from 110 to 125VAC—the exact voltage you will measure depends on the voltage supplied in your area—between the hot and neutral lines.

Between ground and neutral, you should see a voltage that is less than 10 volts. If a larger voltage is present, your house may not have a proper ground system, and you should have an electrician check the circuits. If you see over 100VAC, the socket is probably miswired.

The voltage between ground and hot should measure 110VAC to 125VAC. The voltage between ground and the two DC common terminals should be zero VAC.

Leave the supply plugged in and check the AC voltage on the transformer secondaries (the voltage between the two same colored output wires). The two Peltier 12.6VAC transformers should read from about 11VAC to 15VAC depending on the line voltage. The 25.2VAC transformer should read from 23 to 28VAC.

After you have performed the AC testing, unplug the AC power cord.

5.3.4 Wiring the DC Components

Wire the DC side of the power supply in two stages. In the first stage, you will wire the ±15VDC supply, the pump power supply, and the unregulated portion of the Peltier power supply circuit. These are relatively simple

When you have installed all of the components, your power supply will look something like this. You may wish to place parts differently in your power supply. Note that we had to tilt the large heat sink so it would fit.

jobs that you can complete quickly and then test for proper performance. In the second stage, wire the regulator portion of the Peltier circuit. Note that this supply shares a transformer with the pump power supply; if you test and verify the pump power supply in the first stage, you need not suspect the pump supply if you encounter problems when you wire the remainder of the Peltier power supply.

5.3.4.1 Wiring the ±15VDC and Pump Supplies

Begin the first stage of construction by screwing two five-lug terminal strips to the base near the output jacks of the ±15VDC supply, and one five-lug terminal strip near the pump and Peltier outlet terminals. Also install two terminal strips between the heat sink and the 12.5-volt 3-ampere transformers.

Translating the circuit diagram into actual wiring almost comes as second nature for some people but is difficult for others. The trick is to learn how to transform the junction points in the circuit diagram to solder joints and wires. If you are new to electronic construction, draw a picture of the circuit and sketch in the locations of the components. Trace and mark each wire on your sketch against the equivalent wire on the circuit diagram. When

the sketch and the diagram agree, construct the actual circuit. As you construct the circuit, it helps to mark off each finished connection on the circuit diagram with a colored pencil.

There is no "one way" to construct a circuit. If you are new to electronic work, the nest of wires that you are building may appear messy—but that's okay. Put your effort into checking that the connections are correct and into making good solder joints.

For the pump and Peltier circuits, solder the secondary leads from transformer T2 to the AC inputs on the closest 5-amp bridge rectifier. Connect the 1N4001 diode to the terminal board and solder the center tap of T2 to the anode (the non-striped end) of the diode. (The cathode is marked with a band; the anode is the other end.)

Connect transformer T1 to the AC inputs on the remaining 5-ampere bridge rectifier. (The AC input leads are usually marked on the case with a sine-wave symbol.) The exposed center tap wire should be cut off and the wire end covered with electrical tape to prevent shorting.

Connect the 1000μF electrolytic capacitor and the two 4700μF electrolytic capacitors, C1 and C2, to the terminal strip. The plus end of the 1000μF capacitor (which will be marked by a ring of plus signs on the capacitor) should connect to the striped end (the cathode) of the 1N4001 diode. Connect the minus ends of all the capacitors together with a bridge wire joining the lugs they are soldered to. Solder an 18-gauge wire between the minus output of each 5-amp bridge rectifier and the minus end of the capacitors. Solder an 18-gauge wire between the minus end of the capacitors and the common negative output jack for the Peltier cooler and pump. Solder a second wire from the cathode (the striped end) of the 1N4001 diode to one side of the fuse block, and connect the other end to the positive output jack for the pump.

Strap the two plus leads of C1 and C2 together by soldering a wire between the lugs to which they are soldered. Solder an 18-gauge wire between each plus output of the 5-ampere bridge rectifiers and the plus leads of capacitors C1 and C2. This completes the pump power supply and the unregulated portion of the Peltier circuit.

For the ±15VDC circuit, spread the four leads from the 1.5-ampere bridge rectifier and solder them to four separate lugs on the terminal strip near the ±15VDC jacks. Solder the two secondary outputs from transformer T3 to the lugs which connect to the AC inputs on the bridge. Connect the minus end of one 4700μF capacitor to the minus output of the bridge, and connect the plus end of the other 4700μF capacitor to the plus output of the bridge. Connect the free ends of these capacitors to a lug on the second terminal board and also connect the center tap of T3 to this point.

Solder a wire between the terminal lug to which the center tap of T3 is connected and the ±15VDC common jack. Solder a wire between the plus bridge output and the +15VDC jack. Also solder a wire between the minus bridge output and the −15VDC jack.

To tell you that the power supply is on, add an LED (light-emitting diode) lamp to the circuit. Solder a 10KΩ resistor to one lead of the LED and test the series combination across a 9V battery. If the LED does not light, switch the polarity of the leads on the battery. When the LED lights, note which lead is connected to the positive battery terminal and bend this lead to identify it.

Solder a wire to the free resistor lead and a second wire to the free LED lead. Insert the LED in the 0.203-inch diameter hole. Glue the LED and resistor into the box with epoxy or with hot-melt glue. Solder the positive lead from the LED to the +15V jack and solder the other lead to the −15V jack. This completes the wiring for the ±15VDC circuit.

Visually check all of the wiring to ensure all of the capacitors and rectifiers were connected with the correct polarities. Compare each connection you have wired and mark it on the circuit diagram with a colored pencil. If you find an error, correct it. Double-check the diode and capacitor polarities and make double sure that the capacitors are rated for a minimum of 25VDC.

5.3.4.2 Test the ±15VDC and Pump Supplies

To test the first stage in the construction of the power supply, turn off the power switches. Wear safety glasses during this test. (Don't be afraid; they are only a precaution.) Plug in the power cord and turn on both of the switches. Stand back a little and watch for capacitors which swell, hiss, or sizzle. An electrolytic capacitor that is installed backwards will probably vent hot gasses and may even explode. The process is fairly rapid; if there is no evidence of a problem after several minutes, you can be reasonably sure the capacitors are wired correctly. If a capacitor overheats, vents, or explodes, turn off and unplug the supply *immediately* to prevent a possible fire.

Your first positive indication that the supply is working will be the LED: when you turn on the switch, the LED should light.

Check the output voltages. Whenever you measure DC voltages, check the lead polarity. Always connect the red lead to the positive (plus) terminal on the meter. Always connect the black lead to the negative (minus) terminal on the meter. Always attach the common point on the supply to the black lead.

For the first stage testing, set your meter to the

20-volt DC range and measure the voltage between common and −15VDC. Your meter should read between −15VDC and −19.5VDC depending on the line voltage. Measure between common and +15VDC. It should measure between +15VDC and +19.5VDC.

Measure the voltage between the Peltier common and pump terminal. You should measure a voltage between 6VDC and 9.5VDC. Check the voltage between the Peltier common and the positive (plus) side of the Peltier supply 4700µF capacitor, C1. It should measure between 14.5VDC and 19.5VDC.

Turn the meter to the 20-volt AC range. Measure the same points as above. There should be no more than 0.2VAC on any of the DC outputs. If there is, one of the filter capacitors is not connected, has the wrong value, or is defective. Unplug the supply after testing. Inspect all of your solder joints to be sure that the capacitors are connected, and recheck the values of the capacitors. If the AC voltage persists, it will be necessary to replace the defective capacitor.

5.3.4.3 Complete the Peltier Supply

Once you have verified that the unregulated power supplies work properly, you can wire the regulated portion of the Peltier power supply circuit. Start by connecting a crimp lug to a length of 18-gauge wire. Fasten the lug to one of the #6-32 mounting screws that hold the 2N3055 transistor using another #6-32 nut, and run this wire to the terminal strip holding the minus end of the electrolytic capacitors C1 and C2, and solder the wire to a free lug. To this same lug, solder the two 1Ω ceramic power resistors. Solder the other end of the resistors to the plus end of the electrolytic capacitors, C1 and C2.

Do not allow the 1Ω resistors to touch any other parts because they become hot in operation. Leave plenty of space for air to circulate around them.

Solder a length of 18-gauge wire between the emitter of the 2N3055 transistor and the 6-ampere fuse holder. To identify the emitter, hold the transistor with the bottom facing you so that the leads closer to the mounting hole appear at the top; in this orientation the lead on the right is the emitter. The packaging also usually identifies the leads.

Wire the remaining terminal on the fuse holder to the positive output jack for the Peltier supply.

Mount the remaining resistor and capacitors on the terminal strip near the LM317 regulator. You need not use 18-gauge wire for the last of the regulator circuitry because it does not carry any heavy currents. Wire the ground for the LM317 and its associated parts to the common negative jack for the Peltier and pump.

The input to the LM317 should be wired to the plus leads of the electrolytic capacitors, C2 and C3. The schematic shows one end of the 100Ω resistor connected to the base of the 2N3055 transistor, but it's better to connect the resistor directly to the LM317 regulator and to run a single wire from the regulator to the base lead of the transistor. (View the transistor as you did above; the base is the lead on the left. The case is the collector.)

For normal operation of the $1k\Omega$ potentiometer— that is, to get a voltage increase when you turn the shaft clockwise—hold it so the shaft points away from you and the three lugs point up. Wire the left lug and the center wiper lug together.

Although a voltmeter for the Peltier supply is optional, it should prove very useful when you come to operate your camera, and it is strongly recommended. If you find an inexpensive milliammeter, use it as a voltmeter by connecting it across the power supply in series with a resistor. Determine the value of this resistor by testing the meter across a known voltage. The resistance should be roughly $22k\Omega$.

For a classy job, install a digital voltmeter. You may also wish to add an LED similar to the LED circuit on the ±15VDC supply to indicate when the power supply is turned on. Use a $10k\Omega$ resistor in series with the LED.

Double-check the completed circuit before proceeding. Retrace every wire and check every polarity. Your reward for taking care to check everything at this point will be proper operation the first time you apply power.

5.3.4.4 Test the Peltier Supply

For the second stage of testing, measure the DC voltage between the Peltier common and the positive Peltier output. Install the 6-ampere fuse and plug in the power cord. Observe the same precautions you did for the first stage testing.

Check that the voltage varies. As you turn the potentiometer, you should see the voltage rise smoothly from about +0.5V to about +7.5V. The voltmeter on the power supply should indicate the same voltage you see with your test meter.

Unplug the supply after you have completed your tests and attach the cover with the #8 wood screws.

Resist the temptation to apply power to the Peltier module until your Cookbook CCD camera is completed. If you apply power to the Peltier module without a proper heat sink, the device may overheat and fail. Wait until you have installed it in the camera head with a water-cooled heat exchanger removing waste heat.

However, if you want you can test the pump motor. It should run and, primed with water, show a nice flow. Remember that you are running a 12-volt pump at about half that voltage, so it can't power a fountain!

Of course, you will be using the ±15VDC supply in the next step, the construction and testing of the interface and preamplifier printed circuit cards.

Chapter 6. Building the Camera Interface

This section covers the construction of the two printed circuit cards used in the Cookbook 211 and Cookbook 245 CCD cameras—the interface card and the preamplifier card. The interface card is housed in a small metal project box, and connected by cables to the camera head, your computer, and the power supply. The preamplifier card is mounted on the camera head itself.

Constructing the interface card involves soldering electronic components to a printed circuit board, building a metal enclosure to house the circuit board, and installing the card in the enclosure with appropriate connectors. You will be aided in the soldering by a computer program, CARD.EXE, that is supplied with this book. CARD.EXE virtually guarantees that the interface card will function correctly by having you test the interface card step by step as you build it.

Constructing the preamplifier card involves soldering electronic components to a printed circuit board, again testing the assembly step by step as you build it. An assembly and testing program, PREAMP.EXE, is supplied with this book. Before you can build and test the preamplifier card, you must complete the interface card. (You will assemble the completed preamplifier card into the camera head and connect it to your CCD chip in the next chapter.)

In addition to the two cards and the housing for the preamplifier card, you must construct the cables that connect the cards to each other, to your computer, and to the power supply. By the time you have completed this chapter, you will have tested and verified the operation of all three cables and both cards.

6.1 What the Interface Card Does

The interface serves as the link between your computer and the Cookbook 211 or Cookbook 245 CCD camera head. It translates signals from the computer that tell the camera what to do into voltages that the camera-head electronics understand, and it converts the image from the CCD into a digital format that the computer understands. In addition, it contains circuits that generate voltages necessary for the operation of the CCD.

6.2 How the Interface Works

Your CCD camera has no "smarts" of its own. Software running in the computer serves as the "brains" of the operation. The software sends commands to the camera through the computer's parallel printer port; the camera acts as a slave to the software. This design allows us to keep the Cookbook cameras extremely simple.

However, the printer port was not designed to control a CCD camera. Its signals have the wrong voltages and the wrong signal characteristics. The interface card matches the printer port's capabilities to the requirements of CCD imaging. Specifically, the printer port interface card performs these four functions for the camera:

• Conditions digital signals from the computer's printer adapter. Conditioning involves removing noise and restoring the edges of the signals.

• By means of an analog-to-digital converter on the interface card, translates the analog signal from the CCD to a 12-bit binary representation.

• Breaks the 12-bit output of the analog-to-digital converter into three 4-bit segments for transmission to the computer. The printer adapter in the computer obtains the 4-bit binary number segments from the printer interface card in three passes.

• Generates regulated voltage levels from the unregulated ± 15VDC supply. These voltages are +5V for the digital circuitry, +12V, −12V and −9.5V for the analog circuitry, and +2.3V and −9.5V for the CCD clock drivers.

6.2.1 How Control Signals Reach the Camera

The Cookbook cameras use the PC printer adapter card as the control interface. The printer adapter sends control data to the camera and it receives CCD image data from the camera.

To see how we can use the printer port, let us first consider its normal application: to send character data to a printer using TTL level logic signals. The character data signals consist of eight individual data-bit outputs which form one byte of data. The eight bits for each byte of data are sent simultaneously as voltages.

Each TTL logic signal represents one bit and thus

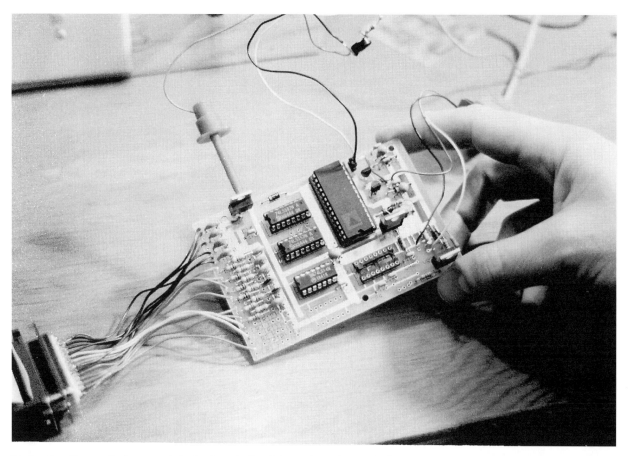

By testing the partially completed printed-circuit boards at the end of every construction step, you are virtually guaranteed that the boards will work perfectly the first time. Here you see the completed interface board.

may be either logic low (0) or logic high (1). The logic levels are defined thus:

Logic low is a voltage between 0.00V and 0.40V.
Logic high is a voltage between 2.40V and 5.00V.

When the printer receives signals from your computer, it senses the voltage levels from the signal cable. Most printers treat any voltage below 1.5V as a logic low level and any voltage above 1.5V as a logic high level.

Standard printer adapter cards use a 74LS374 chip, an octal D-type flip-flop device, to drive the eight data output lines that send information to the printer. The Cookbook camera printer port interface was designed to work with a generic PC printer adapter card that uses the 74LS374 device. Although most printer adapters will drive a CCD camera, there may be a few exceptions. During the assembly and testing of the card, you will test and verify the proper operation of the interface card. In a worst-case scenario, you may need to purchase a generic printer interface card to handle communications with your Cookbook CCD camera.

The printer adapter acquires output data through an I/O bus operation inside of the computer. The control program uses an OUT operation to place data on the computer data bus. An I/O write clocks the D-type flip-flop during the OUT operation. After the D-type flip-flop is clocked, it will hold the bus data and the outputs will not change until the next OUT operation is issued by the control program.

To prevent other devices from responding to I/O data on the bus, the computer uses an address selection bus. The D-type flip-flop on the printer adapter only acquires data when its select address is placed on the address bus. The address of the printer adapter can vary depending on the adapter card. The common printer adapter data port output addresses are:

| LPT1: | 378 hex |
| LPT2: | 278 hex |

You can use either port. If you have a monochrome video adapter card, the output port address of LPT1 is 3BC Hex.

The output signals from the printer adapter are found on a 25-pin female connector on the back of a PC computer. The electrical signals that represent eight data bits are located on pins 2 through 9 on the connector. As in all electrical circuits, the data bit voltage level is meas-

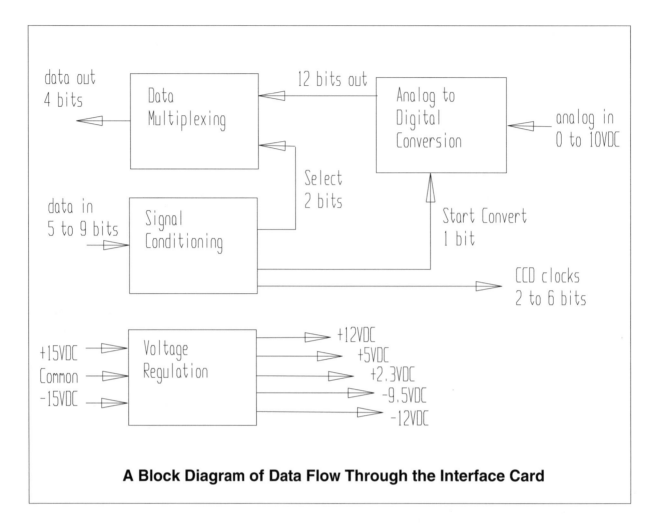

A Block Diagram of Data Flow Through the Interface Card

ured with respect to another voltage level. In the standard PC printer adapter, the reference voltage for the data output is the ground level, pins 18 through 25.

To communicate through the printer adapter, the control program must send data to the output port in a byte format. To simplify coding of the bit positions in the byte data, the bit weight is used as the logic one level for the bit data. The bit weights and the D25 connector pin relationships are given below:

D25 Pin	Bit Weight
2	1
3	2
4	4
5	8
6	16
7	32
8	64
9	128

To send a character, the printer adapter sets the voltage level on each of the pins. To send the character "A," which has an ASCII value of 65, pins 2 and 8 are set to the logic high level. The remaining pins (3, 4, 5, 6, and 7) are set to the logic low level.

To find what character has been sent, the printer sums the bit weights of the logic high levels. Pin 2 has a bit weight of 1 and pin 8 has a bit weight of 64. Their sum is 65, corresponding to the ASCII character "A." Thus a letter has been sent from your computer to a printer.

Let's follow one of the signals from the printer adapter to the camera printer port interface card. The data output from the printer adapter is usually connected to a ribbon cable that may be up to fifteen feet long. Although a wire which carries power can be virtually any length, a cable that carries logic voltage signals from the printer adapter is different because the voltages change so quickly. Most printer adapters can change from a logic one to a logic zero state in 60×10^{-9} seconds, or 60 nanoseconds, and some can change even faster.

When the printer adapter changes a logic level, the electrical transition from a logic one to a logic zero travels down the wire at approximately two nanosecond per foot. When it reaches the end of the cable, the signal is reflected back down the wire with a negative polarity, so that a 3.5V

Electronics for the Cookbook 211 Camera

Capacitors

14 0.1µF 20V monolithic ceramic
5 4.7µF 15V tantalum
3 22µF 15V tantalum
6 100pF 50V ceramic
4 0.001µF 50V ceramic
1 470pF 50V ceramic

Resistors

2 22kΩ ¼W
6 4.7kΩ ¼W
1 2.2kΩ ¼W
1 1.8kΩ ¼W
1 1.5kΩ ¼W
3 1.0kΩ ¼W
2 470Ω ¼W
3 220Ω ¼W
2 150Ω ¼W
6 100Ω ¼W
3 22Ω ¼W
1 15-turn 1kΩ pot

DIP sockets

2 8 pin DIP socket
1 14 pin DIP socket
3 16 pin DIP socket
1 28 pin DIP socket
2 10 pin lengths of 0.1-inch spaced terminal strip
(all DIP sockets are machine tooled solder tail)

Semiconductors

1 TC211-M CCD chip
1 AD1674JN 12-bit ADC
1 74LS14 hex inverter
2 74LS157 MUX
1 LF356 or LF 357 op amp
1 DS0026 dual MOS clock driver
2 2N2907 PNP transistors **(Plastic case only)**
1 2N3904 NPN transistor
1 LM336Z −2.5 voltage reference
1 7805T +5V regulator
1 79L12 −12V regulator
1 78L12 +12V regulator
1 LM337T negative adjustable regulator
1 LM317T positive adjustable regulator
5 1N4001 1 amp 50V diodes

Connectors

1 ribbon to D-25 male connector
1 ribbon to D-25 female connector
1 male D-25 solder cup connector
1 male D-9 solder cup connector
1 female D-9 solder cup connector
1 16 pin DIP component carrier

Wire

17 feet of 25-wire ribbon cable
24 inches of ⅛-inch coaxial cable
15 feet of 18-gauge speaker wire
15 feet of intercom wire (for ±15VDC)
21 4-inch lengths of #26 stranded, insulated
3 6-inch lengths of #26 stranded, insulated

Miscellaneous

1 Melcor CP 1.4-71-06L Peltier module
2 PC boards (make or obtain in kit)
3 ¹³⁄₁₆-inch PC-board standoffs
2 TO-220 heat sinks
1 D-9 plastic hood
1 3 by 5 by 2-inch aluminum project box
1 heat-shrink insulation tube
4-40 nuts and screws

---

signal is reflected as a −3.5V signal. In a 15-foot wire, a signal will bounce back to the source in 60ns.

Signals bounce back and forth through the wire loosing some of their energy at each bounce. The result is that the printer sees a damped oscillation about the final logic level. (This effect is called "ringing.") If the time for the signal to make a round trip through the wire is shorter than the transition time of the logic signal, ringing hardly alters the signal.

However, if the transition time is shorter than the ringing of the signal, the logic gate can respond to the ringing. Each time the signal bounces back, it may cause another logic transition from the logic high to the logic low state. In your Cookbook camera, these signals control the operation of the CCD chip. If the signal normally should cause the CCD to shift one line of data, ringing may cause it to shift twice or three times.

The solution to the ringing problem is to terminate the wire with a circuit that reduces the amount of reflection. By constructing the cable between the computer and printer so that each signal wire has a ground wire on either side, the cable becomes a transmission line with an impedance of about 115Ω. If the end of this line terminates in a circuit with a similar impedance, the signal is absorbed instead of reflected and ringing is minimized.

The termination network, which consists of a 100Ω

Electronics for the Cookbook 245 Camera

Capacitors

17 0.1µF 20V monolithic ceramic
 9 4.7µF 15V tantalum
 3 22µF 15V tantalum
 9 100pF 50V ceramic
 4 0.001µF 50V ceramic

Resistors

 1 39kΩ ¼W
 1 22kΩ ¼W
 8 4.7kΩ ¼W
 1 2.2kΩ ¼W
 1 1.8kΩ ¼W
 2 1.5kΩ ¼W
 3 1.0kΩ ¼W
 6 470Ω ¼W
 3 220Ω ¼W
 6 150Ω ¼W
13 100Ω ¼W
 4 10Ω ¼W
 1 15-turn 1kΩ pot

DIP sockets

 5 8 pin DIP socket
 2 14 pin DIP socket
 3 16 pin DIP socket
 1 28 pin DIP socket
 2 10 pin lengths of 0.1-inch spaced terminal strip
(all DIP sockets are machine tooled solder tail)

Semiconductors

 1 TC245-40 CCD chip
 1 AD1674JN 12-bit ADC
 2 74LS14 hex inverter
 2 74LS157 MUX
 1 LF356 or LF 357 op amp
 4 DS0026 dual MOS clock driver
 6 2N2907 PNP transistors **(Plastic case only)**
 1 2N3904 NPN transistor
 1 LM336Z −2.5 voltage reference
 1 7805T +5V regulator
 1 79L12 −12V regulator
 1 78L12 +12V regulator
 1 LM337T negative adjustable regulator
 1 LM317T positive adjustable regulator
 5 1N4001 1 amp 50V diodes

Connectors

 1 ribbon to D-25 male connector
 1 ribbon to D-25 female connector
 1 male D-25 solder cup connector
 1 male D-9 solder cup connector
 1 female D-9 solder cup connector
 1 16 pin DIP component carrier

Wire

17 feet of 25-wire ribbon cable
24 inches of ⅛-inch coaxial cable
15 feet of 18-gauge speaker wire
15 feet of intercom wire (for ±15VDC)
21 4-inch lengths of #26 stranded, insulated
 3 6-inch lengths of #26 stranded, insulated

Miscellaneous

 1 Melcor CP 1.4-71-06L Peltier module
 2 PC boards (make or obtain in kit)
 3 ¹³⁄₁₆-inch PC-board standoffs
 2 TO-220 heat sinks
 1 D-9 plastic hood
 1 3 by 5 by 2 aluminum project box
 1 heat shrink insulation tube
    4-40 nuts and screws

---

series resistor and a 100pF capacitor to ground, reduces ringing on problem signals with rise times less than 35 nanoseconds. Although a termination network is not required for printer ports with the slower rise and fall times, the network does not interfere. Furthermore, the network adds some protection against electrostatic discharge to the logic inputs.

The signal at the end of the ribbon cable has additional problems which make it unsuitable for use as a logic signal to drive the Cookbook camera electronics. Although the signal wires are separated by ground wires—and thereby partially shielded from other signal wires—crosstalk or noise coupling can occur between the signal wires. Also, the CCD chip requires clocking signals with rise times less than 35 nanoseconds.

To reduce the effects of ringing, crosstalk, and slow signal rise times, the interface incorporates a logic gate, the 74LS14, with Schmidt-triggered inputs. The 74LS14 is a hex inverter, which means the logic output level is high for a low-level input and low for a high-level input.

On the 74LS14 are six inverter gates. Starting with the gate output in a low logic state, the gate will not switch to a high logic state until the input voltage drops below 0.8V. It then switches in about 22ns, restoring the signal edge transition. However, the gate will not switch back to a low logic state until the input rises to 1.7V. (These

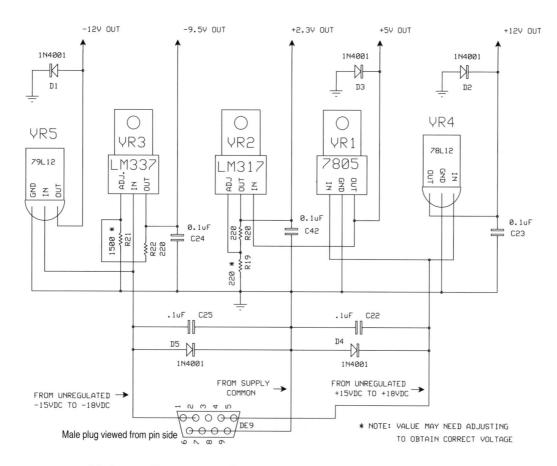

Voltage Regulator Schematic for the Interface Card

switch points vary somewhat from chip to chip.) When we raise the voltage above 1.7V, the gate switches to a low logic state, but it will not return to a high logic state until the input again drops to 0.8V. This effect is called input hysteresis.

Input hysteresis helps make the circuit immune to noise. Consider a signal which also has noise (i.e., a random variation in signal voltage) that varies 0.4V on either side of the signal level. When the input signal falls to 1.2V, the gate will switch to a high logic output because 1.2V − 0.4V = 0.8V. However, the gate will not switch back to a low logic state from the noise since the signal level plus noise is 1.2V + 0.4V = 1.6V. If input hysteresis were not present, then the logic gate would switch at a single voltage point such as 1.5V. In that case, the output of the gate might undergo several transitions from the noise as the input voltage swings past the switching point.

Each of the printer adapter data output bits is assigned to drive a different circuit in the camera. A summary of the function of each of the printer adapter pins is given in the Bit Designations table. The printer port data that comes from the 74LS14 chip is inverted and used as the input signal for the logic chips on the preamplifier

card. The clock driver chips used on the preamplifier card invert the data input yet again, so that a logic low from the printer adapter appears as a low-voltage clock level on the CCD chip. The control signals from the computer thus reach the appropriate pins on the CCD and cause the CCD to capture the astronomical images that you want.

6.2.2 How the Voltage Regulators Work

The power from the ±15VDC power supply contains AC ripple, and when the supply is loaded, the voltage varies. Voltage regulation is required to obtain stable voltages for the Cookbook camera electronics. The necessary regulation is provided by five voltage regulators on the interface card.

Two types of regulators, fixed and adjustable, are present on the card. Fixed regulators VR5, VR1, and VR4 produce −12VDC, +5VDC, and +12VDC, respectively. The two adjustable regulators, VR2 and VR3, can be set to put out virtually any voltage above 1.25 volts. VR2 is a positive voltage regulator and VR3 is a negative voltage regulator.

Although the regulators keep the output voltage constant, the wires that connect the regulated voltages to

Circuit Schematic for the Analog-to-Digital Converter

Nibble Selection

Data Port		Nibble Selected
b5	b4	
0	1	High
1	0	Middle
1	1	Low

Bit Designations

Bit designation in 12-bit word	Pin 1 select Level U3	Pin 1 Select Level U4	D-25 Connector Input Pin
MSB Bit 11	1	X	11
Bit 10	1	X	10
Bit 9	1	X	12
Bit 8	1	X	13
Bit 7	0	1	11
Bit 6	0	1	10
Bit 5	0	1	12
Bit 4	0	1	13
Bit 3	0	0	11
Bit 2	0	0	10
Bit 1	0	0	12
LSB Bit 0	0	0	13

X = Don't care logic level

Addressing the Data

I/O Base address (hex) = 278, 378, or 3BC
Data port address = I/O base address

Cookbook 211 Camera

Data port bit	Function	Data at Device
b0	SRG clock	not inverted
b1	IAG clock	not inverted
b2	ADC convert	inverted
b3	not used	
b4	U4 MUX select	inverted
b5	U3 MUX select	inverted
b6	not used	
b7	not used	

Cookbook 245 Camera

Data port bit	Function	Data at Device
b0	SRG1 clock	not inverted
b1	SRG2 clock	not inverted
b2	SRG3 clock	not inverted
b3	TRG clock	not inverted
b4	U4 MUX select	inverted
b5	U3 MUX select	inverted
b6	IAG clock	not inverted
b7	SAG clock	not inverted

Cookbook 211 and 245 Cameras

Status port bit	Function	Input Data
b0	not used	
b1	not used	
b2	not used	
b3	not used,	
b4	Nibble bit 0	not inverted
b5	Nibble bit 1	not inverted
b6	Nibble bit 2	not inverted
b7	Nibble bit 3	inverted
Status Port Address = Base address + 1		

Cookbook 245 Camera

Control port bit	Function	Data at Device
b0	ADC Convert	not inverted
b1	not used	
b2	not used	
b3	not used	
b4	interrupt enable	must be zero*
b5	not used	
b6	not used	
b7	not used	
Control Port Address = Base address + 2		

* This bit enables the internal interrupt in the computer. The bit is set low to disable interrupts on the printer adapter card.

the chips do not deliver a constant voltage to the device. The devices draw current in surges which have high frequency characteristics. The wires appear as inductive elements at high frequencies, and voltage transients are generated in response to the current surges.

To reduce their inductance, the circuit traces on the interface card are wide. Furthermore, capacitors have been placed across the traces from the regulators and ground to decouple the current surges at the source. Tantalum capacitors are used for this job because they have high capacitance and good high frequency properties. A small-value ceramic capacitor is used in parallel with each tantalum capacitor to extend the range of the frequency decoupling.

The action of a fixed voltage regulator operation is quite straightforward: you apply a voltage greater than the specified output voltage to the regulator and the specified output voltage comes out. If you apply +17.5 volts to a 12-volt regulator, you should get out 12 volts. Within their normal operating range, voltage regulators are wonderful.

Outside their normal range, regulators protect themselves and other circuitry by refusing to deliver too much current. For example, regulator VR1 supplies about 250mA of current to the Cookbook 245. Because the input voltage is 15VDC and the output voltage is 5VDC, the device dissipates 250mA times 10V, or 2.5 watts of power. The chip-to-ambient thermal resistance is 50°C per watt. This means the chip operates 125° Celsius above the ambient temperature. If it gets much hotter, it will not deliver the power that the TC245 requires. This regulator must therefore be attached to a heat sink to reduce its operating temperature.

The adjustable regulators, VR2 and VR3, are set with an external resistor network. The voltages are set as follows:

$$VR3_{out} = -1.25V * (1 + (R21/R22)) = -9.77V$$
$$VR2_{out} = 1.25V * (1 + (R19/R20)) = +2.50V$$

The voltage settings were designed to be somewhat higher than the required values of −9.5V and +2.3V. This allows you to trim the output voltages to the exact values needed in the circuit.

The VR3 regulator dissipates roughly 1.4 watts, so it is a good idea to attach a small heat sink to this device. However, neither the device tab nor the heat sink must touch the grounded metal case because the tab is connected to the input voltage for the device.

To protect the camera electronics against being accidentally connected to the ±15VDC supply incorrectly, diodes D4 and D5 are connected across supply inputs. Three additional diodes—D1, D2, and D3—placed across the three fixed regulators preclude regulator start-up problems and protect the regulators against probe slips during testing.

6.2.3 Digitizing Signals from the Camera

Data from the CCD passes through the preamplifier card and reaches the interface card as an amplified voltage with a nominal range of zero to ten volts. This information is converted by an analog-to-digital converter (ADC) to a twelve-bit binary integer that ranges from zero to 4095.

The ADC, an AD1674JN, is designed to interface to a microprocessor bus. The device is used in a stand-alone 12-bit mode that requires just one control signal to initiate conversion. When a conversion is completed, 12-bit data appears on the ADC's output pins.

A conversion cycle begins when the input goes from a logic high level to a logic low level on the read/convert-not line, R/*C. This ADC has an integral sample-and-hold circuit that samples the input voltage at the start of conversion and holds it stable for the conversion cycle. Internally, the ADC operates by making a successive approximations of the input voltage until the last approximation matches the input voltage.

When the conversion cycle is initiated, the ADC outputs change to a high impedance (high-Z) mode. This special logic state allows the converter to be attached to a microprocessor bus with other devices. Although it is not important in the Cookbook CCD cameras, you should be aware that the outputs from the converter appear as a logic high or intermediate level when the R/*C input is low. Accordingly, the outputs will pulse high during normal operation of the camera even with a constant input voltage. Following the high-to-low transition of the R/*C input, the conversion cycle requires 10 microseconds. Digital data appears on the output pins after R/*C input returns to a high level.

In the Cookbook 211, bit 2 ($2^2 = 4$) of the printer interface data output controls the ADC conversion. This line is inverted by the 74LS14 U2 chip, so the software uses a low-to-high transition to start a conversion. To read data, the computer raises bit 2 high and waits 10µs for the conversion to complete. The data is then sent through the multiplexer circuits to the computer. (Multiplexing the data is discussed in the following section.)

Operating the multiplexer and clock lines on the TC245 CCD chip requires all eight of the regular printer data bits. To start the ADC conversion requires finding a ninth bit; this is obtained from an output control bit on the printer adapter called the strobe-not, represented on pin 1 of the D25 connector. The control port resides at the data port address plus 2 and the data bit location is bit zero.

The strobe-not output differs from the other data outputs in the printer adapter because it has an open-collector driver. Although an open collector output can pull the signal to a logic low level, it requires a resistor to pull the signal to a logic high state. The output has a 4.7kΩ pull-up resistor and a capacitive load of 0.0022µF in the printer adapter. However, the rise time of the signal is slowed to 5 µsec. by the capacitive load. To speed the rise time of the output, a 1.5kΩ pull-up resistor, R1, is placed on the input to the 74LS14 inverter. Because the strobe-not output in the printer adapter inverts the data, the start convert sequence is a high-to-low transition. The slower rise time on this data line means that a delay of at least 1.5μs must occur before the strobe-not output returns to a low state. The control program generates this delay in the software.

6.2.4 How the Interface Returns Images

Once the voltage from a pixel has been digitized to 12-bit precision, this information must be sent to your computer. Unfortunately, because of the limitations of the printer adapter, only four bits are available to transmit a 12-bit number to your computer. To send the data, the interface card sends the 12 bits as three successive 4-bit transmissions.

Transfer of the 12-bit intensity data from the camera is accomplished by sending select data out of the printer adapter then reading the printer adapter status bits which contain the selected multiplexer data. The printer adapter uses pins 10 through 13 as logic inputs. On the interface card, a multiplexer circuit breaks the data into three 4-bit nibbles. (In the logic of engineering lingo, 8 bits make a byte, so 4 bits is half of a byte, or a nibble.)

The multiplexer circuit on the interface card is based on two quad 2-input 74LS157s. Each of these chips has four separate multiplexer switches. The switch selects data from one of two inputs and sends the selected data to its output. The multiplexer select lines are driven by inverters in the 74LS14 chip U2 connected to the printer adapter data bits b4 ($2^4 = 16$) and b5 ($2^5 = 32$). In this way, the multiplexer circuit is controlled by the control program in your computer.

If the select input to the chip is low, all four of the multiplexer switches transfer data from their n0 input to the Zn output (where n may be A, B, C, or D). When the select input is high, all four of the switches transfer data from their n1 input to their Zn output. By cascading two multiplexer chips, the circuit forms a quad 3-input multiplexer. The Nibble Selection table shows the relationship between states of b5 and b4 and which nibbles the multiplexer select will select.

With the data converted to 4-bit nibbles, it is sent to the computer. Although ringing is a problem in sending data to the interface card, it is far less critical on data sent to the computer. The outputs of the 74LS157 are capacitively loaded to slow down the logic level transition rates to about 150ns. Not only do the slower signals ring less, but they also reduce the amount of radio interference emitted by the wires. (As astronomers, we don't want to interfere with ham radio operators any more than we want them to leave their outdoor lights on all night.)

The computer control program reads camera data through the status inputs on the printer interface, available from the I/O bus address select for the status port. The address for status port is one greater than the data port address; that is, if the output data port address is 378 hex,

To solder parts to your circuit boards, you'll need a grounded 15-watt soldering iron and .032-inch 60/40 rosin-core solder. Each lead should take just a few seconds, and leave neat, clean, and shiny solder joints.

the status port input address is 379 hex. The I/O system status port read instruction, INP, returns a full byte of data even though it needs only the four upper bits of the byte. Because the printer adapter inverts the most significant bit of each byte, the program inverts this bit in the software and thus restores the original nibble.

With all three nibbles received from the status port, the control program combines the data to a 16-bit integer format. The high nibble and the mid nibble are AND masked with F0 hex to remove the lower four bits. Multiplying the high nibble by 16 shifts the nibble four binary places to the left. Dividing the low nibble by 16 shifts the low nibble four binary places to the right. Summing the three nibbles combines the data into the correct integer format.

6.3 Constructing the Interface Card

To construct the interface card, you will use the CARD.EXE software included in every copy of this book. CARD.EXE contains step-by-step instructions for installing the components and testing the interface. Because the program prompts you at every step of the way, the opportunity for error is greatly reduced. After you have completed the interface card, you can go on to construct and test the preamplifier card using the PREAMP.EXE program that is also supplied with this book.

The CARD.EXE program assumes that you will use the PC boards shown in the chapter. You can buy these ready-made, or make boards for your personal use only (they are copyrighted and as such you may not sell or give them away) from the artwork in this chapter.

Before you actually build the interface card, step through the CARD.EXE program several times so you are familiar with the program and the technical terms it uses. Set up a well-lighted static-free work area. You will need space in your work area for the power supply, a grounded soldering station, a volts/amps/ohms multimeter, all of the standard electrical tools, and, of course, your computer. Remember to wear a grounding strap when you work with electronic components.

6.3.1 The Printer Port Ribbon Cable

Although the CARD.EXE program prompts you to construct the 15-foot cable that connects your computer to the interface card, you may wish to build it ahead of time. Measure 15 feet of 25-conductor ribbon cable and cut it with scissors or wire cutters. (You will also need a 20-inch length of ribbon cable to connect the interface card to the preamplifier card.) Note that one side of the cable is marked on the insulation; this is usually the pin 1 side.

To attach the connectors to the cable, you will squeeze them between two pieces of brass shim stock or wood in a vise. (The shims are to prevent damage to the connectors.) Slide the ribbon between the cutter pins and the plastic backing plate. The marked side of the ribbon should be on the pin 1 side of the connector. Allow the end of the ribbon to extend slightly out of the connector and set the ribbon square with respect to the connector.

Press down hard on the plastic backing plate until the cutter pins push through the cable. Slide the assembly into the vise between the wood or brass shim plates and compress the assembly until the backing plate is flush with the connector. (If a vise is not available, you can compress the connector using vise grips.) Fold the cable over the back and compress the stress-relief clip.

6.3.2 The ±15VDC Power Cable

As with the ribbon cable, instructions for the power cable are in CARD.EXE, but you may wish to complete this cable in advance. Cut a 15-foot length of three-wire intercom cable. Strip the outer jacket back about 1.5 inches on one end. Strip off $1/16$ inch of insulation from each end of the wire and tin the ends of the stranded wires.

Solder three short lengths of 26-gauge solid wire across the solder cups of a female 9-pin solder-cup D-connector. Connect the following pins: pin 1 to pin 2; pin 4 to pin 5; and pin 6 to pin 7 to pin 8 to pin 9.

Solder the yellow intercom wire to pins 1 and 2. Solder the red intercom wire to pins 4 and 5. Solder the black or green wire to pins 6, 7, 8, and 9.

For strain relief, tie a knot in the cable about an inch below the connector and assemble the plastic hood over the connector.

From the free end of the cable, strip off 3 inches of jacket. Strip off $1/4$ inch of insulation from each of the wires and tin the wires. The wires will connect to the ±15VDC jacks as follows: the red wire to +15VDC, the yellow wire to −15VDC, and the green wire to the ±15VDC common.

6.3.3 Prepare the Interface Card Box

To prepare for the last step in the construction of the printer interface—placing the card in the box—you must first drill some holes. Make these holes and cut outs *before* you solder any components to the interface card. See the drawing titled Aluminum Housing for the Interface Card for the locations of these holes and openings in the aluminum project box.

Center the card on the outside bottom of the box with the solder side of the card facing you. Mark the positions of the three card mounting holes on the bottom of the box. Center punch the marks and drill the holes with a $9/64$-inch (0.141-inch) drill. Cut and drill holes for the D-connectors, and then use a nibbling tool to shape the openings.

A slot in the side of the box accommodates two ribbon cables and a coaxial cable that connect the interface card and the preamplifier card. Make this opening with a nibbling tool.

6.3.4 Building the Interface with CARD.EXE

Components for the interface card for each of the Cookbook cameras were listed earlier in this chapter. Assemble the components and tools in your work area. On the hard disk of your computer, create a directory containing the following files:

CARD.EXE
CARD1.EXE
CARD2.EXE
CARD3.EXE
PREAMP.EXE
PREAMP1.EXE
PREAMP2.EXE
PREAMP.HLP
CARD.HLP
BRUN45.EXE

You will also need to know whether you are using LPT1 or LPT2 on your computer for the printer interface card.

Run each test sequence in order. You will be prompted on which components to install. Take care when you solder because the pads on the printed circuit board are small. If you are new to electronics, check out Appendix B for tips on good soldering technique. It should take 2 seconds or less to form a good solder joint.

Some of the passive components require lead bending to fit. To bend component leads without stressing the

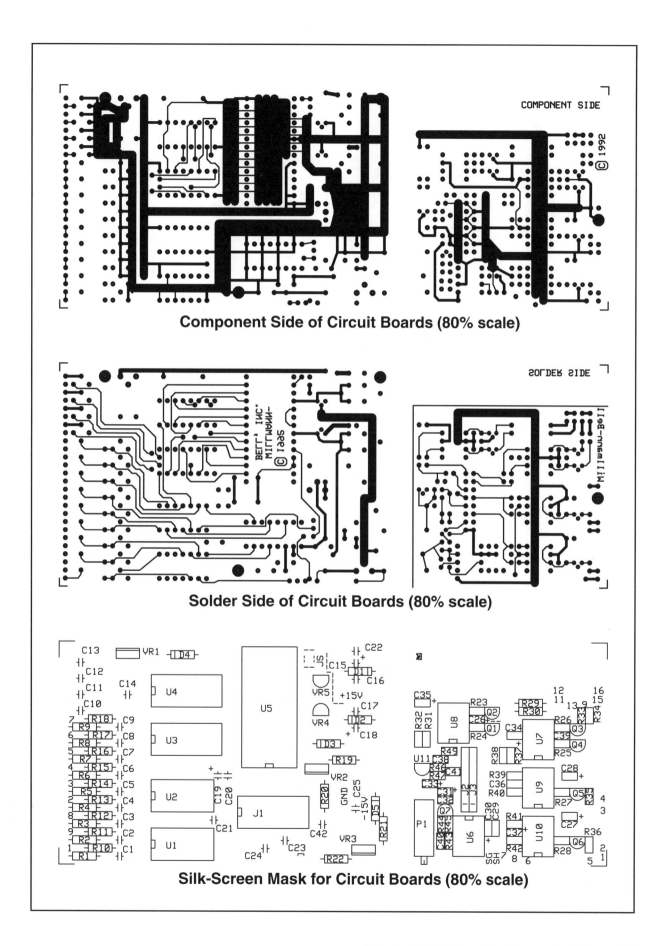

Component Side of Circuit Boards (80% scale)

Solder Side of Circuit Boards (80% scale)

Silk-Screen Mask for Circuit Boards (80% scale)

With CARD.EXE and PREAMP.EXE software to guide you, it's unlikely you'll make a mistake. But even if you do, you will catch and correct it because after each step you test the board. Result: an error-free board!

parts, hold the lead with needle-nose pliers close to the body of the component and bend the wire on the far side of the pliers. If you are new to electronic assembly, may have some trouble determining which parts are which. CARD.EXE aids you by specifying components by their color bands (for example, red-red-brown-gold identifies a 220Ω resistor) and numerical identification codes (102K designates a .001μF ceramic capacitor), and you will find a table listing resistor color codes in Appendix B.

First-time builders may find tantalum capacitors a troublesome component. These devices are polarized, that is, their plus side must always be connected to the positive potential. Tantalum capacitors can withstand about 10% of their rated voltage in the reverse direction—any more and they short out. The real trouble comes about because they may not short immediately if they are installed backwards. Instead, the circuit may operate perfectly through testing and then suddenly fail. Because shorted capacitors get very hot, you can detect the bad part by carefully touching each capacitor.

The only components with height requirements are the LM317, LM337 and the 7805 regulators. The tops of the regulators should be set about 0.75 inch from the card. The 7805 regulator needs to be perpendicular to the card. When you install the 7805 regulator in the box, you will use a small heat sink as the spacer. The LM337 regulator needs a heat sink but the heat sink must not be grounded to the case because the package is at a negative potential.

6.3.5 CARD.EXE Test Sequences

There are five sequences in the CARD program. These are (1) the resistance tests, (2) the regulator tests, (3) the logic level test, (4) inverter and MUX tests, and (5) analog-to-digital converter tests. When the card has passed all its tests, it is fully functional.

Sequence 1: Printer Port Interface Card Resistance. You are asked to stuff and solder the passive components, that is, to insert resistors, capacitors, and sockets and to solder each pin to the solder side of the card. The silk-screened mask on the circuit board identifies where each component should be placed. Three tests check that you have installed these components correctly. In Test 1 you check for correct wiring to ground and for correct resistances to ground, and you ascertain that circuits connected to ground through capacitors have high resistance.

As you step through the tests, if the measurement you make does not agree with the expected result, press the H key to summon a help screen. Suppose that a test step specifies that you expect a resistance of 450Ω, but you actually measure 240Ω. Press H. The help screen prompts you to check resistors R19 and R21. If these resistors have the correct values, you can proceed down a list of suggestions until you find the problem.

Test 2 asks you to perform resistance testing to the +5V supply line, and Test 3 steps you through continuity and resistance tests between pairs of circuit nodes, checking for wiring and correct resistance values.

Sequence 2: Card Supply Regulator Test. This short test sequence asks you to attach five voltage regulators and three supply wires the interface card, then prompts you to connect the wires to the power supply and verify that the unregulated voltages are reaching the card. You then check that the voltage regulators are working properly and making the proper voltages.

Sequence 3: Computer-to-Interface Card Logic Levels. In this sequence, the real interfacing begins. In a set of three tests, your computer will start to "talk" to the interface card. After you have wired the D25 socket to the card, you carry out Test 1 to check the continuity from each pin on the D25 connector to the card itself.

If you have not done so before, you must construct the power supply cable and the printer port ribbon cable. In Test 2 you connect your computer to the card and verify that the expected logic-level voltages appear on the card. This checks for the cable wiring from the computer to the card and for correct logic drive levels. Finally, in Test 3, you check the printer port data input path. CARD.EXE forces the input bits to a high and low state, and one by one, you verify that the correct voltages are present.

Sequence 4: Card Function Test #1, Inverters and MUXs. You now install the hex inverter chips and multiplexers in their sockets on the interface card. Test 1 is a powered test that checks for incorrect voltages at the D25 connector. This checks for any miswiring that could place an undesired voltage on the D25 cable. This test prevents the interface card from damaging your computer.

In Test 2, you check the logic level outputs from the 74LS14 inverters and trace the signal path to the J1 connector to the analog-to-digital converter input. Test 3 verifies that the input data path from the ADC socket through the 74LS157 multiplexers is correct.

Sequence 5: Card Function Test #2, Converter. You now plug the analog-to-digital converter (ADC) into its DIP socket and construct a test circuit—a simple voltage divider that lets you produce a variable input voltage—so that you can test the ADC. As you perform Test 1, you confirm that an input voltage to the ADC generates a digital output. Your work on the interface card electronics is complete when the card passes this final test.

6.3.6 Install the Interface Card in Its Box

When the interface card is done, install the three threaded standoffs into the bottom of the box. Align the card on the standoffs and mark the location of the 7805 regulator hole. Remove the card from the box and drill a $\frac{9}{64}$-inch hole. Carefully deburr all of the holes and openings, and then clean the box to remove grease and metal chips.

Mount the card on its standoffs. Fasten the D25 and D9 connectors in their holes with #4-40 machine screws and nuts. To do this you will find that you must bend the wires between the sockets and the card; take care that you do not break any of the wires in the process.

For the 7805 regulator, use a #4-40 machine screw to attach a small heat sink and the 7805 regulator to the box. Place the heat sink between the metal tab on the regulator and the box; use a flat washer against the regulator tab so that you do not bend it. Before bolting the tab, heat sink, and box together, apply heat-sink compound to the mating surfaces.

Attach a small heat sink to the LM337 negative regulator. If a standard size TO-220 heat sink is too high to fit inside the box, cut it down. The heat sink must not touch the box because it would short to the box. If necessary, you can make an adequate heat sink from a $\frac{1}{2}$-inch aluminum angle bracket—just make sure the mating aluminum surface is flat. Spread enough heat-sink compound between the mating surfaces to completely fill the tiny volume between them. The amount required is small; if more than a tiny bead of heat-sink compound oozes out, you've used too much. Wipe up the extra before it gets spread around.

6.4 Constructing the Preamplifier Card

You should construct the preamplifier card with the aid of the PREAMP.EXE software included with this book. (See Section 6.3.4.) Before you construct the preamplifier card, step through PREAMP.EXE so you are familiar with it. PREAMP.EXE walks you through installing the components and testing the card at each stage of assembly.

PREAMP.EXE program assumes that you will use the PC boards shown in the chapter. You can buy these ready-made, or make boards for your personal use only

When the interface board checks out fully, you can install it in its box. The board is held securely on small metal standoffs. The box does double duty because it serves as a heat sink for one of the voltage regulators.

(they are copyright and as such you may not sell or give them away) from the artwork in this chapter.

6.4.1 What the Preamplifier Does

The preamplifier card has two circuits: the clock driver circuits that drive the CCD chip and the preamplifier circuit that amplifies the raw signal from the CCD. To drive the CCD, the clock driver circuits convert the TTL clock signal levels from the printer interface card to the signal levels that the CCD requires. The CCD requires clock signals with voltage levels of −9.5V for the logic low level and +1.75V for the high level.

To minimize interference, the wires from the CCD to the preamplifier must be short, so the preamplifier card attaches directly to the body of the Cookbook 211 or Cookbook 245. The preamplifier circuit performs two functions: it removes the bias voltage from the raw signal and it amplifies the signal for the ADC chip located on the interface card.

6.4.2 How the Clock Drivers Work

The clock drivers generate voltage inputs that the CCD chip requires. These voltage levels differ from the TTL gate outputs on the interface card, and to further complicate things, each gate input on the CCD nominally requires a different voltage range. However, the levels overlap and a range can be defined for all of the gate inputs. The high-level clock input is defined as a voltage between 1.5 and 2.0 volts. The low-level clock input is defined as −9.0 to −10.0 volts.

The gate input clock levels must also switch rapidly between the states. The serial gates on both the TC211 and the TC245 CCD chips and the transfer register gate on the TC245 CCD chip should have rise and fall times of 15 nanoseconds, that is, they must switch between logic

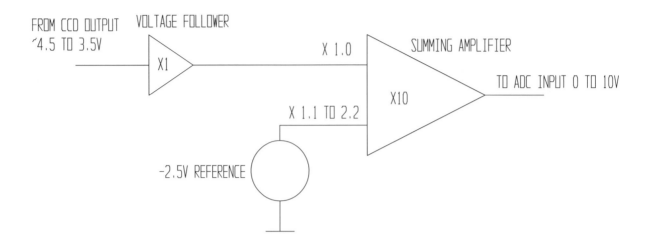

FROM CCD OUTPUT   VOLTAGE FOLLOWER
´4.5 TO 3.5V

X1

X 1.0

SUMMING AMPLIFIER

X10

TO ADC INPUT 0 TO 10V

X 1.1 TO 2.2

-2.5V REFERENCE

How the Preamplifier Works

levels in 15 nanoseconds. The rise time is measured starting when the voltage has covered 10% of the voltage difference and ending when it has covered 90% of the voltage difference. For your CCD to work optimally, its gate input clock levels must switch from −8.38V to 0.63V in 15 nanoseconds.

The image area gates and storage area gate should have typical rise times of 150ns and fall times of 90ns. The clock driver circuitry has been designed to operate with the proper clock timing parameters, so you need not measure the clock signal speeds. When you build the circuit according to plan, it works.

The circuit translates the TTL DC level to the CCD clock levels with a common-base level shifter and a MOS clock driver chip, the DS0026. Here the logic low input to the DS0026 is referenced with respect to the −9.5V supply instead of ground. The ground reference point is moved to −9.5V with a common-base transistor circuit formed with Q1, R30, and R24 on the card.

When a TTL low level (about 0.1V) is applied to the input-to-emitter resistor R30, transistor Q1 is in cut-off, that is, the emitter-to-base voltage is less than the turn-on point of approximately 0.7 volts, and there is no collector current. With no collector current, the input to the DS0026 chip remains at −9.5V. The output of the DS0026 chip is at 1.75V because the DS0026 inverts the logic state.

However, when the TTL input to R30 goes to a high state around 2.5V, an emitter current of (2.5V −0.7V)/R30 = 12mA is forced by the TTL gate on U2. The collector current and the emitter current are approximately equal

when the transistor is biased on with the TLL high input. The collector current generates a voltage drop across R24 and the DS0026 input, which can be modeled for the high input level as a 150Ω load tied to −8.3V. The 12mA of collector current pulls the input to the DS0026 up by 2.3V (to a voltage of −7.2V referenced to ground) and this drives the output of the DS0026 to −9.5V.

This clock driver circuit makes use of properties of the 74LS14 TTL chip (on the interface card) which are not defined parameters: this chip is not specifically designed to drive 12mA of current. However, we have used 74LS14 devices from different manufacturers and they have worked without problems.

The DS0026 devices are capable of switching faster than the desired rise and fall times on most of the gate inputs. The CCD gates appear as capacitive inputs and this slows the switching speed. The serial gates have small capacitances which vary from 25pF for the TC211 to 120pF for the TC245. To counter this, we use series resistances and RC networks. The series resistance helps to damp ringing and overshoot on the clock signals.

The capacitance of the image area gate is higher than the serial gate capacitance. The TC211 has a gate capacitance of 1600pF, and the TC245 has gate capacitances of 6400pF for the image area and 6800pF for the storage area. Although a single gate on the DS0026 can drive the image area gate on the TC211, the DS0026 must provide almost an ampere of current when switching the image area gate on the TC245. To provide the potential for larger chips such as the TC241, and to improve the switching waveforms, two gates work in parallel to switch the image area and storage area gates.

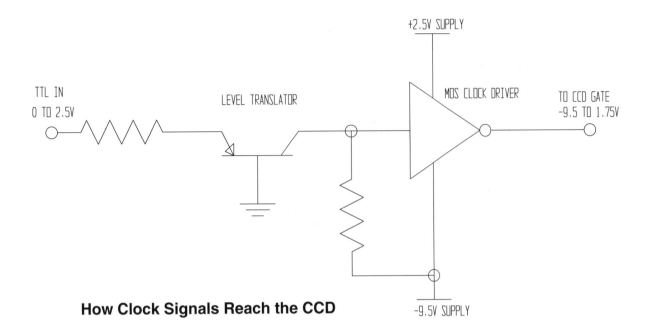

+2.5V SUPPLY

TTL IN
0 TO 2.5V

LEVEL TRANSLATOR

MOS CLOCK DRIVER

TO CCD GATE
-9.5 TO 1.75V

-9.5V SUPPLY

How Clock Signals Reach the CCD

6.4.3 How the Preamplifier Works

The output signal from the CCD becomes more negative as the image signal increases, but the ADC needs image signals which are more positive for higher light levels. Furthermore, the output signal from the chip has a DC bias level of about 4 volts. To buffer the raw signal from the CCD chip, the preamplifier uses a unity-gain voltage follower, transistor Q7. To send a correct signal to the ADC, an operational amplifier, U6, inverts the CCD signal and subtracts the voltage offset.

The output from the CCD chip is buffered by a unity-gain voltage follower, transistor Q7. The transistor serves two functions. The first is to lower the output impedance of the CCD from 700Ω to about 10Ω. This allows you to have a second amplifier stage with a low input impedance. Q7's base-to-emitter drop of 0.7V also provides some level translation of the output signal. Although its base-to-emitter voltage increases about 2mV for each 1 degree Celsius drop in temperature, the temperature of this transistor is fairly stable because the camera housing is water cooled. The transistor temperature drift is less than that of the CCD chip, and it is in the opposite direction of the CCD drift. As a result, they tend to compensate.

The TC211 and the TC245 chips generate a signal of about 4µV for each electron. From the TC211, the maximum useful voltage output is about 1V, and from the TC245, about 0.5 volts due to the smaller pixel size. To yield the maximum dynamic range, we kept the amplifier gain as low as possible.

The gain of the U6 amplifier is set with the ratios of R43/R45. For the TC211, we used a gain of −10. R43 is 22kΩ and R45 is a 2.2kΩ resistor. For the TC245 chip, we used a gain of −17.73. R45 is the same, and R43 is a 39kΩ resistor.

Maintaining the largest possible dynamic range is particularly important with the TC211 to allow for subtraction of its electroluminescence and to allow measurement of its reset voltage, which is about 100mV lower than the dark level.

The DC offset is subtracted from the CCD output by placing a reference voltage at the second input to the operational amplifier. This voltage comes from a circuit that includes a resistor, R44, and a potentiometer, P1, connected to a stable −2.5V reference voltage from U11. Changing P1 adjusts the offset level. The range of adjustment is the reference voltage times the ratio of resistor R45 to the P1-plus-R44 combination, that is, from 5.5V to 2.75V. Taking into account the base-to-emitter drop of Q7, this circuit can zero voltage offsets between 6.1V and 3.5 volts.

The U11 reference voltage circuit operates like a Zener reference diode. Resistor R47 provides 7mA of current from the −9.5V supply. To reduce high frequency noise on the −2.5V reference, U11 is decoupled with tantalum capacitor C33 and C40. Both the TC211 and the TC245 chips require a −2.5V level applied to the anti-blooming gate. This voltage is conveniently supplied by the same reference circuit.

6.5 Assembling the Preamplifier Card

Continue working in the same well-lighted static-

The interface box protects the circuitry inside from mechanical damage and electrical noise, and provides a solid place to plug in the power wire and the ribbon cable from the computer. It's not beautiful–but it works!

free area that you have used for the interface card. As before, you must have your computer in the work area to run the PREAMP.EXE test software.

Remember to wear your grounding strap. As you complete the preamplifier, you will connect it to the interface card through three cables. If you construct these cables before they are required, you will complete the preamplifier more efficiently.

6.5.1 Construct Connectors and Cables

A special plug mounted on the preamplifier card connects the card to the CCD, and three short cables connect the preamplifier card to the interface card. You should prepare the J2/J3 plug and solder it to the card before you solder any other components to the preamplifier card.

Two of the connecting cables are eight-conductor ribbon cables that connect to the J1 socket on the interface board, and the third is the coaxial cable, JS. The ribbon cables carry timing signals and power from the interface

card to the preamplifier, and the coaxial cable returns the CCD signal from the preamplifier to the interface card. In addition, you will need to construct a simple test circuit to supply a voltage to the input transistor Q7.

Because they are fussy and time-consuming to construct, prepare the socket and cables before you begin work on the preamplifier card itself. Having the socket and cables ready when you are ready will speed you through the construction of the card.

The J2/J3 Plug: To build the J2/J3 plug, break off two 8-pin lengths of the 0.1-inch spaced solder tail machine tooled sockets. Cut sixteen $\frac{3}{4}$-inch lengths of 26 gauge solid wire (the trimmed-off leads from resistors are perfect for this job) and insert the wires into the sockets of the strips. Solder the wires into the sockets. Apply as little heat as you can because the plastic socket material melts quickly. Do not get any solder on the gold plated solder tails because these tails form the plugs. Clean residual flux off the tails with alcohol.

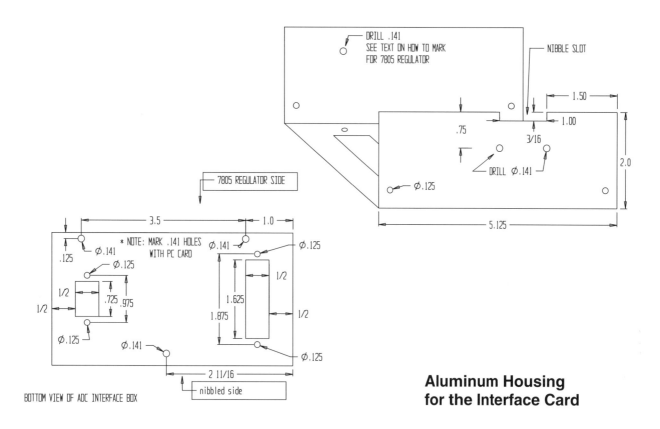

**Aluminum Housing
for the Interface Card**

Apply a thin strip of quick-set epoxy to one side of one of the 8-pin strips and glue the two strips together. To maintain an accurate 0.1-inch spacing between pin centers, insert them into two short lengths of machine-tooled socket.

Insert the wires for J2/J3 through the bottom of the preamp card (that is, from the solder side) and solder the wires on the component side. (This means that you must solder the socket in "the wrong way" compared to every other component.)

The socket strips should be flush with the card and perpendicular to it. Start by soldering one of the wires into the card to align the socket. Use solder sparingly on the wire-to-card joints. The solder pads are very close and excess solder could flow on the bottom of the card and short pins together. Solder one pin at a time then inspect the bottom of the card to see if you are using too much solder. If a joint flows together, use solder removal braid to soak up the solder, then resolder the connection.

The J1 Ribbon Cable: From a 20-inch length of 25-conductor ribbon cable, cut two eight-conductor strips. A pair of scissors works well for this operation. Cut along the grooves in the insulation and be careful not to expose the wire conductors. Using the scissors, cut back the end of each wire along the grooves to separate the wires. At one end, separate the wires for 3 inches; at the other end, separate them for 1 inch. Once again, be careful not to expose the conductors.

Strip $\frac{1}{16}$ inch of insulation from the ends of each conductor. If the stranded wires of the conductor splay apart, twist them together. Place the end of each wire against the soldering iron tip. Apply solder to the tip until the wire has a thin coating of solder. The insulation will melt slightly so the actual length of the exposed wire will be about $\frac{1}{8}$ inch. The solder operation is called tinning. It makes it easier to form a good solder joint to the wire.

Insert a 16-pin component carrier into a spare 16-pin socket to prevent soldering from displacing its pins. Clamp the socket in a pair of vice grips or a small vice to hold it during subsequent operations. Touch the soldering iron tip to the solder terminals on the dip plug and apply a small amount of solder to the terminal to tin it. Tin all sixteen of the terminals. The flux and solder on the wires and the DIP plug terminals should be adequate to form good solder joints.

Circuit Schematic for the Preamplifier Card

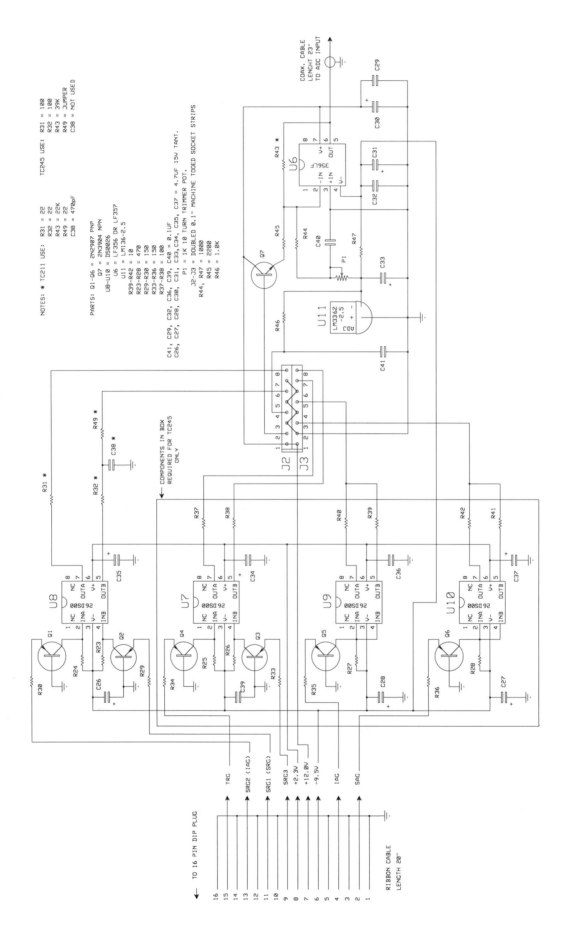

The preamplifier board rides piggyback on the camera body. This board conditions ingoing control signals and amplifies the small signal coming from the CCD before passing it to the interface board to be digitized.

Solder the one inch end of each eight-conductor ribbon cables to the DIP plug. One cable is soldered to pins 1 through 8 and the second cable is soldered to pins 9 through 16. Place the wire end to be soldered on the terminal of the DIP socket and touch the soldering iron to the top of the wire. The solder should fuse and the wire will drop into the split terminal slot. Inspect the solder connection after each wire is soldered. There must be no solder bridging between pins and the insulation must not melt back enough to expose a length of conductor that might short to an adjacent pin at a later time.

At the appropriate time, the instructions in the PREAMP.EXE test program will ask you to solder the free wire ends on the cable to the pads designated on the preamp card.

The JS Coaxial Cable: Coaxial cable is made of a stranded outer shield and an insulated central conductor. Cut about 24 inches of cable. Strip off approximately $\frac{1}{2}$ inch of the outer insulating jacket. Twist the stranded wire

shield together and tin it with solder. Keep the solder tinning operation as short as possible so that you do not melt the polyethylene or polypropylene insulation. If you see any stray shield wires after tinning, clip them off. They could touch a nearby conductor and short it to ground.

Strip off about $\frac{1}{8}$ inch of the center conductor insulation. Twist the center conductor stranded wires together and tin the wires with solder. Prepare both ends of the cable in this way.

You are now ready to form the JS plug. Cut a two-pin section of the 0.1-inch machine tooled solder tail strip. Check that the twisted and tinned wires "press fit" into the sockets. If they do not, trim the wires a little until you can press the center conductor into one socket and the shield into the other. Solder the wires into the sockets.

It is a good idea to test the cable to ensure that the shield is not shorted to the center conductor. On the free end of the cable, separate the wires and measure the resistance between the shield and the center conductor.

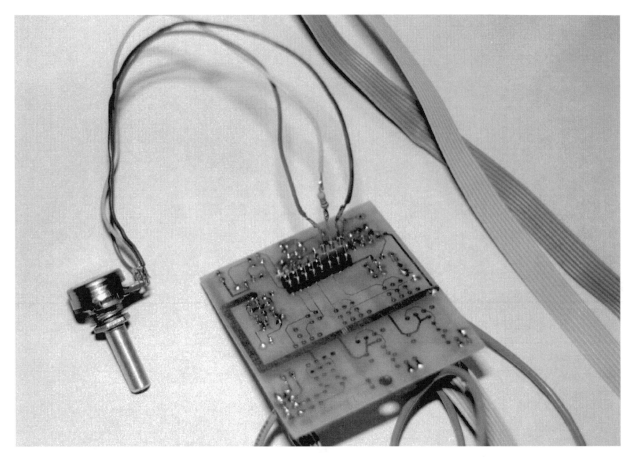

The assembled preamplifier undergoes a critical test when a voltage is applied to the CCD signal pin. On the screen of your computer, you see the digitized voltage readout, you know that the electronics are working!

The resistance should be greater than 1MΩ. If you measure 20kΩ to 1MΩ, you might be measuring the resistance of your fingers across the wires. If the resistance is near zero ohms, the shield is shorted to the center. Cut off both ends of the cable and start over.

You will solder the free end of the wire to the preamp card per the instructions in the PREAMP.EXE test program. After the preamp card is tested, place a drop of hot glue on the end of the cable to insulate the wires. Stressed coaxial cables sometimes expose additional shield wire which can short to nearby conductors.

The two-pin plug goes into the two-pin JS socket strip on the card. When you insert the JS plug into the socket, double check to make sure you have the shield wire (ground) and the signal wire (center conductor) correctly oriented, with the signal wire closer to the edge of the card.

Amplifier Test Circuit: The test circuit is a simple voltage divider from three components: a 3-pin length of wire-wrap socket strip, a 10kΩ resistor, and a 1kΩ potentiometer. Solder a wire from each of the outside pins on the socket strip to the outside terminals on the potentiome-

ter. Solder the 10kΩ resistor to the center pin and extend a wire to the center (wiper) pin on the potentiometer.

6.5.2 PREAMP.EXE Test Sequences

PREAMP.EXE checks the operation of your preamplifier card with four test sequences. These are (1) checking resistance in the passive components, (2) testing the voltage levels and connections to the interface card, (3) checking the operation of the chips that drive the CCD, and (4) verifying the correct function of the input transistor. When the preamplifier card passes its tests, you have finished the electronics.

Sequence 1: Preamp Resistance Testing. Use the silk-screen mask to locate and orient each set of components. After you have installed the resistors, capacitors, and sockets on the board, the three tests in this sequence verify that you have installed components correctly. In Test 1 you carry out continuity testing with respect to the ground and the –9.5V, +12V and +2.3V connections. The test checks for correct wiring and resistance values.

The second test verifies that those circuits which should be open with respect to ground check out properly as open, and that circuits with capacitors in them capaci-

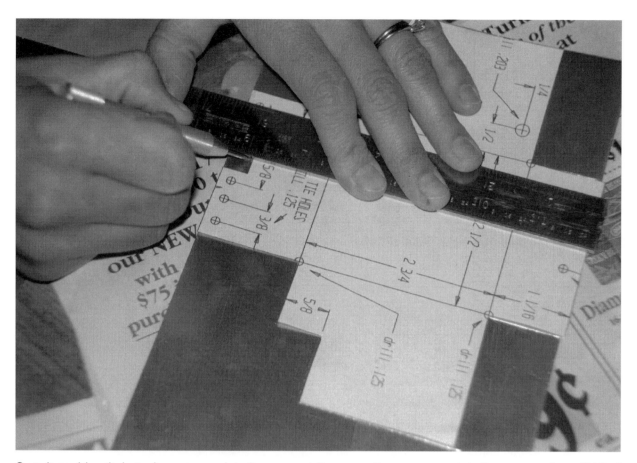

Sure it could wait—but why not complete its cover at the same time you complete the preamp board? That way, you'll have another small but vital task behind you when you are ready to test the completed camera.

tatively charge to an open reading. In Test 3, you perform continuity and resistance tests between pairs of circuit nodes. This checks the wiring and looks for correct resistance values. If at any time the meter shows the board is outside specs, press the H key to call up a list that you can use for troubleshooting.

Note that many of the resistors on the preamp card must be installed "end on," as shown in the photograph on page 75.

Sequence 2: Voltage and Logic Level Input Test. This sequence consists of two tests. The first checks the continuity of the wiring between the J1 DIP plug socket and the preamp card. In Test 2 connect the preamplifier to the interface card and attach both to the printer port of your computer. You then check that all of the supply voltages are correct. You also check the logic input levels for abnormal loading.

Sequence 3: Clock Driver Functional Test. You now install the DS0026 driver chips and check for abnormal supply loading with the drivers in place. You also verify that the drivers on the preamplifier card produce the correct high-level and low-level outputs.

Sequence 4: Operational Amplifier Functional Test. This short sequence shows that the input transistor, Q7, is correctly connected and working. For this test, you must make a test circuit to supply a voltage to the transistor. You also check that the zero-point shifter for the operational amplifier and the coaxial cable are functional.

If your preamplifier and interface boards pass these tests, you have every reason to think that both boards are functioning properly. Your camera should run properly the very first time.

6.5.3 Fabricate the Preamp Cover

To protect the preamplifier, construct a cover from an aluminum sheet. The cover is a box 2.5 inches wide by 2.75 inches long; it stands 2 inches high. Although you will not need it until you have mounted the preamplifier on the camera body, it is best to make the cover now.

Trace the pattern shown in the Preamplifier Cover drawing onto a sheet of 0.030 aluminum. Drill holes at the marked locations. Cut the pattern with sheet-metal shears, and nibble the opening at the back end of the cover. Bend the box with a sheet-metal brake, in a vise, or over a block of wood 2.5 by 2.75 inches on a side. Deburr the holes and

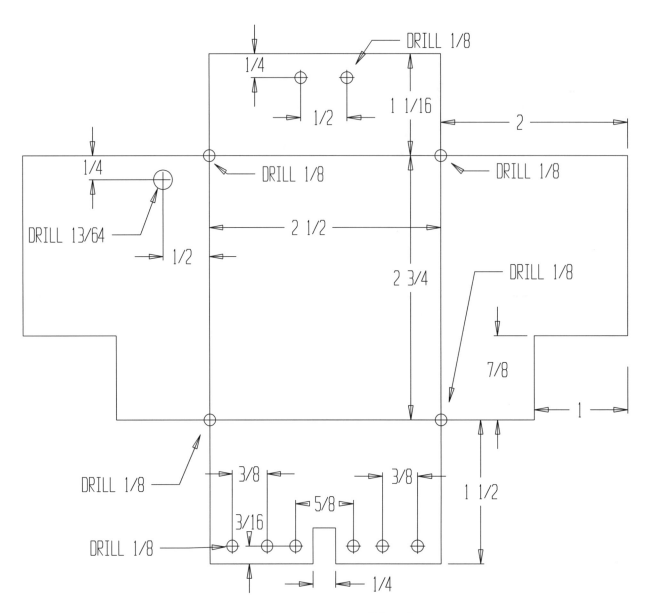

Pattern for the Preamplifier Cover

smooth all sharp edges.

Wash the completed box in strong detergent to remove grease and metal chips, and then set it aside for later installation.

6.6 Package the Interface Card

You can now close the box that contains the interface card. Line the cable exit slot on the box with tape to prevent the edges of the box from cutting the ribbon and coaxial cable. If the negative regulator extends too high and might short to the box cover, bend it down or install a shorter heat sink on it. As a further precaution, line the top of the lid with masking tape to prevent an accidental short from the regulator.

Route the ribbon cable and the coaxial cable through the exit slot and slide the lid over the box. Mark the lid edge where the cable exit is and lift off the lid. With a pair of pliers, bend the edge outward about $1/16$ of an inch at the marks. Loop a tie wrap through the two holes in the box. Place a piece of double-sided foam tape behind the wires, then fasten them tightly with the tie wrap. Finally, fit the lid in place and secure it with sheet-metal screws.

6.7 What Comes Next?

After the preamplifier has passed all of its test sequences, the electronics are done. Congratulations! As you turned the knob on the test circuit potentiometer, you

Lest you forget: the point of playing with all these tinsnips and soldering irons is astronomy. This 60-second exposure with a Cookbook 245 CCD on a 4-inch f/5 Genesis refractor shows the Cocoon Nebula in Cygnus.

were simulating the voltages that will soon be coming from your CCD. Before you run the CCD you must complete the camera housing.

The next chapter guides you through building the camera housing. You will machine and clean the parts, prepare the cold finger and socket for your CCD chip, seal the heat exchanger, bond an airtight window into the housing, install the thermoelectric cooler, construct the electrical feedthroughs that connect the TC211 or TC245 to the preamplifier, wire the socket and feedthrough, install the CCD chip (!!!), close the camera body, and finally attach the preamplifier card and its cover to the camera body. The chapter ends with a functional test of the camera on the lab bench.

As you work on the camera housing, never forget the possibility of electrostatic discharge. Store the completed circuit boards and their connecting cables in a conductive plastic bag where they will be safe from electrostatic discharge.

You have made substantial progress toward your goal of a working CCD camera. If during construction you have doubted, take heart! You can now see the light at the end of the tunnel.

7. Building the Camera Head

The camera head is the most important part of your Cookbook 211 or Cookbook 245 CCD camera. The camera head houses the CCD chip and provides a cold, dry environment so that you can operate the CCD at maximum sensitivity. The other camera components support operation of the camera head, and the camera head, of course, supports the CCD chip mounted in it.

Because of its complexity, the camera head requires the greatest effort to construct and calls on the greatest range of skills. These include lathe and milling-machine skills to fabricate the metal parts of the CCD housing, fine soldering skills to connect the wires that carry signals to and from the CCD chip, and small-parts assembly skills to mount the CCD on its cold finger. You will also learn how to clean and then bond a glass window to the metal housing of the camera to form an environmental seal and how to mount the preamplifier circuit board on the side of the camera body.

Depending on your background and experience, you may opt to build the camera body on your own or work as a team with others to build one or more Cookbook cameras. You may be able to contribute electronics assembly skills, for example, while a friend machines the metal parts for housings for two or more cameras. However you do it, by the time you have completed this chapter, your CCD camera will have seen "first light."

7.1 What the Camera Head Does

The camera head provides a controlled environment for the CCD chip. In operation, the chip must be dry, cold, free of stray light, and shielded from electrical noise. Inside the camera head, the CCD stays dry because the chamber is sealed from the outside environment, and it stays cold because it is mounted on a "cold finger" affixed to a solid-state Peltier cooling module. The only light to reach the CCD is light that comes in the front window from your telescope. Finally, the chip receives signals from the preamplifier card mounted just outside the camera head.

The CCD must be cooled to reduce thermal noise generated in the chip itself. The colder the chip, the longer your exposures can be, and the fainter the stars and galaxies you can detect. However, the cooled CCD chip must be protected from the atmosphere because in operation the chip is cooled well below the dew point. If moist air touches the chilled CCD, frost forms on the chip. Although no permanent harm results, you cannot take images when the face of your CCD is covered with ice!

The rear end of the camera body is a fluid-filled heat exchanger which removes the heat that the Peltier cooler takes from the CCD. Although you can run the Peltier at low power without it, the camera performs best with fluid circulating.

On the side of the camera head, the preamplifier card is mounted piggyback. This circuit card must be close to the camera body to reduce the length of the wires that carry CCD chip driver signals from the card to the CCD and image signals from the CCD chip to the card. Keeping the wires short minimizes interference and insures proper operation of the CCD.

7.2 How the Camera Head Works

Each component of the camera head carries out a specific task. As you build your camera, try to visualize what each component does and how it fits into the overall operation of the camera. The following names each of the major components of the camera head and what each does.

Tube Cap. The front end of the housing is covered with a cap that contains the eyepiece tube and the optical window. Light from your telescope should come to focus approximately 0.89 inches behind the top of the cap.

Eyepiece Tube. The tube adapts the camera to a standard 1.25-inch focuser. Depending on your machining skills, you may opt to glue the eyepiece tube into the tube cap or cut threads in the eyepiece tube and tube cap so that these components can be screwed together.

Optical Window. This thin, glass window is glued to the inside of the tube cap. The window allows light to reach the CCD chip inside the camera housing.

Camera Housing. An aluminum tube houses the CCD, Peltier cooler, and cold finger. Openings in the camera housing allow wires to pass signals and power to the CCD and power to the Peltier cooler inside the camera housing. The wires that supply the Peltier cooler pass

The camera head provides a cold, dry, electrically quiet environment so the CCD can do its best. Here you see a wired TC245 mounted on its cold finger in the open camera head. The tube cap will close the camera.

through milled slots in the tube. These holes are sealed with hot-melt glue in the completed camera. All wiring to the CCD is soldered to a socket strip that is epoxied into a milled slot in the side of the camera housing.

J2/J3 Connector. Constructed from two lengths of socket strip material, this air-tight connector links the CCD inside the camera body with the preamplifier circuit board outside the camera body.

Preamplifier Card. The preamplifier circuit card is mounted piggyback on the camera head. Multi-pin socket strips on the card plug into the socket strips that are epoxied into the side of the camera housing. In Chapter 6, you built and tested the preamplifier card.

Preamplifier Card Cover. A thin sheet metal box that covers the preamplifier card. The construction of this cover was described in Chapter 6.

Cold Finger. The cold finger supports the CCD and cools it. The base of the cold finger is mounted on the cold side of the Peltier thermoelectric cooling module. When the Peltier cooling module is turned on, the entire cold

Tools and Materials Checklist

Tools

- Grounded 15-watt soldering iron
  or temperature-controlled soldering iron.
- Screwdriver.
- Small adjustable crescent wrench.
- Scissors.
- Drill and $\frac{1}{8}$-inch bit.
- Marking pen.
- Eye loupe.
- Wire wrap tool with an integral wire stripper.
- Small diagonal cutters.
- Tweezers.
- Hot-glue gun.

Materials

- Several feet of Kynar 30AWG wrap wire.
- Rosin-core Sn60 or Sn63 solder.
- Q-tips.
- Non-chlorinated cleanser (Bon Ami).
- Toothbrush.
- Acetone.
- Isopropanol (rubbing alcohol).
- Deionized water.
- Household ammonia.
- Disposable gloves.

Adhesives

- Duro Mastermend extra strength quick-set epoxy.
- J.B.-Weld epoxy.
- Thermogrip Caulk/Sealer sticks.
- G.E. Silicone adhesive.
- Gasket-sealing compound.

Plumbing Materials

- 4 $\frac{1}{8}$-inch hose to $\frac{1}{8}$-27 NPT male
  brass fittings.
- 2 $\frac{1}{8}$-inch compression to $\frac{1}{8}$-27 NPT female
  brass fittings.
- 25 feet of $\frac{1}{4}$-inch O.D. $\frac{1}{8}$-inch I.D.
  clear vinyl hose or model airplane
  fuel-line tubing.
- Automotive windshield wiper pump
  such as Autozone WP10 12V universal
  pump replacement.
- 20 feet of $\frac{1}{4}$-inch copper tubing.
- One 3 by 3-inch rubberized sheet
  of $\frac{1}{16}$" cork.
- Teflon pipe tape.

Fasteners

- 5 #6-32 by $\frac{3}{8}$" round head machine screws
- 1 #6-32 by $\frac{1}{4}$" round head machine screw
- 5 #4-40 by $\frac{1}{2}$" long.
- 3 #4-40 nuts
- 20 5-inch Nylon tie wraps.
- for the Cookbook 245 only:
  2 #2-56 by half-round machine screws.
  2 #2-56 nuts and flat washers.

Sockets

- 2 Eight-pin lengths of 0.1-inch spaced
  machine tooled wirewrap socket strips.
- 2 Three-pin lengths of 0.1-inch spaced
  machine tooled soldertail strips.

---

finger cools. The cold finger becomes cold before the CCD does, and in operation the cold finger is colder than the CCD. As a result, any water vapor present in the sealed body of the camera condenses and freezes on the cold finger, leaving the CCD itself dry.

Cold Finger Socket. For the Cookbook 211 camera, you form a socket for the CCD and bond it to the side of the cold finger. For the Cookbook 245, you solder wires directly to the leads on the CCD.

Peltier Cooler. The Peltier cooler acts like a pump, moving heat from one of its faces to the other. This electronic component is sandwiched between the cold finger and the heat exchanger. When current is passed through the Peltier cooler, the side against the cold finger becomes colder than the side against the heat exchanger.

Heat Exchanger. To remove heat from the Peltier cooler, the hot side of the Peltier cooling module is mounted on a fluid-filled heat exchanger. When a mixture

of alcohol and water is pumped through the heat exchanger, the hot side of the Peltier remains cool, allowing the cold side to reach a temperature well below freezing. The alcohol and water mixture enters and exits the heat exchanger though two $\frac{1}{8}$-27 NPT male to $\frac{1}{8}$-inch hose brass fittings.

End Plate. The end plate covers the bottom side of the heat exchanger and retains the coolant mixture. The heat exchanger is sealed with a rubberized cork gasket and the end plate.

7.3 Constructing the Camera Head

By the time you have finished this chapter of The CCD Camera Cookbook, you will have powered up your CCD and seen "first light." The camera will be ready to shoot test images and, when everything checks out properly, you will be able to mount the camera on your telescope to take astronomical images. Here is a summary of the steps that you must take toward those goals:

Machine all parts of the camera body. The eyepiece tube, tube cap, camera body, cold finger, heat exchanger, and end plate must be machined from aluminum stock. Many of the components are turned on a lathe and subsequently milled. These operations are detailed in sections 7.3.1.1 through 7.3.1.10.

Planarize thermal transfer surfaces. To insure efficient flow of heat between parts, you must make the bottom surface of the cold finger and the top surface of the heat exchanger as flat as possible. This operation is described in section 7.3.2.

Clean all components. With the completion of the previous step, the basic character of the work changes from "messy" to "clean." Grease, oil, dust, and metal chips are the natural accompaniments of turning, milling, and filing. From now on, you must strive for clean, degreased surfaces. Basic cleaning techniques are covered in section 7.4.1.

Glue the J2/J3 socket into the camera body. After a thorough cleaning, you construct an airtight 16-pin socket from socket-strip material and epoxy it into a milled slot in the camera body. Surface preparation is essential to forming a good bond. This operation is described in section 7.4.2.

Install a socket for the TC211. Construct a socket from socket-strip material and epoxy it to the cold finger. The TC245 is not socketed; for the Cookbook 245 the wires are soldered directly to the leads of the CCD. Section 7.4.3 describes how to do this.

Bond the optical window. Silicone bond a thin glass window to the tube cap. You must pay strict attention to cleaning both the glass and the aluminum to obtain a good bond. Section 7.4.4 covers this operation.

Assemble the heat exchanger. Assemble the heat exchanger, cork gasket, end plate, and tubing connectors to form a sealed unit. This assembly procedure is outlined in section 7.4.5.

Install the Peltier cooler. You now sandwich the Peltier cooler between the heat exchanger and the cold finger. Heat sink compound insures proper transfer of heat. Assemble the camera housing to the heat exchanger. Section 7.4.6 gives you the details.

Wire the CCD socket or chip. Working inside the confined space of the camera body, you solder each wire to the appropriate socket pin or lead on the CCD. For the Cookbook 245, this is the most difficult step in the assembly of the camera. Test every connection to insure that everything is wired correctly and that there are no short circuits. If you are building the Cookbook 211 camera, consult section 7.5.1; for corresponding steps on the Cookbook 245, see section 7.5.3.

Mount the preamplifier card. Install the preamplifier card on the side of the camera using the J2/J3 plug and a bracket at the back of the camera body to support the card. See section 7.5.1 if you are building a Cookbook 211 and 7.5.3 for a Cookbook 245 camera.

Socket-test the TC211. For the Cookbook 211, test that each pin in the socket receives the correct voltages. The Cookbook 245 cannot be checked in this way. Section 7.5.2. describes the test procedure for the Cookbook 211.

Turn on the camera; see first light. Vindication that the CCD operates and is sensitive to light! See section 7.6.

Clean the camera and close it. Clean away all residues with swabs and solvent. Install the tube cap on the camera and seal the camera head closed. These operations are covered in section 7.7.

Install the preamplifier cover. Install a sheet-metal cover to protect the electronics from any damage. Section 7.8 describes this step.

When you have completed the steps above, you will know that the camera head works and can transfer an image to your computer. After you complete the cooling sytem, the camera is ready to use for imaging.

7.3.1 Machine the Camera Head

Anyone with a small lathe and mill—nothing fancier than you could find in any high school metal shop—can make a CCD camera body. Only the mating parts and surfaces perpendicular to the optical axis are critical. These parts are the end cap, eyepiece tube, housing, cold finger, and heat exchanger. When you make parts on a lathe, it is easy to make the critical surfaces precisely perpendicular to the axis of rotation.

If you do not have a home machine shop, look around for someone who does. You can probably have an amateur machinist turn out the job for a favor or a couple of beers. The lathe work takes about 4 hours and the drilling, milling and tapping operations take about 3.5 hours. (Perhaps you'd better change that to a big favor and a case of beer!)

If you belong to an astronomy club, someone in the club is likely to have a home shop. If you and several other members of the club team up, you can make several cameras for just a little more effort than making one takes. One member can do the machining while others build the circuit boards, power supplies, cooling system, and tune up the clock drive and optics of the club telescope to meet the demands of CCD imaging.

The material you use for the camera body is not critical. The novice machinist will find 6061-T6 aluminum easy to machine. More experienced machinists may select the material of their choice.

7.3.1.1 Turn the Cap and Heat Exchanger

The tube cap and heat exchanger have the same outside diameter, and can be turned from a single length of 2.38-inch outside diameter solid round stock at least 3.75 long. The work itself requires 2.25 inches of material, and you will need about 1.5 inches to hold in the chuck. Clamp the work in a three-jaw chuck.

Machine Tools for the Cookbook Camera

Lathe
- 6-inch swing minimum, threading capabilities optional.
- 5-inch three-jaw chuck able to clamp 2.5-inch O.D.
- Tail-stock $3/8$-inch drill chuck.

Turning Tools
- Center drill.
- $3/8$-inch bit.
- $3/4$-inch carbide-tipped masonry bit.
- Tail-stock center.
- 0.1-inch cut off tool and tool holder.
- Boring bar for $3/16$-inch tools.
- Straight tool holder for $1/4$-inch brazed tungsten-carbide tools.
- Square cutting tool, style C4, carbide type 2A5, aluminum turning.
- V-threading tool, carbide, style E4. For boring V-threads, gauge $3/16$-inch tool against V-thread alignment tool.
- general-purpose cutting tool, steel. Back rake, 35 degrees; side rake, 15 degrees; end relief, 8 degrees; side relief, 12 degrees.

Milling Machine
- 15-inch swing, spindle stroke 4 inches, X-Y table travel 6 inches.
- 2.5-inch machinist's vise.

- $3/8$-inch drill chuck,
- Drills: 0.109, 0.156, $1/4$, 0.343 inches; for Cookbook 245, 0.070 inches.
- $1/8$-inch end mill and collet.
- $3/8$-inch end mill and collet.

Measuring Tools
- Dial caliper.
- Square for marking.

Marking Tools
- Center punch.
- Scribing tool or razor knife.
- Dividers.

Taps
- 6-32
- $1/8$-27 NPT
- for Cookbook 245: #2-56.

Additional Tools
- General-purpose bench vise.
- Saber saw.
- Saber saw metal cutting blade, 18 TPI.
- Safety glasses or goggles.
- Earmuff or earplug ear protection.
- 400 or 600 grit silicon carbide paper.
- Kerosene or mineral oil cutting fluid.

Begin by facing the free end of the stock using a square cutting tool. Next, turn the outside diameter of the stock to 2.373 inches. Note that this diameter can lie anywhere between 2.370 and 2.376 inches. Rough the diameter with the general-purpose cutting tool then follow up with the square cutting tool.

The first component you will turn is the heat exchanger. On the end of the stock, turn a new diameter of 2.083 inches by a nominal 0.260 inches in length. To produce a smooth finish, use a square tool and tilt the cutting face of the tool $1/2$ degree with respect to the work, so that the gap opens in the direction opposite the feed. This helps prevent chattering. Hold the finishing cuts to 0.010 inches or less and use cutting fluid such as kerosene.

Face the work to a nominal 0.250 inches length on the 2.083-inch diameter. For facing, cut from the outside edge towards the center. Make only one pass over the surface. The last pass should result in a mirror-like finish. Do not worry if a small hump at the very center remains;

you can remove it later during planarization. Because the Peltier module must mate with this surface, it is important to generate a flat surface perpendicular to the axis of the camera housing. Try to hold the surface tilt to 0.001 inches across the work.

Use a parting tool to cut free a blank 0.950 inches thick. This piece of metal will become the heat exchanger. Because some aluminum alloys may cold-weld to the tip of the parting tool, use plenty of cutting fluid and make shallow (0.020-inch) passes at the work. Keep the drive-belt tension low enough that the belt will slip if the work jams during parting. Set the unfinished heat exchanger aside.

You can now cut the tube cap. Face the workpiece and cut another 2.083-inch diameter to a nominal length of 0.250 inches. Part a disk 0.600 inches long. This disk is the tube cap. Remove the work piece from the lathe.

Clamp the heat exchanger in the chuck and face the large 2.373-inch diameter end to a nominal length of 0.600-inch. This dimension is not critical; and it can be long by 0.050 inches and work perfectly well. Face this surface as you did the reverse side of the heat exchanger. This surface must be flat and but it need not be exactly perpendicular. Remove the heat exchanger blank from the chuck.

Next you must make the tube cap. Reverse the cap in the chuck and clamp the work on its 2.083-inch diameter. Face the larger diameter end to a length of 0.25 inches. Take care that this diameter is flat and smooth. Leave the work in the chuck.

Using a center drill, make a start hole in the cap at a small depth of about $\frac{1}{4}$ inch. Drill through the work with a $\frac{3}{8}$-inch drill, then open the hole larger with a standard twist drill of $\frac{3}{4}$-inch diameter. Alternately, bore the hole with a carbide masonry bit. These bits act as double-bit boring bars and they cost $\frac{1}{10}$ as much as a twist drill.

Using a boring bar, bore the hole to a diameter of 0.800 inches. Countersink a square bore hole 0.300 inches deep with a diameter of 1.115 inches for a threaded eyepiece tube or 1.250 inches for a straight eyepiece tube. You can use a square tool to bore this diameter, but remember that the tool requires adequate side clearance to prevent running into the hole diameter. When the hole is completed, chamfer the edge with a width no more than 0.050 inches at 45 degrees.

For the threaded hole option, set the lathe for right-hand threading at 32 threads-per-inch feed. Because of the small thread size and the tight space in the I.D. of the cap, you may prefer to disengage the belt drive and turn the threads by hand. Align the V-thread tool on the boring bar and set the cut depth to 0.007 inches on the 1.115-inch diameter. Engage the half nut at a selected mark and coat the interior of the workpiece with cutting fluid.

Turn the chuck to advance the carriage and place friction with the other hand on the carriage crank to remove the backlash on the half nut. Turn the chuck by hand; thread until the threading tool contacts the face of the smaller 0.8-inch diameter. Back out the tool and set the cut depth 0.007 inches deeper. Make four cuts until you reach a total depth of 0.028 inches. This completes cutting the threads.

Reverse the cap in the chuck and place the 2.373-inch diameter against the back of the chuck. Use the square tool to countersink the 0.8-inch hole on the 2.083-inch diameter side to a diameter of 1.020 inches and a depth of 0.100 inches. The countersunk hole is used to seat an optical window that is nominally 1.0 inch in diameter. If you have a 1-inch square piece of slide glass for the optical window, open the countersunk hole to a diameter of 1.430 inches.

7.3.1.2 Machine the Eyepiece Tube

Clamp a piece of 1.25-inch diameter tubing into the chuck leaving a working length of about two inches. Face the end of the tube square. Turn the outside diameter of

---

Metal for the Cookbook Camera

Aluminum Tubing
- 2.373-inch O.D., 2.073-inch I.D., 0.150-inch wall, 1.8-inch length minimum if ends are square.
- 1.25-inch O.D., 1.0-inch I.D., 2.5-inch length.

Aluminum Rounds
- 2.373-inch O.D., 3.75-inch length.
- 1.75-inch O.D., 2.50-inch length.

Aluminum Sheet
- 2.5-inch diameter, 0.1- to 0.15-inch thick.
- 6.5-inch square, 0.030-inch thick.

Aluminum Angle
- $\frac{1}{2}$-inch angle, 2-inch length.

Material Selection

If possible, use precipitation hardened and stabilized 6061-T6 temper aluminum stock. If you obtain your materials at a scrap yard, you may not be able to choose a material. If this is the case, turn a sample of the material before committing to use it. You will need material that turns well and does not "chatter" in small diameters.

---

the tube to 1.248 inches for a length of 1.75 inches.

You have two options in making the eyepiece tube: you may thread the tube so that it screws into the tube cap, or you may leave it straight-sided and epoxy the tube to the tube cap. If you are a novice machinist, the straight tube is the easier route.

For the straight tube option, chamfer the end of the tube at 45 degrees with a 0.050-inch chamfer. You may wish to thread the interior of the tube to accept standard filters, but if you have opted not to thread the tube, you probably won't want to cut threads for filters either.

For the threaded tube option, turn a 0.350-inch length on the end of the tube to a diameter of 1.140 inches. Turn a second diameter, starting at the end of the tube, to 1.100 inches for a 0.100-inch length. Chamfer the outer edge on the end of the tube.

To cut threads, align the V-thread tool and set the feed for a right-handed thread with 32 threads per inch. Because of the small thread size, you may prefer to disengage the belt drive and turn the threads by hand. Start threading at the end of the tube and thread until you reach the 1.248-inch diameter.

Increase the depth by 0.007 inches per cut until you

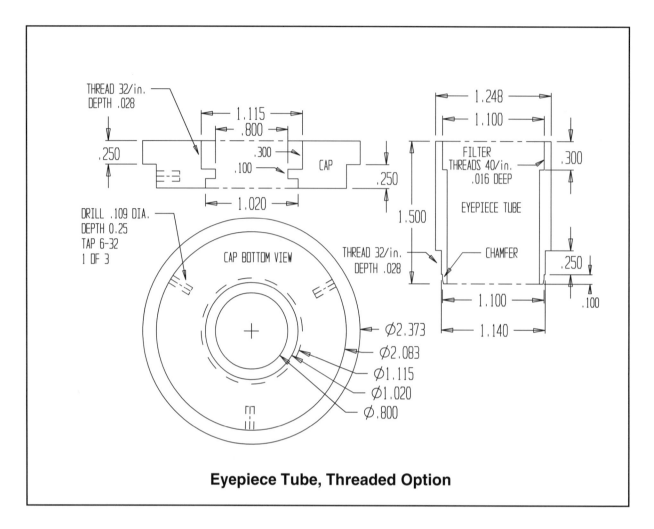

Eyepiece Tube, Threaded Option

reach a depth of 0.021 inches. Test the end cap on the threads for fit. Aluminum tends to extrude a few mils when machined with a single-point cutting tool, so continue increasing the depth of the cut by 0.002 inches until you get a good fit between the cap and tube. Make sure to clean particles off of the threads before you test the fit and do not force the threads because the pieces may seize. If they do seize, you may find it impossible to separate them.

Cut the tube length to 1.600 inches using a parting or cut-off tool. Clamp the tube in the chuck with the cut-off end facing out. Face the end of the tube square and reduce the tube length to 1.5 inches. Cut a 0.050-inch 45-degree chamfer on both the inside and outside edges.

If you want to be able to insert filters into the eyepiece tube, bore the tube end to an inside diameter of 1.100 inches along a nominal length of 0.300 inches. Align the V-threading tool on the boring bar and set the feed to 40 threads-per-inch right-hand threading. Set the cut depth to 0.016 inches and make one threading pass. Most standard filters fit these threads, but if your filters do not, make a second pass a few thousandths of an inch deeper.

If you are making the straight tube option, test the fit of the eyepiece tube in the 1.250-inch hole in the cap.

The tube should slip in and seat squarely on the bottom of the hole. If it does not, turn the tube diameter a few thousandths of an inch smaller and try again.

Prepare the outside surface of the eyepiece tube and the inside wall of the 1.250-inch hole in the tube cap. (Surface preparation techniques are described in section 7.4.1.) Mix a small amount of J-B Weld epoxy and apply a thin film to both surfaces. Press the tube into the hole and allow the epoxy ample time to cure.

7.3.1.3 Turn the Camera Housing

The camera housing is made from a length of aluminum tubing. Because most extruded tubing is slightly out-of-round, the inside diameter must be bored to fit other parts. The tube cap fits into this bore at the front end and the heat exchanger fits into the bore at the back end.

Clamp a 2-inch length of 2.375-inch outside-diameter tubing in the three-jawed chuck. To avoid deforming the tube, clamp the tube lightly in the chuck. Face the end of the tube square and bore the inside of the tube to a diameter of 2.085 inches over a length of about 0.4 inches. Check that the tube cap slips into the bore.

Reverse the tube in the chuck and seat the end of the

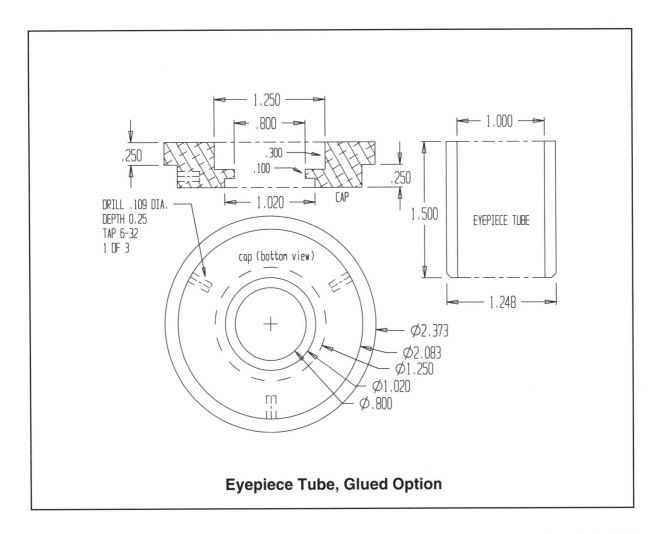

DRILL .109 DIA.
DEPTH 0.25
TAP 6-32
1 OF 3

cap (botton view)

CAP

EYEPIECE TUBE

Ø2.373
Ø2.083
Ø1.250
Ø1.020
Ø.800

Eyepiece Tube, Glued Option

tube firmly against the back of the three-jaw chuck. Face the end of the tube square. As you face the tube, reduce its length to exactly 1.750 inches. Bore a 0.4-inch depth of the inside of the tube to a diameter of 2.085 inches. Check that the heat exchanger makes a slip-fit with the end of the tube.

7.3.1.4 Drill and Mill the Camera Housing

After you have turned the camera housing, you must drill three radial holes in each end to hold the tube cap and heat exchanger in place, and then you must mill a large slot for the CCD signal plug and two small slots to accommodate the Peltier cooler wires in the tube wall.

Begin by drilling the holes to hold the tube cap and heat exchanger. Because you will later use the housing as a template to locate holes in the tube cap and heat exchanger, minor errors in the positions of these holes do not matter.

The drilling template for the heat exchanger shows the locations of three equally spaced radial holes. Place the camera housing over this template and scratch the outer edge of the tube at these three locations. Use a square to extend the marks up the tube vertically. Set a caliper to

0.125 inches and locate the center of each hole 0.125 inches from each end of the tube. Mark three holes at each end, for a total of six marks. Center punch the six marks.

Select one of the marks as a center reference. Select one end of the tube as the end that will hold the heat exchanger. From that end, measure along the center line 1.010 inches and punch the tube. This is the location of the center of the slot for the CCD leads.

Clamp the tube lengthwise in a machinist's vise and mount it on a milling machine. With a 0.156-inch twist drill in the milling head, drill each of the seven marked and center-punched locations. Remove any burrs around the holes with a larger bit.

If you wish to, scribe the location of the slot into the tube. The top and bottom ends of the slot are 1.115 inches and 0.905 inches from the heat exchanger end of the camera body. Because the slot is 1 inch long, the ends of the slot are located 0.5 inch to either side of the center.

Place a 0.125-inch milling bit in the head of the milling machine. Clamp the tube ends in the vise with the center mark facing up. Align the 0.125-inch bit at the center line of the heat exchanger end of the tube. Set the zero point of the mill carriage to this location.

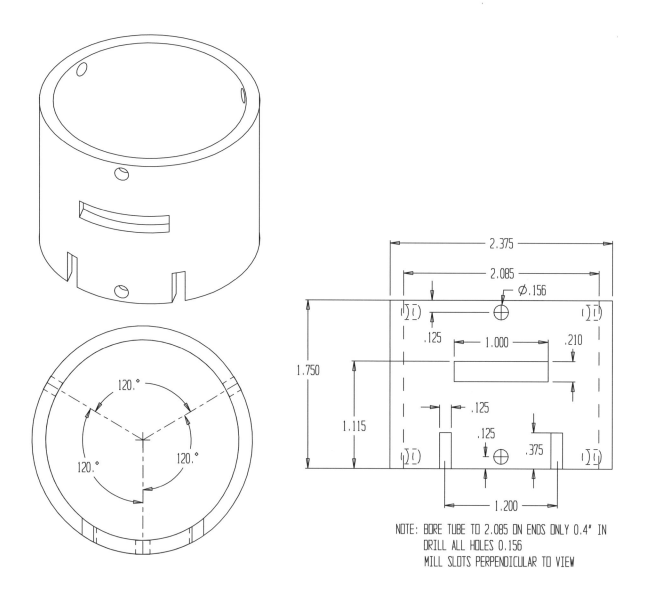

Cookbook Camera Housing

Move the workpiece +0.6 inches across the direction of the tube face. Mill a slot 0.375 inches into the tube. Back the tool out and then move the work −1.2 inches and mill a second slot 0.375 inches into the tube. These two slots allow the wires from the Peltier cooler to exit from the camera head.

Lower the 0.125-inch milling bit into the center of the 0.156-inch starting hole. Mill a slot 0.5 inches long across the tube. Reverse the direction of the cut and mill for a total slot length of 1 inch. Enlarge the slot to a width of 0.21 inches with 0.043-inch-deep cuts along each edge of the 0.125-inch slot. This gives you a slot across the tube 1 inch wide by 0.21 inches high to hold the J2/J3 plug that

connects your CCD to the preamplifier.

7.3.1.5 Mark the Heat Exchanger Drill Holes

The tube cap and heat exchanger each have a large face (with a diameter of 2.373 inches) and a small face (with a diameter of 2.083 inches.) In both parts, the small face fits into the camera housing. Before proceeding, check that each of these fits squarely into its end of the camera body.

The heat exchanger goes on the end with the open milled slots, and the tube cap goes on the end without slots. Press the tube cap and exchanger firmly into the tube with a C clamp. With a pencil inserted through the holes in the camera body, mark the location of each of the hole

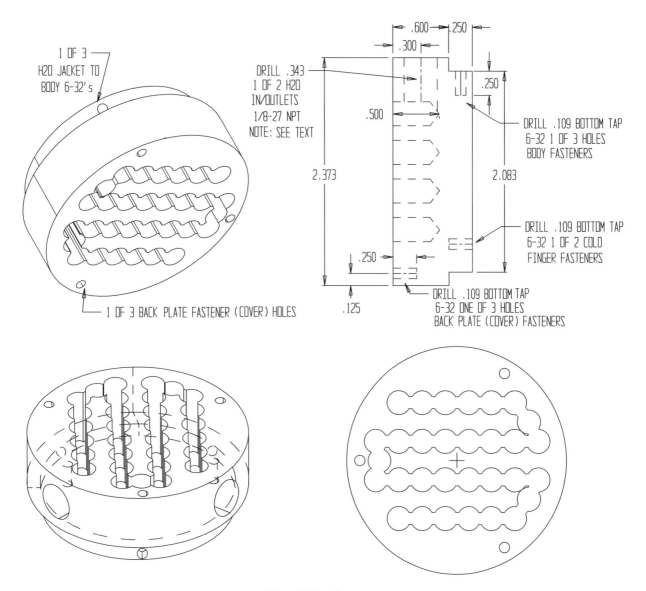

Heat Exchanger

on the cap and heat exchanger. To help you orient the parts later, on the J2/J3-slot centerline of the camera body and on the corresponding side the tube cap and heat exchanger, make a dimple with the center punch.

Remove the cap and heat exchanger and center punch each of the six penciled hole locations. Color code the holes with a marker to avoid confusion when drilling at a later time. These marks locate 0.109-inch #6-32 body drill holes for the screws that will hold the tube cap and heat exchanger.

On the large and small diameters of the heat exchanger, scribe a center line through the drill hole punch mark. (This is on the hole next to the locator punch mark.)

Continue the scribe lines from the edge to the center on both end faces. These lines define the orientation of the heat exchanger.

Now locate holes for the brass fittings that bring coolant to the heat exchanger. Place the heat exchanger large-end down on heat-exchanger drill template and align it so that the center line you scribed is aligned with the center line on the drawing. Mark the edge of the heat exchanger at the $^{11}/_{32}$-inch holes. Continuing from these marks, scribe a line on the outside diameter of the heat exchanger. At a distance of 0.3 inches from the large end of the heat exchanger, mark the line and center punch the two marks. This locates the $^{11}/_{32}$-inch holes for the brass tube fittings.

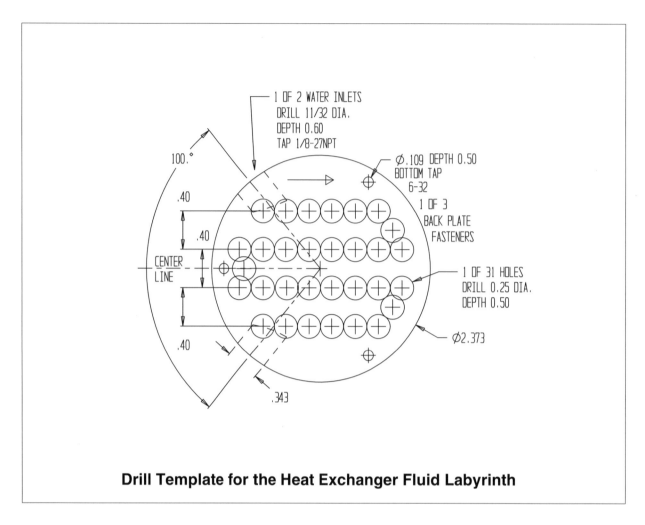

Drill Template for the Heat Exchanger Fluid Labyrinth

Next, mark the drill points for the fluid chamber in the heat exchanger. Photocopy the heat-exchanger drill template for the labyrinth side and with scissors cut out the template. Align the template along the center line and tape the cut-out template to the large face of the heat exchanger. Center punch the heat exchanger at each of the hole marks. There are three 0.109-inch drill locations and 31 0.250-inch drill locations. After punching, remove the template and identify the 0.109-inch holes with a colored marker. The small holes will hold the end plate that closes the heat exchanger.

Finally, photocopy the hole template for the Peltier side of the heat exchanger. This shows where to drill the holes in the Peltier face. Cut out the template and tape it to the smaller face of the heat exchanger. Align the template along the center line mark. Center punch two locations for 0.109-inch holes. These holes will secure the cold finger to the heat exchanger.

7.3.1.6 Drill and Mill the Heat Exchanger

The next step is to drill and tap the radial holes that hold the tube cap, heat exchanger, and camera body together. After that, you will drill out the heat-exchanger labyrinth and then drill and tap holes for brass tube fittings. These bring the coolant fluid to the heat exchanger.

Clamp the tube cap in a machinist's vise. Align the cap so that the punch mark is straight up, making the drill hole radial. Chuck a tap drill for #6-32 threads—a 0.109-inch bit—and set the drill depth to 0.25 inches. Drill the three housing screw tap holes.

Repeat this process for the heat exchanger. Drill the three housing screw tap holes on the small diameter lip. In addition, drill two holes 0.25 inches deep for the cold finger on the small-diameter face and three holes 0.50 inches deep on the large face for the end plate holes.

Now drill out the fluid labyrinth. Clamp the heat exchanger with the large-diameter face up. For each of the holes in the labyrinth, drill a 0.109-inch pilot to a depth of 0.5 inches. The pilot hole will help keep the large bit from drifting especially where 0.250-inch holes overlap.

Switch to a 0.250-inch diameter drill. Set the drill hole depth to 0.500 inches and drill the 31 labyrinth holes. Drill the holes at the ends of the labyrinth last because these holes have a larger overlap than the other holes.

Change to a $\frac{1}{8}$-inch end-mill bit. Set the cutting

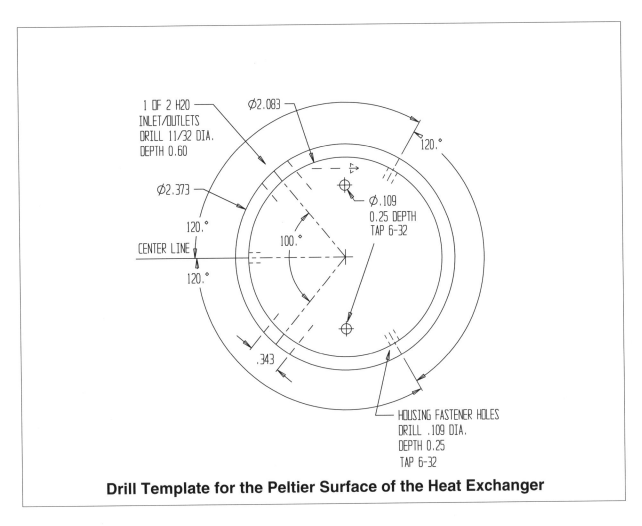

Drill Template for the Peltier Surface of the Heat Exchanger

depth to 0.4 inches and mill connecting slots between the ¼-inch holes. The heat exchanger drawing shows the connecting paths. Clean out any burrs from the labyrinth.

Clamp the heat exchanger on edge across the flat faces in a bench vise using wood or brass shims to protect the faces of the heat exchanger. Place an $^{11}/_{32}$-inch drill in the chuck. Drill the two ⅛-inch pipe thread tap holes. These holes should be 0.6 inches deep. Tap these two holes with a ⅛-27 NPT tap. Use mineral oil as a cutting fluid.

After you start the tap and take a couple of turns clockwise, back out ½ turn counterclockwise to clear the cutting chips. Continue tapping by advancing the tap clockwise ¾ of a turn, then backing off counterclockwise ½ of a turn to clear the chips. (Each cycle produces ¼ turn of new thread.) Continue this process until the tap reaches the bottom of the hole. Remove the tap and brush off the chips.

Tap the eight #6-32 tap holes in the heat exchanger and three tap holes in the tube cap. Use a T-handle tap holder. Start tapping by cutting two or three turns, then back out the tap and clear the chips. Reinsert the tap and continue to tap by advancing ¾ of a turn and then backing out ½ a turn.

Take your time. Taps are quite brittle and snap easily. If a tap does break, you may have to drill along each side of the broken tap to remove it. Clean the hole out with water and detergent, and then with solvent. Fill the hole with JB-Weld, and when this epoxy has cured, drill a new hole in the JB-Weld and tap it.

All of the #6-32 holes should be bottom tapped, that is, threaded to the bottom of the hole. Hardware stores do not generally stock bottoming taps. Take an old #6-32 tap and snap the end off using two pairs of pliers (wear safety glasses). Use a stone or grinder to square the end and to taper the last few threads. After tapping each hole, run your makeshift bottoming tap to the end of each hole. Use the same ¾ turn forward, ½ turn back action and enough cutting fluid to keep cutting free and easy.

When you have finished tapping all of the holes, the tube cap and the heat exchanger are complete.

7.3.1.7 Cookbook 211 Cold Finger

If you are making the Cookbook 211 CCD camera, you must make a TC211 cold finger. This cold finger is

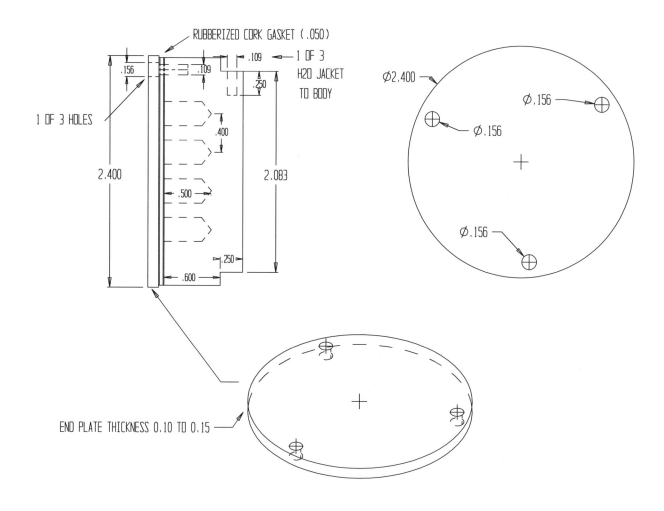

RUBBERIZED CORK GASKET (.050)

.156
.109
.109
1 OF 3
H2O JACKET
TO BODY
.250
1 OF 3 HOLES
.400
2.400
.500
2.083
Ø2.400
Ø.156
Ø.156
Ø.156
.250
.600

END PLATE THICKNESS 0.10 TO 0.15

Heat Exchanger End Plate

thinner than the cold finger for the Cookbook 245. If you ever replace your TC211 chip with a TC245, you will need to replace the cold finger also.

Begin work by clamping a 2.5-inch length of 1.75-inch solid round aluminum in the three-jaw chuck of a lathe. Leave about 1.5 inches of stock free. Use a square tool to turn the face of the workpiece flat.

Turn a 0.6-inch length of work to a diameter of 0.60 inches. The step from this diameter to the full diameter of the stock must be square and have a smooth finish. Face the small diameter to a length of 0.500 inches. This face must be flat and smooth. Part the work at the 1.75-inch diameter leaving a lip 0.2 inches in width.

Clamp the small-diameter end in the chuck. Face the 1.75-inch diameter end to a thickness of 0.125 inches. Use a tilted square tool to generate a smooth finish. Lubricate the work with kerosene, and make the final cut very shallow: 0.005 inches. Make just one pass over the surface, and cut from the outside toward the center. The last pass should result in a mirror-like finish. Because it mates with the Peltier module, this surface must be flat and perpendicular to the axis of the cold finger.

Transfer the job to a milling machine. Photocopy the diagram of the TC211 cold finger and cut out the top view. Place the pattern on the bottom of the 1.75-inch diameter and center it. Transfer the pattern from the

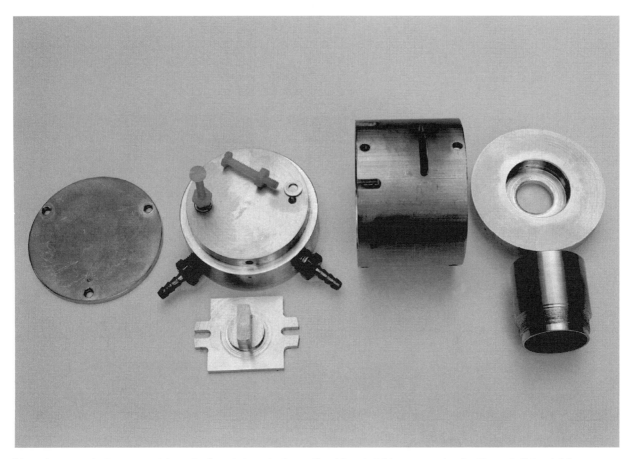

Here is a ready-to-assemble set of metal parts for a Cookbook 211 camera body. From left to right you see an end plate, a heat exchanger and TC211 cold finger, a camera housing, a tube cap, and an eyepiece tube.

diagram with a scribe.

Clamp the cold finger in the vise across the two faces of the 1.75-inch diameter and place a $\frac{3}{8}$-inch end mill in the chuck. You are going to mill the 1.75-inch circle to a 1.25-inch square that has mounting ears on opposite sides. Mill away the areas labeled a, b, and c on the diagram, then turn the workpiece over and remove d, e, and f.

Clamp the work in the vise along the two flat edges with the base down. Avoid using more clamping force than necessary so that you do not distort the cold finger. Set the mill depth to cut 0.375 inches from the top of the small-diameter face and mill the sides of the round to obtain a cold finger that is 0.210 inches wide.

Chuck a $\frac{1}{8}$-inch end mill. Turn the cold finger over in the vise and clamp the work with the base facing up. Mill two 0.156-inch slots in the mounting ears.

This completes the TC211 cold finger.

7.3.1.8 Cookbook 245 Cold Finger

If you are making the Cookbook 245 camera, you must make a TC245 cold finger. This cold finger is wider than the cold finger for the TC211. If you plan to replace your TC211 with a TC245 some day, it would be smart to make the cold finger now, while you're all set up for it.

Clamp a 2.5-inch length of 1.75-inch solid round aluminum stock in the three-jaw chuck of a lathe. Leave about 1.5 inches of working length. Face the end of the work square with the square tool.

Turn a 0.500-inch length of the cold finger to a diameter of 1.250 inches. The surface between the 1.25-inch diameter and the 1.75-inch diameter should be square and have a smooth finish. Face the 1.25-inch diameter to a length of 0.400 inches. The end must be square, flat, and have a smooth finish. Using a parting tool, cut off the work at the 1.75-inch diameter, leaving a lip of 0.35 inches.

Reverse the cold finger in the lathe. Face the surface to a thickness of 0.250 inches. The surface should be flat with a smooth finish. To achieve this, lubricate the work with kerosene, and take off only 0.005 inches on the finish cut. Remember that because it mates with the Peltier module, this surface must be flat and perpendicular to the axis of the cold finger.

Transfer the cold finger to a milling machine. Photocopy the TC245 cold finger print and cut out the top view. Center the pattern on the bottom of the 1.75-inch

To cut interior threads for the tube cap, place a 60-degree thread cutting tool in a tool-holder. Use the thread-cutting drive to make a set of progressively deeper cuts until you reach the full depth of the threads.

diameter and trace the pattern with a scribe.

Place a $^3/_8$-inch end mill in the chuck. Clamp the work in the vise across its faces with an earless side up. Mill the 1.75-inch diameter to remove the areas marked a, b, and c on the diagram. From the top of its radius, mill the top edge of the 1.25-inch diameter down 0.350 inches. Rotate the cold finger and remove areas d, e, and f. From the top of its radius, mill the top edge of the 1.25-inch diameter down 0.350 inches. This leaves a land 0.55 inches thick.

Note that the drawing shows radii around the mounting ears at sections b, c, d, and f. These radii are optional and are not generated by the procedures described.

To transfer the proper shape for the upper section of the cold finger, cut out the cold finger pattern and scribe the pattern on the top of the partially milled 1.25-inch diameter. Center punch the two holes in the top surface. Clamp the work bottom-side down along the two long, straight edges. Do not use excessive clamping force or it will distort the work. Install a $^1/_8$-inch end mill in the mill's chuck and mill the sides of the cold finger to obtain the cold finger pattern. Change to a 0.070-inch diameter drill and drill the two CCD

clip fastener holes to a depth of 0.25 inches.

Turn the cold finger over in the vise and clamp the work along the long, straight edges with the bottom up. Mill two 0.156-inch wide slots in the mounting ears.

Remove the cold finger and tap the holes for #2-56 machine screws. Be very careful because small taps can snap off in the tap hole with a very small amount of force. Tapping completes the TC245 cold finger.

7.3.1.9 Turn the End Plate

The end plate seals off the coolant chamber of the heat exchanger. It is a very simple piece to make. On a sheet of 0.10- to 0.15-inch aluminum stock, mark a 2.5-inch-diameter circle. Cut out the circle with a saber saw and a metal cutting blade.

Using the heat exchanger drill template, center punch the three hole locations and at each of the punched locations drill a clearance hole for a #6-32 machine screw with a 0.156-inch drill. Clean the burrs off the work.

With three #6-32 screws, fasten the plate to the back of the heat exchanger. Clamp the heat exchanger in the three-jaw chuck of a lathe on the larger diameter with the end plate facing out. Be sure to leave a gap between the

Mark and punch the location for each of the 31 ¼-inch holes in the labyrinth for the heat exchanger.

Drill each ¼-inch hole to the same depth. After the holes are drilled, mill out the path between the holes.

end plate and the jaws of the chuck. Turn the end plate to a diameter of 2.40 inches. Remove the end plate.

7.3.1.10 Make Two Cover Brackets

To hold the preamplifier card and its metal cover to the camera body, make two cover brackets from ½-inch aluminum angle. Drill the #6-32 clearance holes and drill and tap #4-40 holes as shown in the Preamplifier Cover Bracket plan. Note that you should not drill the single #4-40 hole in the rear bracket until you can determine the actual position of the circuit board in section 7.5.2.

7.3.1.11 Make Two Chip Clips

To hold the TC245 firmly against the cold finger in the Cookbook 245, make two chip clips from Nylon plastic. These are small and hard to handle parts. Mill a strip of Nylon to dimension and slice off ¼-inch lengths.

7.3.2 Planarize Mating Surfaces

The top and bottom of the cold finger, both sides of the heat exchanger, and the inside of the end plate may require sanding to remove raised edges and the small center bump left after you have faced them on the lathe.

Place a sheet #400 to #600 silicon carbide emery

cloth on a flat surface such as the bed of a table saw. Tape one end of the cloth to this surface.

While you apply even pressure, stroke the piece away from the taped end of the paper. Use single strokes, rotating the work when necessary. Sand just enough to remove the surface irregularities.

7.4 Integrating the Components

With the components of the camera body machined and cleaned, you can begin assembly. This includes the following key steps: (1) Gluing the J2/J3 socket into the camera body; (2) for the Cookbook 211, installing a socket on the cold finger; (3) bonding the optical window to the tube cap; (4) closing the heat exchanger; (5) installing the Peltier cooler; (6) wiring the CCD socket for the Cookbook 211 and for the Cookbook 245, possibly wiring the CCD chip itself; (7) mounting the preamplifier card; (8) for the Cookbook 211, testing the socket; (9) turning on the camera and seeing first light; (10) cleaning and closing the camera body, and finally (11) installing the preamplifier cover. Now that you have machined the camera body parts, you've passed the halfway point to completion!

7.4.1 Camera Body Assembly

With the components made, you pass from the

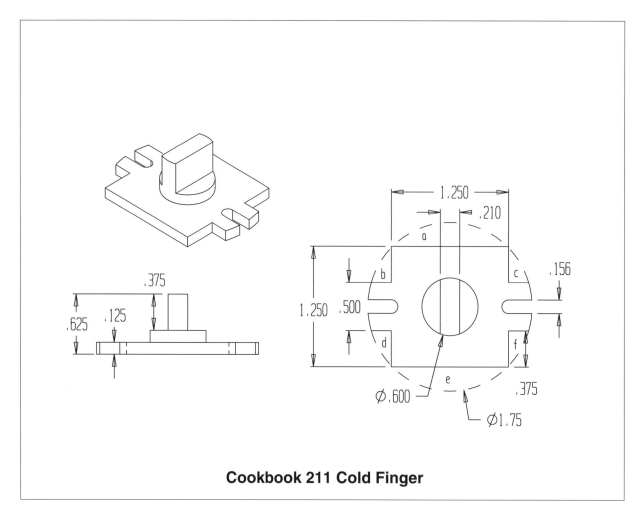

Cookbook 211 Cold Finger

"messy" work on your camera to the "clean" work. The grease, oil, and cutting fluids so necessary to machining must be removed. Chemically clean, dry surfaces are required to build a successful CCD camera. This is necessary not only because the interior of the camera must be clean, but also because the adhesives that you will use to assemble the camera will not properly adhere to greasy or oily metal surfaces.

For aluminum, wash each part with a dish detergent such as Joy, then clean it with acetone and scrub it down with an old toothbrush and an abrasive non-chlorinated cleanser such Bon Ami. The clean surface should have a dull gray appearance, and water should coat the area evenly without beading. After the aluminum parts are cleaned, rinse them in tap water and then, if possible, with deionized or distilled water. Pat each piece dry with a clean paper towel.

Because organic materials readily contaminate surfaces, you should apply adhesives as soon as possible after you have cleaned a piece. If you wet a piece and water beads up, repeat the cleaning. The bottom line is this: if the metal is dirty, the adhesive won't stick.

Plastic surfaces such as the sockets require degreasing with a solvent. Use a Q-tip and acetone to remove

finger oils from the bonding surfaces. Wear polyethylene disposable gloves to keep solvents off your skin and to handle the cleaned parts. The gloves also prevent your fingers from contaminating surfaces. Bond the parts as soon as practical after you have cleaned them.

Glass surfaces, such as the optical window, must be cleaned by soaking the part in an ammonia solution. Rinse and dry the glass, then bond it to the tube cap. Any delay between cleaning and bonding virtually guarantees recontamination with organic materials.

Whenever you handle any semiconductor device, remember to employ good electrostatic discharge (ESD) procedures. Avoid non-conductive plastic surfaces; instead, work on a non-static surface such as newspaper or unpainted wood.

Use a grounded soldering iron for all semiconductor work. ESD precautions are important on the TC245 CCD chip especially, because small wires are soldered directly to the pins of the chip. Do not solder to the CCD chip with an ungrounded soldering iron.

To bleed electrostatic charges from your body, wear a grounded wrist strap with a $1M\Omega$ resistor to ground. Keep all semiconductor devices in protective antistatic

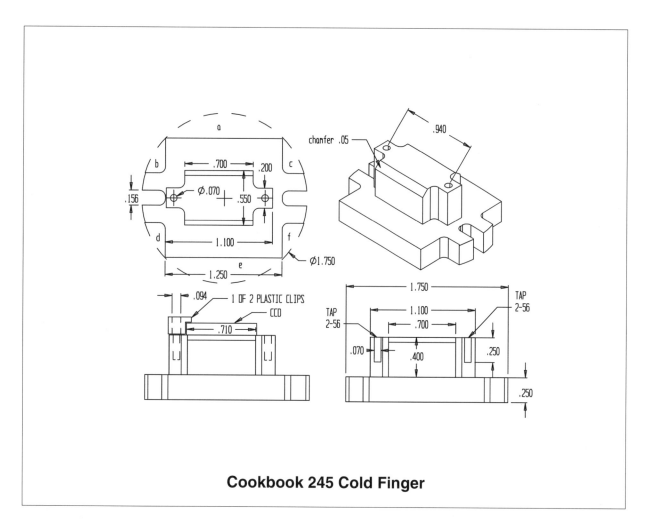

Cookbook 245 Cold Finger

containers until they are ready for installation.

As you assemble the camera, you will use certain "messy" materials. It is important that you apply adhesives such as epoxy only to surfaces that you wish to bond. Handle and apply heat-sink grease very carefully; it is extremely difficult to remove silicone grease, and nothing will bond to a contaminated surface.

7.4.2 Install the J2/J3 Electrical Sockets

Your CCD communicates with the outside world through an electrical "window" in the side of the camera body. The purpose of the sockets is to make possible good electrical connections while at the same time producing a tight environmental seal. To do this, you must insure that the sealing material, in this case quick-setting epoxy, forms a tight bond between the aluminum body and the plastic sockets.

You can construct this connection made from standard plastic terminal strips. Terminal strips consist of a plastic matrix with pass-through gold socket pins on 0.1-inch centers. You can use a section cut from an eight-pin wire wrap socket or from a 0.1-inch spaced wire wrap strip. The socket or strip should be a high quality machined tool type of contact.

Although only one strip of sockets is necessary for the Cookbook 211, two strips are needed for the J2/J3 socket pair. For the Cookbook camera, we recommend using two strips because this allows you an easy upgrade path to the Cookbook 245 CCD.

Glue the two strips together with quick-setting epoxy. To align the two strips during bonding, have a punched perf board on hand. With holes on 0.1-inch centers, the perf board will serve as an alignment fixture. To bond two socket strips, mix a small volume of epoxy. With a toothpick, apply a thin film of epoxy to one side of each strip and clamp the sides with the adhesive together. Be careful to keep the epoxy out of the socket holes. Allow the epoxy to cure fully.

Next, solder a short length of wire-wrap wire to the pin side of the J2/J3 socket as shown in the CCD Wiring Schematic. This wire zigzags from J3 pin 2 to J2 pin 3 to to J3 pin 4 to J2 pin 5 to J3 pin 6 to J2 pin 7. This wire keeps all of these pins at ground potential. Use your multimeter to check that these pins are all shorted, and that every other pin connection is open.

Before gluing the double socket-strip into the cam-

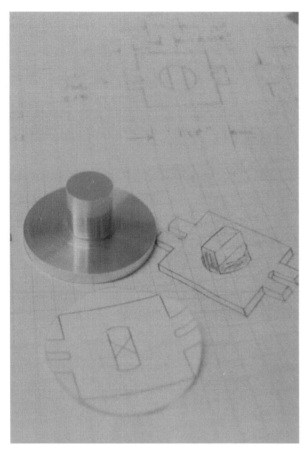

The cold finger is first turned to generate the correct outer dimensions. The one shown is for the TC211.

The flats on the cold fingers are made on a milling machine. Here you see the first cut with an end mill.

era body, prepare the metal and plastic surfaces for bonding. First make sure the socket strip fits into the slot on the camera housing, and if there is any problem, file away some of the plastic so that it does fit. Pin 5 of J2/J3 must be aligned with the center of the slot when it is bonded in. If you cannot see the original scribe line across the center of the slot, scribe it clearly. Use the end fastener holes as center line guides.

Next, rinse the area around the slot with acetone and then scrub it thoroughly with Bon Ami on a cotton swab. Rinse with water or deionized water. If the area in and around the slot on the inside and outside of the tube is free of grease and organics, water should wet the surface without beading. Clean the socket strip with acetone.

Put on polyethylene gloves to keep finger oils from the surface you are about to bond. Mix about a half of a teaspoon of the quick-setting epoxy. Using a toothpick, coat the inside of the slot with a thin film of epoxy. Apply a thin film of epoxy around the edge of the J2/J3 strip.

Slip the socket strip into the housing slot. The wire wrap pins must point in. Set the socket flush with the tube at the center of the strip. If the fit is loose, use a toothpick or a piece of paper to wedge the strip in the hole.

With quick-setting epoxy, fill in the slot around the pins and form a small fillet of epoxy around the outside of the strip. Take care not to get epoxy in the socket holes and do not coat the pins except for a small meniscus around the slot in the housing.

Quick-setting epoxy sets in 5 to 15 minutes. To prevent the epoxy from running out of the slot, turn the camera body end over end until the epoxy sets. If possible, cure the epoxy in a 150-degree Fahrenheit oven for 15 minutes. An ordinary household oven set to "warm" works well, and, of course, the oven should be relatively clean. (Your spouse will appreciate your CCD activities more fully if you clean that greasy oven.)

If you cannot cure the epoxy in an oven, wait a full day before handling the camera body. Epoxy does not cure well at temperatures below room temperature. Place the parts in a warm area to insure that the epoxy cures fully.

Because quick-set epoxy is transparent, light can leak into the camera around the J2/J3 socket slot. After the epoxy has cured, paint the epoxy black to eliminate light leakage. Any flat black enamel should work well. Do not get paint into the socket terminal holes.

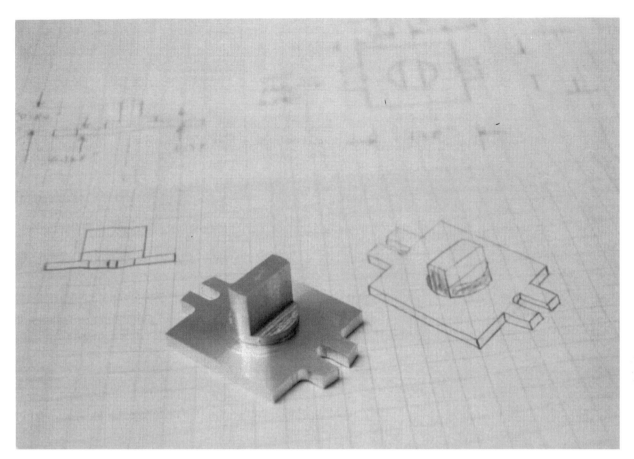

The completed cold finger draws heat from the CCD to the Peltier cooler under it. Silicone heat-sink grease will speed heat flow from the CCD to the cold finger to the Peltier module. Shown is a cold finger for TC245.

7.4.3 Bond a Socket to the Cold Finger

The Cookbook 245 chip does not fit well in non-standard 0.07-inch sockets but you may try using a socket if you can find one that works. Otherwise, you must solder the wires for the TC245 directly to the pins on the chip.

Cut two three-pin lengths of machine-tooled solder-tail terminal strips, or alternatively, cut a standard machine-tooled solder-tail socket into two three-pin segments. Cut six 2-inch lengths of wire-wrap wire and strip both ends back $\frac{1}{8}$ inch with a wire-wrap stripping tool.

Strip each wire with a wire wrap/stripper tool to avoid damaging the conductor. Bend one end of each wire into a small hook and solder the hooked end of the wires onto the strips. All three wires on each strip should come off the same side of the socket strip.

Remove any residual flux from connectors with trichloroethane, isopropanol, or acetone. Because some solvents tend to move flux around, it may take you several cleaning steps to remove the flux. Try to prevent solvent from entering the connector holes on the socket strips.

Check your work carefully to make sure that your connections will not short to the cold finger. Place each of the strips on a flat surface. Make sure the solder connections are good and that there is a gap between them and the surface. If they touch the surface, redo them or shave them down until they do not touch. This prevents shorts from the pins to the cold finger.

Plug the two strips onto a "dummy" DIP chip, a six-pin plastic DIP package. The wires leading from the strips should point outward from the DIP package. After you insert the strips fully, pull them back out about 0.030 inches. This ensures that the CCD will seat without leaving a gap between the chip and the cold finger.

Prepare the sides of the cold finger with a cleanser scrub. Apply a thin coat of JB-Weld epoxy to the sides. Slip the six-pin dummy chip with the strips over the center of the cold finger and set the chip firmly against the top of the cold finger. Center the strips and check that the DIP is flat on the top of the cold finger.

Using a toothpick as your applicator, add a fillet of epoxy to the socket strips. Do not get epoxy on the cold finger or the soldered pins. These must be free of epoxy to prevent the dummy chip from bonding to the cold finger or in case a wire breaks and you need to replace it.

Allow the epoxy to set for one hour, then cure it in

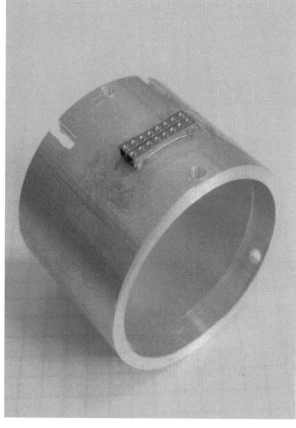

To make the J2/J3 socket, bond two eight-pin machine-tooled socket strips with quick-setting epoxy.

After you have glued the J2/J3 socket into the camera housing, the camera body should look like this.

an oven for 15 minutes at 150 degrees Fahrenheit or allow the epoxy to cure for 24 hours.

7.4.4 Mount the Optical Window

The optical window serves as a barrier to moisture and dirt, while letting light from your camera reach the CCD. Select a piece of glass for the window of your camera that is approximately 1 inch in diameter. A reticule with marking gratings that will not obstruct the central view for the TC211 will work quite well. Glass microscope slides also work well for the window. Because it is easiest to make straight cuts in glass, cut a 1-inch square or an octagon for your window.

If you have adhesively bonded the eyepiece tube to your tube cap, it is best to paint the inside diameter of the eyepiece flat black before you install the window. Prepare the interior aluminum surface of the eyepiece tube with Bon Ami cleanser and then mask the outside with tape prior to painting. Allow the paint to dry thoroughly.

Prepare the window for bonding by soaking the glass in an ammonia solution and rinsing it with deionized water. Prepare the inside ledge on the camera cap by wiping it with acetone then scrubbing with Bon Ami and a cotton swab. Be sure the window and tube cap are fully dry before you proceed.

Apply a thin coating of silicone adhesive to the mounting ledge. Change to a new pair of polyethylene gloves before handling the optical window or the silicone adhesive may spread to the window. Drop the window onto the adhesive and press it down lightly with a Q-tip. Let the silicone adhesive cure overnight.

7.4.5 Assemble the Heat Exchanger

You must now join the heat exchanger with its coolant labyrinth to the end cap. Work carefully and make sure that you leave no voids in the seal that might allow coolant to leak.

Start by cleaning the bottom of the heat exchanger with acetone, and then apply a thin coat of gasket compound to the surface. Apply a thin coat of gasket compound to the rubber or cork gasket. Let the gasket compound dry on both surfaces.

Press the coated face of the cork firmly against the coated surface of the heat exchanger. Fasten the end plate with the three $\frac{3}{8}$-inch #6-32 machine screws. Tighten the screws just enough to insure a tight seal.

For the Cookbook 211, you will construct a socket for the CCD on the cold finger. Here you see two three-pin lengths of machine-tooled socket strip epoxied to the cold finger. A dummy chip holds the strips in place.

Wrap two turns of Teflon pipe tape around the $\frac{1}{8}$-27 NPT to $\frac{1}{8}$-inch hose brass fittings. Thread each fitting into one of the two tapped holes in the heat exchanger and tighten it. The heat exchanger is now a sealed unit.

7.4.6 Install the Peltier Cooler

The Peltier module acts like a heat pump, removing heat from the cold finger and pumping it into the heat exchanger. In this step, you will assemble the cold finger and heat exchanger, placing the Peltier cooler between them.

To facilitate the flow of heat, it is necessary to coat the thermal joints with silicone heat-sink compound. Before you use the heat-sink compound, rehearse the assembly without using heat-sink compound so that you are familiar with every step. If you take this precaution, you will be less likely to smear silicone grease on a clean surface. Silicone heat-sink grease is very hard to remove and it tends to spread.

Start by checking which side of your Peltier module is the hot side and which is the cold side. Connect the red lead on the Peltier cooler to the positive (+) terminal of a 1.5-volt D-cell battery and connect the black lead to the negative terminal. Hold the module so that you can feel both sides. One side will soon become hot and one side will become cold. With a graphite pencil, write the letter "C" on the cold side and the letter "H" on the hot side.

Using a razor knife or small file, remove any remaining sharp edges from the slots in the housing to prevent any damage to the wires of the Peltier module. Slip the camera housing over the heat exchanger and align the three #6-32 machine-screw holes. With a pencil mark the location of the two slots on the side of the heat exchanger. (These marks should be between the two $\frac{1}{8}$-inch hose outlets on the heat exchanger.) Remove the camera housing and set it aside.

Center the Peltier module on the cold plate and align its wires with the exit slot marks. (The hot side of the Peltier module should be against the heat exchanger.) Gently bend the wires of the Peltier module so that they pass right over the exit slot marks, taking care not to stress the solder connections on the module.

Put on polyethylene gloves. When you handle the cold finger and the cold plate, your hands should be free of silicone grease. The idea is to keep silicone grease away

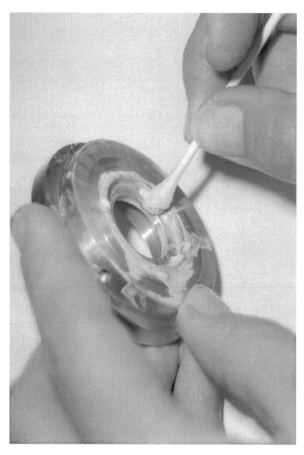

Before bonding the window, prepare the aluminum by scrubbing with cleanser and rinsing with water.

After cleaning it in an ammonia solution, dry and then seat the glass window in a bed of silicone adhesive.

from everything except the mating surfaces of the module, cold finger, and heat exchanger.

Place a small spot of heat-sink compound on the hot side of the Peltier module. Press the module against the heat exchanger with its wires over the marks you made for them. Holding the module by the edge, spread a thin film of grease between the surfaces. Don't get it on the sides. Work the Peltier module around until it is seated.

Place another small spot of silicone grease on the cold side of the Peltier module, and then press the base of the cold finger on the module. Work it around until the grease spreads to a thin layer between and the cold finger feels seated.

Slide the cold finger to its final location. The wires must exit at the locations you have marked previously, the screw holes must be aligned, and the cold finger must be centered on the heat exchanger. If your polyethylene gloves have any silicone grease on them, switch to a new pair of gloves.

Thread a Nylon nut onto each of the 1-inch Nylon machine screws. Slip a steel flat washer onto the screw, and then thread each of the screws into the heat exchanger. Tighten the nuts against the ears of the cold finger until it

is firmly held in place. For a neat job, cut off the heads of the machine screws to form Nylon studs.

Slip the camera housing over the heat exchanger. Check that the cold finger appears centered in the optical window and that the Peltier wires pass through the slots in the camera housing. Your camera is fast approaching completion. Only a few steps—admittedly tricky ones—remain before you will be making images.

Stretch-wrap the 2.083-inch diameter of the heat exchanger and its lips with two to three turns of Teflon pipe thread tape. Place the heat exchanger on a solid surface. Gently force the camera body over the Teflon-wrapped heat exchanger. Insert the three #6-32 housing to water jacket screws and tighten them.

7.5 Final Assembly of the Camera Body

In the Cookbook 211 camera, the last steps in assembling your CCD camera are installing the wires leading to the CCD and installing the CCD itself. In the Cookbook 245 camera, you must solder connecting wires directly to the pins of the CCD chip. Once the chip is wired in place, you can check the wiring, and if everything seems to be okay, turn on the power and check that it is

To close the fluid labyrinth of the heat exchanger, coat the cork gasket with a layer of gasket sealant.

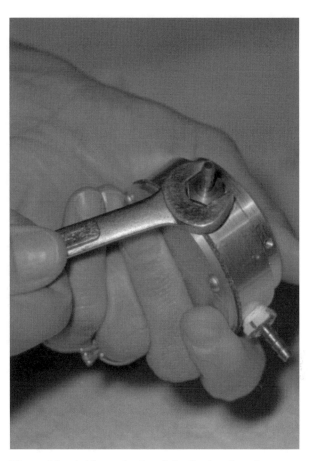

Thread the tubing adaptors into the heat exchanger. Teflon tape on the threads seals the joint watertight.

sensitive to light. Once you know that, close the camera body, install the preamplifier card and its protective cover, and proceed with taking your first images.

7.5.1 Install the TC211 CCD

Study the socket wiring schematic for the Cookbook 211. In the schematic, the sockets are shown as you see them from inside the camera housing. Connector J2 is the top set of pins. Note that this pin order is a mirror image of the view shown in the preamplifier schematic.

When you are wiring the CCD socket or chip, use the socket wiring diagram to identify the pins. When you test for continuity, identify the pins from the preamplifier schematic. Double-check the order of these pins; getting them right is necessary for successful camera operation.

Using a pair of tweezers, hook the stripped ends of the cold-finger socket wires. Connect and solder the wires to the J2/J3 sockets one at a time. Inspect each solder connection. Make sure all solder joints are good and make sure that solder does not short adjacent pins.

Inspect the wire-wrap wire insulation. If you accidentally burn away a small section of insulation with the soldering iron, the exposed wire could short at a later time

if it touches a metal part inside the camera. You must either route the damaged wire so that it cannot short or repair the burned section with a piece of Mylar tape.

Using the ohm measurement setting on your multimeter, check the continuity of your wiring. When you probe J2/J3 from the outside and the socket, the housing, and the cold finger from the inside, you should measure the following resistances:

From Connector	To CCD Socket	To Housing	To Cold Finger
Pin J2-1	Pin 3 Short	Open	Open
Pin J2-2	Pin 4 Short	Open	Open
Pin J2-3	Pin 2 Short	Open	Open
Pin J2-4	Pin 1 Short	Open	Open
Pin J2-5	Pin 2 Short	Open	Open
Pin J2-6	Pin 5 Short	Open	Open
Pin J2-7	Pin 2 Short	Open	Open
Pin J2-8	Pin 6 Short	Open	Open

If your meter reads between 0 and 2Ω, you have a short. If it reads 1MΩ or more, the circuit is open. Between

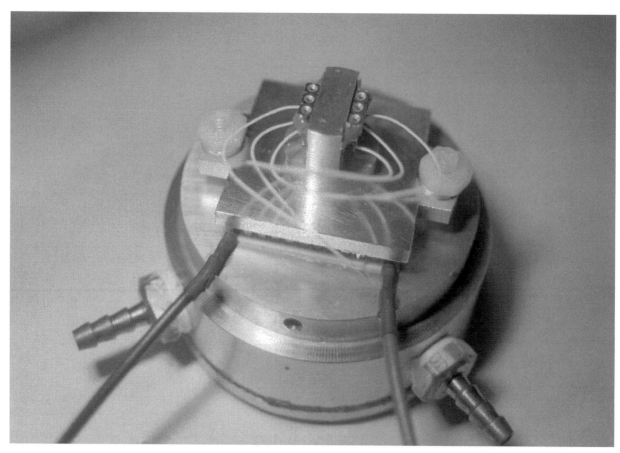

The leads of the Peltier cooler extend from beneath the Cookbook 211 socketed cold finger. Two Nylon nuts on Nylon studs hold the cold finger firmly without adding the danger of crushing the Peltier module.

every pair of adjacent pins on J2, you should measure an open circuit.

If you find an open where a short should be, look for a miswired pin or a poor solder joint. If a short is present where an open should be, look for miswiring, a solder bridge, or a bridge between wires. If you see no obvious problem and a pin is shorted to the case or to the cold finger, remove the socket associated with the short and replace it.

After the wiring has tested good, wet a cotton swab with a small amount of solvent. Remove any residual flux that you find around the soldered connections. You may find droplets of flux spattered on the inside of the housing; clean them off with solvent.

7.5.2 Socket-Test the TC211 CCD

To guard against damaging the TC211 when you apply power to it, test the voltage on every pin of the socket that the TC211 is plugged into. If the voltages are correct, you probably cannot harm the chip when you apply power. Remember, however, that throughout socket testing you must continue to use static-safe handling procedures whenever you handle any electronic compo-

nent or assembly.

Plug the preamplifier connectors J1 and JS into the printer interface card. Make sure the JS connector has the ground shield in the correct pin position.

Plug the preamplifier into the J2/J3 socket on the camera housing. Inspect the pins carefully to ensure the plug is seated and that it is not shifted over by one pin. Remove the centerline end plate screw on the heat exchanger to temporarily install the back preamplifier cover bracket. Mark the place on the bracket where the circuit board hole aligns, and then remove it and drill and tap this location for a #4-40 thread. After cleaning the bracket, replace it on the camera body.

Thread a nut onto a #4-40 machine screw and insert it into the mounting hole on the preamplifier card. Thread another nut on the end of the screw and turn the screw into the bracket. The card is captured between the two nuts and the height of the card is adjusted with the nuts.

At this point the TC211 is ready for socket testing. Connect the interface box to the power supply and the printer cable between the computer and the interface box.

Start the AP211.EXE program and turn on the ±15VDC power supply. Although you will see an error

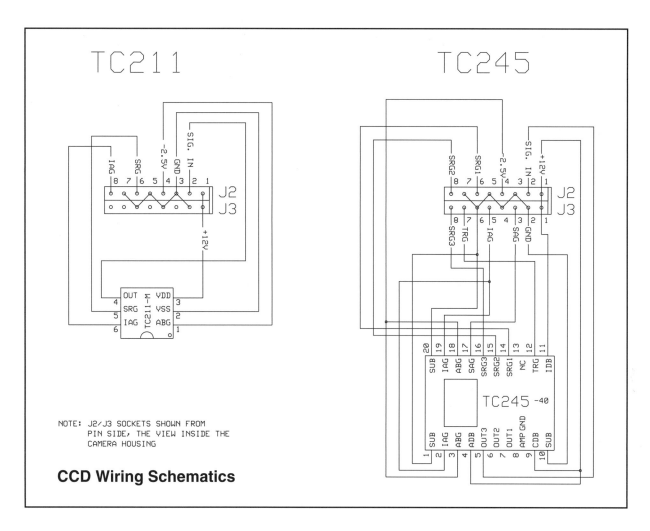

CCD Wiring Schematics

NOTE: J2/J3 SOCKETS SHOWN FROM PIN SIDE, THE VIEW INSIDE THE CAMERA HOUSING

message because the program will not find a SETUP.DAT file, you can safely ignore this message. Exit to the Main Menu by pressing any key. This will cause the program to begin continuously clearing the CCD chip, and in so doing to activate the voltages you are about to check.

Connect the negative lead of your digital multimeter to the case of the interface box and set the meter to a 20VDC full scale range. The voltages on the socket pins should measure as follows:

Pin 1	−2.7 to −2.1 VDC
Pin 2	−0.1 to +0.1 VDC
Pin 3	+11.5 to +12.5 VDC
Pin 4	−2.7 to +1.0 VDC
Pin 5	-9.8 to +2.2 VDC
Pin 6	−9.8 to +2.2 VDC

Note that the voltages on pins 5 and 6 are clock signals, and they will change. If a voltage reads outside the range specified, check the ±15VDC supply. If the power supply is okay, then you may have wired the socket

incorrectly or installed the preamplifier card incorrectly in the J2/J3 socket. Check that each pins from the preamplifier card are properly plugged into the J2/J3 socket.

If you see no obvious problems, turn off the power and unplug the preamplifier card. Check the voltages on the J2/J3 pins on the preamplifier card. Correct voltage levels at the card indicate a wiring problem between the J2/J3 socket and the CCD socket.

If you get incorrect card voltage levels, troubleshoot by first checking that you have plugged the J1 DIP plug into the printer interface card correctly. Next retest the preamplifier using PREAMP.EXE, the preamplifier test program. Start at the level with all of the chips removed from the preamplifier card. The most likely cause of failure is that a tantalum capacitor installed with the wrong polarity has shorted. If the preamplifier card checks out, test the printer interface card for this problem.

When the socket passes its test, quit the AP211.EXE program and turn off the ±15VDC power. Wait a minute for the supply to discharge.

Two very small square dots on the top edge of the TC211 ceramic package identify pin 1. Use a magnifier to ensure you know where pin 1 is. Apply a small amount

Soldering the CCD leads in the Cookbook 211 is a delicate job. Each of the six wires from the socket must be soldered to the appropriate soldertail of the J2/J3 socket. Completing this task takes roughly 20 minutes.

of heat-sink compound to the top of the cold finger. Clean your hands thoroughly before you insert the CCD chip because silicone grease is extremely difficult to remove from the CCD window.

Press the TC211 CCD chip firmly into the cold finger socket. The chip should fit flush against the surface of the cold finger. Use a magnifier to check that the chip is installed with pin 1 in the correct location.

Your Cookbook 211 is now ready for first light!

7.5.3 Install the TC245 CCD

Wiring the TC245 chip in the Cookbook 245 may be the most difficult process of the camera assembly. It involves delicate handling of many fine wires in a very small space while using electrostatic discharge precautions. The installation takes about two hours. Take the procedure step by step and relax. After all, installing a CCD is still a lot easier than brain surgery.

If you are converting a Cookbook 211 to a Cookbook 245, you must make the appropriate changes on your preamplifier card and your printer interface card prior to wiring the TC245 chip. Refer to Appendix D for the details of making this upgrade.

To install the TC245, cut nine $1\frac{3}{8}$-inch lengths and seven $2\frac{1}{8}$-inch lengths of wire-wrap wire. Strip $\frac{1}{16}$ inch of insulation off each end of each wire.

Next, cut a $\frac{5}{8}$-inch wide by $1\frac{1}{4}$-inch long piece of black conductive foam. Using static-safe handling procedures, wrap the foam in aluminum foil and insert the foiled block of conductive foam between the leads of the TC245 chip. The idea is to short all of the leads, so that no stray voltage can harm the CCD.

A small triangular index mark denotes pin 1 on the TC245. To leads 11, 12, and 14 through 20 on the TC245, solder one of the short wires. To leads 1 through 5, and leads 9 and 10, solder one of the long wires.

Each wire you solder must lie flat against the outer face of the lead on the CCD, and the wire should continue straight downward from the lead. Do not wrap the wires around leads or there may be too little clearance between the wires and the cold finger. Inspect each solder connection with a magnifier: look for cold solder joints and solder bridges.

Shape each of the free ends of the wires into a hook and solder the wires to the J2/J3 socket pins. Follow the

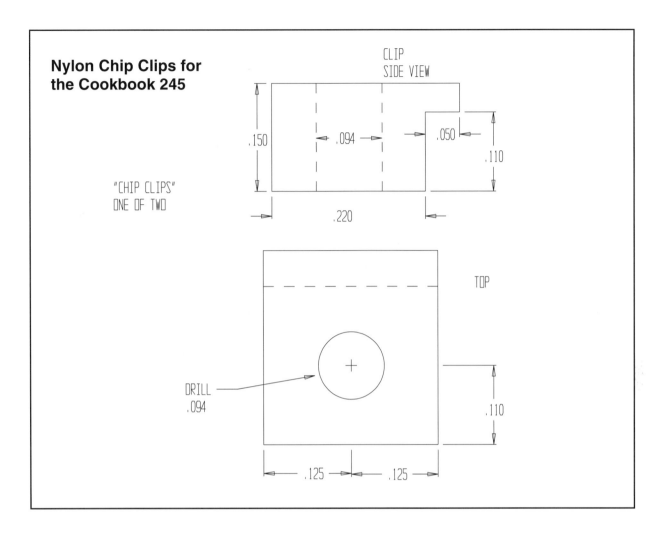

Nylon Chip Clips for the Cookbook 245

CLIP
SIDE VIEW

"CHIP CLIPS"
ONE OF TWO

.150   .094   .050   .110

.220

TOP

DRILL
.094

.110

.125   .125

CCD-to-socket wiring diagram. Remember that this diagram shows the pin numbers as they appear from inside of the camera body.

Soldering these tiny wires can be very frustrating. It may be best to have a partner hold the wire with a pair of tweezers while you solder the connections. It helps to tin each of the pins and wires beforehand; a light touch of the soldering iron then usually serves to join them. You may also wish to practice your soldering technique on a discarded op amp or logic circuit before you start to solder wires to a $150 CCD chip.

Inspect the final job with a magnifier for pin-to-pin solder bridges and cold solder joints. As an ESD precaution, tape a piece of aluminum foil over the J2/J3 socket then remove the foil block from between the CCD leads.

Wrap the sides of the cold finger with an insulating tape, preferably a Mylar film tape such as the Rubylith tape that lithographers use. This prevents the leads of the TC245 from shorting to the cold finger.

Stretch-wrap the 2.083-inch diameter of the heat exchanger and its lips with two to three turns of Teflon pipe thread tape. Brace the heat exchanger against a solid surface while you gently force the camera body over the heat exchanger. Insert the three #6-32 housing to water jacket screws and tighten them.

Coat the top of the cold finger with a thin film of heat-sink grease. Slip the housing over the water jacket and route the CCD chip wires around the cold finger as in the chip wiring diagram.

Press the CCD onto the cold finger and fasten the chip at each end with the Nylon plastic clips that you made. The two Nylon clips prevent you from exerting a too-strong force and thereby damaging or cracking the CCD. Fasten each clip using a #2-56 screw as a stud, with a #2-56 nut and a flat washer to press against the plastic clip. The clips can press on the ceramic but must not press on the glass window.

On the CCD is a protective plastic shield over the chip. Leave this on until the first light test is done.

Lift the aluminum tape off of the J2/J3 socket strip and perform continuity testing. Every pin should test open circuit to the housing and open circuit to the cold finger. If you find a short to the cold finger, check for a break in the tape insulation. A short to the housing usually means

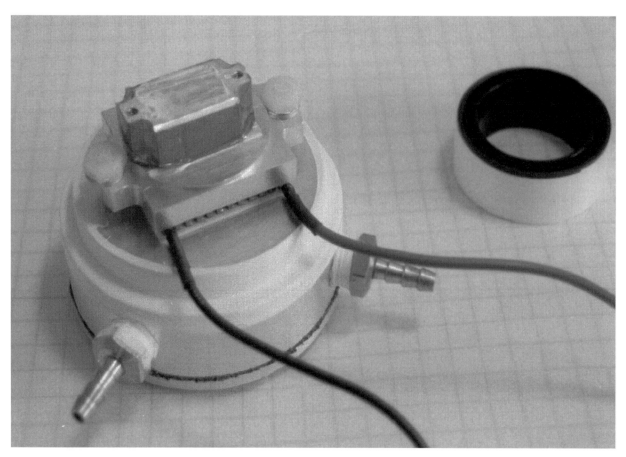

The cold finger and Peltier module in the Cookbook 245 are similar to the Cookbook 211. However, unless you can find a socket to match the non-standard pin spacing, you must solder wires directly to the 245 chip.

solder splashes or a wire end shorting to the housing. Test for *zero ohms* between these pins:

J2 Pin 1 to CCD Pins 4, 9 and 11
J2 Pin 2 to CCD Pin 5
J2 Pin 3 to CCD Pins 1, 10 and 20
J2 Pin 4 to CCD Pins 3 and 18
J2 Pin 6 to CCD Pin 14
J2 Pin 8 to CCD Pin 15
J3 Pin 3 to CCD Pin 17
J3 Pin 5 to CCD Pins 2 and 19
J3 Pin 7 to CCD Pin 12
J3 Pin 8 to CCD Pin 16

If any pin combination tests out incorrectly, first check that you are probing the correct socket and CCD pins. (It is easy to get flustered and confuse the pins.) Next, trace the wiring to find the error. Wiring errors must be fixed before you apply power to the CCD chip.

7.5.4 Testing the TC245 CCD

Unfortunately, you cannot socket-test the Cookbook 245 camera before you install the CCD because the TC245 is not mounted in a socket. The camera must be powered up with the TC245 chip on line. Unless you encounter a problem in its operation, you are better off not to measure the voltages on the pins of your TC245.

To prepare the camera for operation, plug the preamplifier connectors J1 and JS into the printer interface card. Make sure the JS connector has the ground shield in the correct pin position.

Plug the preamplifier into the J2/J3 socket on the camera housing. Inspect the pins carefully to ensure the plug is seated and that it is not shifted over by one pin. Remove the centerline end plate screw on the heat exchanger to install the back bracket. Thread a nut onto a #4-40 screw and insert the screw into the mounting hole on the preamplifier card. Thread another nut on the end of the screw and turn the screw into the bracket. The card is captured between the two nuts and the height of the card is adjusted with the nuts.

7.6 First Light!

Your first functional test of the CCD chip requires a dark environment. The chip is very sensitive to light. Place the tube cap on the camera and cover the eyepiece

Painstaking attention to electrostatic safety is the key to installing the TC245 in the Cookbook 245. During installation, the CCD's pins press into conductive foam and the J2/J3 pins are grounded with aluminum foil.

tube with an opaque cover. It is also a good idea to dim the room lights before you turn on the camera.

Start the image acquisition software, AP211.EXE or AP245.EXE, and turn on the ±15VDC power. Move to the Main Menu and check the reset voltage level. Adjust the P1 potentiometer until the reset level measures about 500 counts for the Cookbook 211 and 1000 counts for the Cookbook 245 camera. (These are good starting points and the values can be adjusted later.)

If the reset level remains at 4095 no matter what you do with the potentiometer, there may be a light leak in the camera body. If the reset level remains at zero, the camera may be malfunctioning. Try shining a bright light on the chip, and if the reset count remains at zero, power down. Check that the CCD chip you installed has the correct orientation, and recheck the pin voltages on the CCD socket. It is very unlikely that a problem would suddenly arise in the completed circuitry, so look for recent problems such as the preamplifier card shorting out on a pair of pliers on the bench.

After you have adjusted the reset level, uncover the CCD chip and expose it to light. The reset count should increase with exposure to light.

Shield the chip from light and enter the Find/Focus display menu. Go to the Set Option sub-menu and set the high stretch level to 4095. Exit to the Find/Focus display menu. The quarter-frame display should appear gray. When the chip is exposed to light, the display will become entirely white. When this test is completed, power down the system and exit the image acquisition program.

That's it! Your CCD camera has passed its first functional test. It has detected light. To use it on your telescope, you must now complete a few tasks and neatly package the camera for outdoor use.

7.7 Clean and Close the Camera Body

With the camera now functional, it's time to ready everything for use on a telescope. Unplug the preamplifier from the socket and cover the J2/J3 pins with aluminum-foil-lined tape. The foil must press against the J2/J3 contacts and the exposed aluminum on the housing. This protects the CCD from electrostatic damage when you handle the housing.

Air-dust the inside of the camera housing to remove dirt particles or metal chips. Clean the CCD window with isopropanol on a cotton swab; finger oils may require

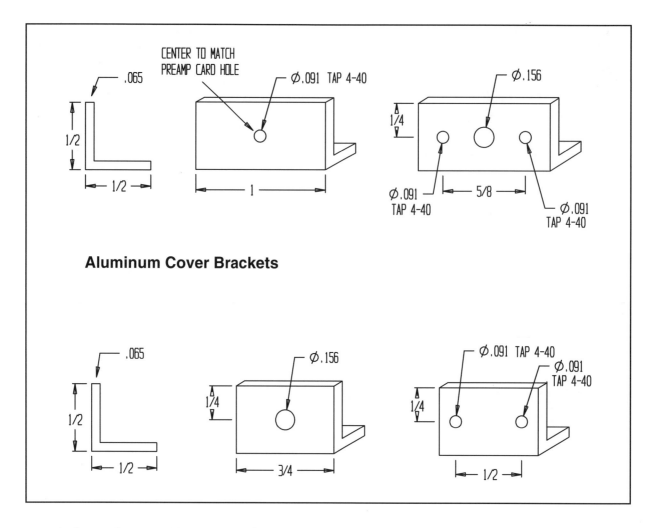

Aluminum Cover Brackets

several wipes to clean away. Dust away any lint or cotton fibers that remains with lintless lens paper and air.

Next, close the top of the camera. Mark the orientation of the tube cap and then stretch-wrap two turns of Teflon pipe tape over the large and small diameters of the cap. Press the cap onto the housing and insert the two #6-32 machine screws in the holes away from the preamplifier side.

The hole on the preamplifier side is the fastener location for a cover bracket. Insert the remaining #6-32 machine screw through this bracket and attach the bracket to the camera. Tighten all three screws.

Next, seal the wires to the Peltier cooler. Squeeze hot-melt glue caulking compound around the Peltier wires where they enter the machined slots in the housing. If the caulk does not adhere to the cold surface of the aluminum, heat the housing with the tip of the glue gun before you apply the hot-melt glue.

When the hot-melt glue cools, paint it black. If you leave the glue white or clear, unwanted light can enter the camera body and fog your astronomical images.

Remove the aluminum tape cover from the J2/J3 socket and install the preamplifier card just as you did earlier for testing. Attach the card to the bracket at the bottom end of the camera.

7.8 Install the Preamplifier Cover

The preamplifier cover protect the preamplifier from mechanical damage and absorbs tugs and pulls that might otherwise harm the wires.

You made this cover, described in section 6.5.3., from sheet aluminum. Attach it to the cover brackets with $\frac{1}{8}$-inch #4-40 machine screws. (If you cannot find such short screws, cut off longer ones.)

Tape the edges of the cover to prevent cuts on cables. Run tie-wraps through the holes in the cover and tighten them over the ribbon cables, the coaxial cable, and Peltier wires. When you tug at these cables, the tie-wraps should take up all of the stress.

7.9 What You Have Done and What Remains

Take stock of the entire project: where are you now? The power supply is done and working, the electronic circuits are finished and working, and you know that your CCD is light-sensitive and that it "talks" to your computer. So far so good.

Where do you go from here? For astronomical

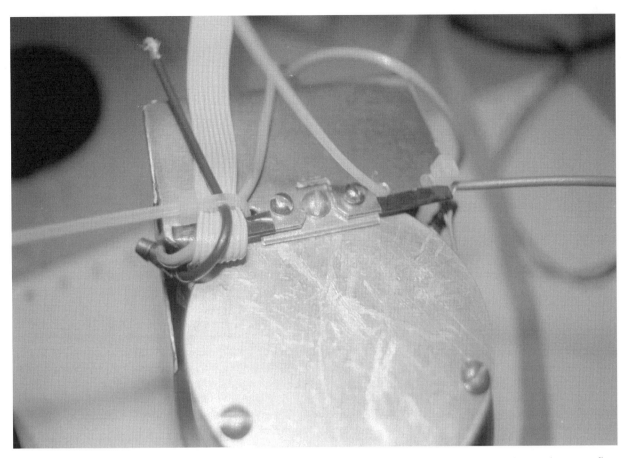

Installing covers and securing wires may seem like a waste of time when you can't wait to take your first image—but do it right. Here the ribbon cable and coaxial cable are being tie-wrapped to the rear of the cover.

operation, you must now complete the cooling system and fill it with coolant. This is covered in Chapter 8. You must also become familiar with the image acquisition software, which you will begin to learn in the course of taking your first indoor images. The use of the image acquisition software is covered in Chapter 9.

You will receive your reward when you integrate the entire system and begin to take images with it. Section 10 describes how to integrate and test the camera indoors, and Chapter 11 gives hints and tips for using your Cookbook 211 or Cookbook 245 for the best possible astronomical images.

Chapter 8. Building the Coolant System

To get the best possible performance from your Cookbook CCD camera, the chip should operate at a temperature of –30° Celsius or cooler. During operation, the chip should stay as close to the same temperature as possible. Stability in the operating temperature means that the thermal signal generated in the chip remains constant, allowing you to shoot less frequent thermal frames and therefore make more efficient use of your observing time.

The liquid cooling system is the most effective way to maintain a low and stable temperature at the CCD chip. Although well designed air-cooled CCD cameras may attain the same temperature as a liquid-cooled camera, most air-cooled designs are less stable.

Without a doubt, the liquid-cooled camera requires more effort to transport, set up, and use than an air-cooled camera would. Once you have it operating on your telescope, however, the liquid-cooled camera repays your extra effort with superior results.

8.1 What Cooling a CCD Does

Cooling your CCD dramatically reduces the thermal signal from the chip, and greatly increases the length of the exposures you can make with your CCD camera. Section 3.4 covers the effects of thermal noise.

In your camera, the Peltier cooler "pumps" heat from the cold finger that holds the CCD, making the CCD cold. To work efficiently, all the waste heat pumped through the Peltier cooler should be removed. This is the first job of the liquid coolant system.

Other things being equal, the Peltier cooler maintains a constant temperature difference between its two sides, so the key to maintaining a *constant* temperature at the chip is to maintain a constant temperature on the hot side of the Peltier cooler. This is the second job of the liquid coolant system.

8.2 How the Liquid Coolant System Works

The coolant system is a simple closed-loop heat exchanger that ultimately derives its stability from the heat capacity of a water bath. The coolant system consists of the heat exchanger in the camera head, a second heat exchanger in the form of a coil of copper tube immersed in a bath of water, a large tub to hold the copper coil in the bath, an automobile windshield-washer pump to circulate a coolant fluid through the system, and roughly 30 feet of tubing to carry the coolant between the heat exchangers.

In the camera head, a coolant made of isopropanol and water enters and flows through the labyrinth in the heat exchanger. Because of the high thermal capacity of the coolant and the high thermal conductivity of aluminum, the temperature of the hot side of the Peltier module remains very close to that of the coolant fluid.

When it exits the heat exchanger in the camera head, the coolant has absorbed almost all of the 40 watts of heat from the Peltier module. The coolant transfers this waste heat through the copper coil to the water in the tub.

The large heat capacity of a water bath prevents rapid changes in the temperature of the circulating coolant. The more water, the greater the thermal stability. We recommend five gallons, though as little as one gallon of water does a good job.

As tempting as it sounds, cooling the Peltier with extremely cold water does little to help the camera's performance. This is because, as the hot side of a Peltier module gets colder, its efficiency drops. For each 2.5 degrees you drop the temperature of the water, the temperature of the CCD chip drops only 1 degree. Furthermore, if you use coolant that is below the dew-point of the air, condensation forms on the camera and fogs the window.

The optimum results come with a water bath that is about 5° Fahrenheit (3°C) above the dew point. In dry climates, cool the water bath with ice. In moist climates, keep the water bath at the ambient air temperature.

You can enhance the temperature *stability* of the system by adding an ice cube to the water bath every four minutes. The energy needed to melt the ice offsets the heat input from the Peltier and keeps the water bath at a constant temperature. (This rate assumes 40 watts from the Peltier and 28-gram ice cubes.)

8.3 Building the Coolant System

In this design, the liquid coolant system serves to cool the CCD. A significant side benefit of the coolant system is that you can route the wires between the inter-

Buy an automotive windshield-washer pump, 30 feet of plastic tubing, a coil of copper tube, a few plumbing parts and—*voilà*—you've got what you need to remove unwanted heat from your Peltier-cooled CCD camera.

face box and the power supply alongside the coolant tubes. The construction of the coolant system therefore includes assembling a complete harness of wires and tubes to carry power and coolant between the camera and the cooling system and power supply that support it.

The design of the coolant system is quite flexible. If you plan to use your CCD in a small observatory, you can shorten the coolant tubes, use a quieter coolant pump, and route the ribbon cable separately to the computer. No problem! The only constraint in changing the cooling system is that you *must* keep the water bath well separated from 120VAC electrical equipment. Water and house current should *never* mix.

8.3.1 Form the Copper Coil

By passing the coolant through 20 feet of copper tubing immersed in a bath of ice and water, you will insure that the coolant that enters the heat exchanger in the camera body remains at very nearly the same temperature as the bath, and thus insure that your CCD operates at a low and constant temperature.

Purchase 20 feet of $\frac{1}{4}$-inch copper tubing. Copper tubing usually comes wrapped in a loose coil 12 to 18

inches in diameter. If you don't buy the tubing new, make sure that the tubing has no kinks or bends, and that nothing harmful or corrosive has flowed through the tubing.

Select a form for winding the copper coil. The form should be a cylinder roughly 2.5 inches in diameter and 6 inches long, ideally made of a solid material such as wood or aluminum. In a pinch almost anything round will work as a form, even an unopened drink can!

Leaving 6 inches of tubing free, wrap ten turns around the form. This will take about 7 feet of tubing. Tie the first ten turns of the coil together with heavy string, then wrap another ten turns back up over the copper spiral that you have already formed and tie the double coil together with heavy string. You will have about 3 feet of tubing left over.

Bend the free ends of the tubing so that they are parallel to the axis of the coil. With a tubing cutter, trim the tubing so the free ends protrude about 3 inches beyond the end of the coil. On each free end of tubing install a $\frac{1}{4}$-inch compression to $\frac{1}{8}$-27 NPT female fitting. Over the threads of a $\frac{1}{8}$-27 NPT male to $\frac{1}{8}$-inch hose adapter, wrap Teflon tape. Thread the two tubing adaptors into the fittings installed on the coil.

8.3.2 Assemble the Cable Harness

Although you might be able to use your camera with wires and cables snaking every which way indoors, when you're outdoors and trying to shoot images you'll need to keep all of the wires and cables that connect the camera under control. Because the tubes that carry coolant to the camera are strong and stiff, the coolant tubes conveniently form the backbone of the cable harness connecting the camera to the computer and power supply.

From the camera end of the cable harness, you will route the Peltier cooler wire and the ±15VDC power wire into the harness with the coolant tubes. By cinching these wires to the coolant tubes with wire ties, you'll relieve stress on these connections and prevent any sudden tugs or jerks from damaging the Peltier cooler wire.

At the power-supply end of the harness, the Peltier cooler wires and ±15VDC power wire split away from the coolant tubes about 2 feet from the copper coil. At the same point, the pump power wire joins the harness and continues down the harness to the pump. The harness ends where the coolant tubes enter the copper coil.

To carry power to the Peltier cooler, cut a 15-foot length of 18-gauge speaker wire. Separate the wires about 3 inches from one end and strip the insulation from $\frac{1}{2}$ inch on each wire. Slip a one-inch length of $\frac{3}{8}$-inch heat-shrink tubing over each speaker wire. Twist the copper or striped wire together with the red Peltier wire and solder them together. Do the same for the silver or non-striped speaker wire and the black Peltier wire. Slip the shrink tubing over the exposed wires and shrink the tubing with a match or a cigarette lighter.

For the coolant tubes, buy a 30-foot length of $\frac{1}{4}$-inch outside diameter by $\frac{1}{8}$-inch inside diameter plastic tubing. Model airplane fuel line is expensive, but it stays flexible. Cut two 12.5-foot lengths and set the remainder aside in the event that you later need it. Press one end of each tube over the $\frac{1}{8}$-inch fittings on the camera head.

On a large table or a clean floor, make up the camera end of the harness. Pull the interface box away from the camera head so that the ribbon cables and coax cable are straight. Plug the ±15VDC cable into the interface box and run it side-by-side to the camera head. Using nylon tie wraps, bundle the ±15VDC cable, the Peltier wire, and the two coolant tubes into one group about 5 inches below the camera head. Leave a little slack in the Peltier wire and ±15VDC wire so that the tubing carries the weight of the wires. The tubing should absorb any stress on the wires.

At 6-inch intervals, tie-wrap the tubing and wires into a tight bundle. Stop putting on tie-wraps when 2 feet of vinyl tubing remain free.

At this point, 2 feet from the end of the coolant tubing, the Peltier wire and the ±15VDC wire should exit

Form the copper coil heat exchanger by wrapping 20 feet of $\frac{1}{4}$-inch copper tube over any cylindrical form.

from the harness. In addition, a wire to the pump should exit the cable at this point.

Cut one of the coolant tubes in the free section of the harness 6 inches from the last tie-wrap. Insert the cut tube into the pump fluid input port and connect the 18-inch length to the pump output port.

To serve as the pump power wire, cut a 4-foot length of speaker wire. Split and strip one end of the wire, and solder them to the pump terminals. Make sure that you solder the "marked" or copper conductor in the speaker wire to the positive terminal or lead on the pump. Solder a 0.1μF 50V film capacitor across the pump input terminals.

Run the pump power wire along the tubing. Stress relieve the tubing and wire by tie-wrapping them to the pump mounting ears. Bundle the pump wire, the ±15VDC wire, and the Peltier wire together and tie-wrap them every 6 inches.

Cut the ends of all the wires to the same length as the ±15VDC wire, then strip the ends and attach the Peltier wires to the Peltier power supply. Also strip the ends of the pump power supply wire. Connect the pump positive

Five gallons of water absorb heat from the Peltier and ensure a low, stable temperature for your CCD.

the pail, and nail small wooden blocks to the bottom side of the disk to center the disk on the pail. You may wish to seal or paint this wood before using it.

Drill or cut a radial slot 1 inch wide from the edge to the center of the disk. Using sheet-metal screws, mount the pump on the top of the disk and route the tubing to the copper coil through the slot.

To simplify filling the system with coolant, add a coolant reservoir. A one-pint plastic container will serve well. Purchase a $\frac{1}{8}$-inch plastic tubing connector and cut it in two. Drill two holes that fit the cut ends of the tubing connector near the base of the reservoir container, and then seal the tubing connectors in place with hot-melt adhesive.

Glue the reservoir to the top of the disk with hot-melt adhesive. Cut the tubing and route the fluid circuit into the reservoir. Finally, tidy the job by cinching the tubing harness to the wooden disk with wire ties.

8.4 Test the Liquid Coolant System

Before you conduct an all-up test of the camera, test the coolant system for proper operation. Arrange the power supply, camera, and coolant system and connect the wiring.

Pour two cups of deionized water into a clean one-quart container. Turn the Peltier voltage to the minimum level and then turn on the Peltier supply. The pump should start immediately.

Immerse the end of the coolant tubing that is connected to the pump inlet side in the deionized water. The pump will draw in air, but if it does not start to draw coolant, suck on the free tubing end until it starts pumping. Make sure that the end of the copper coil is over the container so that coolant doesn't squirt out.

Once the pump has been primed and is running, add one cup of isopropanol to the coolant water. Allow the pump to run until all of the air bubbles are out of the system. (If you have put a reservoir in your system, the bubbles will clear automatically.) You may need to tip and turn the camera head and the copper coil to get all of the bubbles out. After you have a steady flow established, slip the free end of the tubing over the fitting on the copper coil and allow coolant to circulate in the closed system.

If you have added a coolant reservoir to your system, you need only fill the reservoir with coolant. As the fluid circulates, the reservoir will trap all the bubbles.

The pump may sound pretty rough at first. Remember that you are running an intermittent duty 12-volt pump in continuous duty on 5 volts, so forgive its idiosyncrasies as long as it continues to run. Windshield-washer pumps sound better after they have run a few hours.

As you run the system, check for leaks and monitor the pump for proper operation. If a few new bubbles appear, you can unhook the tubing and work them out, but don't worry about them. A few bubbles will cause no harm. When the coolant system checks out, you are ready to fire up the camera!

wire (the marked or copper conductor in speaker wire) to pump positive (+) out, and connect the pump minus connection (use the non-marked or silver conductor) to the Peltier/pump common. Connect the Peltier positive red wire (the marked or copper conductor) to the Peltier positive (+) output. Connect the Peltier negative wire (the non-marked or silver conductor) to the Peltier/pump common.

As you build the ±15VDC cable, check that the red wire goes to +15VDC, the green or black wire goes to the common, and the yellow wire goes to −15VDC.

Press one of the two free ends of the coolant tubing onto the copper coil but leave the other end free until you are ready to fill and test the coolant system.

The cable harness should keep all of the wires neat and tidy. Inspect the harness: if you see any loose or sloppy areas, tie-wrap them together.

8.3.3 Mount the Pump and Coil

As an optional step, you can mount the pump and copper coil on the container for the water bath. For your water bath, purchase a heavy-duty plastic pail that holds 12 to 20 quarts. Cut a plywood disk to fit over the top of

Chapter 9. Using the Camera Software

Before you can make images with your camera, you will need to install the appropriate image acquisition program and become familiar with using it. Two image acquisition programs, AP211 and AP245, are provided with this book. AP211 runs the Cookbook 211 camera and AP245 runs the Cookbook 245. The image acquisition programs will run on virtually any PC—from a humble XT to the fastest 486. You will find them on the diskettes bound into the back of this book.

To install the image acquisition software, make a directory for it on your computer's hard disk. Use a name that you can easily remember, such as C:\COOKBOOK. Copy the ZIPped files from the distribution disk into this directory, then follow the instructions you find in the READ.ME file on the distribution disk to unZIP the files.

Please note that the image acquisition programs and the other software included with this book are copyrighted works, and that the purchase of this book grants you license to use the software with your Cookbook camera. You may copy the image acquisition programs onto any computer that you use with your Cookbook camera, but your license does not grant you the right to lend, give, or sell copies of this software to any other person.

9.1 What the Software Does

The acquisition program is designed to make taking images with the Cookbook cameras fast and easy. The program controls the Cookbook camera through your computer's parallel port. When you run the program, you make choices from a screen menu that tells your camera what to do. The software takes care of all the technical details of communicating with the camera.

To find a celestial object, you press the F key to start the finding mode. When you see finder images on the screen, you press the A key to automatically adjust their brightness. You can see faint objects in exposure times of 1 or 2 seconds. To begin an integration—that is, to capture an image with your CCD—you press the I key and then select the length of the integration, typically several minutes. When the integration is complete, you press the D key to display the image and A to automatically adjust its brightness. If you wish to save the new image, you press

the S key and type in a filename. In a few moments, your image is stored safely on the computer's hard disk.

The acquisition programs are very flexible. They allow you to make full-frame exposures of any desired length, to take dark frames, and to take half- and quarter frames. Full-frame images naturally give the largest field of view, but they also take the most disk space. With the Cookbook 211, you can take pseudo-shuttered half-frame images of the planets. Quarter-frame images can be used for rapidly reading out part of the chip when you are focusing, or in a special "binned" mode for finding faint celestial objects with short trial exposures.

These programs also allow you to display and save the images that you have acquired. Although you can set the brightness of the image automatically, if you want to you can manually select low and high pixel values. You can remove a dark-frame from your image display in real time. Finally, you can save an image using any valid 8-character DOS file name. The acquisition programs add the PIX, PI2, PI4, PA, PB, PC, or FTS extensions to your filenames to identify the image formats.

The job of the AP211 and AP245 programs is to *acquire, display, and save* images. The acquisition software is not designed to perform dark subtraction, flat-fielding, or image processing. You can perform these operations with software designed specifically for calibration and image processing. For information on image calibration, refer to *Choosing and Using a CCD Camera*. With a Cookbook 211 camera, you can use the *QwikPIX* software included with *Choosing and Using a CCD Camera* for calibration and the *AstroIP* software included with *Introduction to Astronomical Image Processing* for calibration and image processing.

To calibrate and process images from the Cookbook 245 camera, you can use any image processing software that can read FITS files, such as *Hidden Image, Epoch 2000, Imagine 32, MIRA, CB245PIX*, or *Astronomical Image Processing for Windows*.

9.2 How the Software Works

The image acquisition software operates from simple menu-driven screens. The menus allow you to navi-

```
___245_MAIN MENU___          RESET: 4095
I: Integrate Image          REF:   4095
M: Multiple Images
D: Display Image
F: Focus
C: Copy as Dark Frame
A: Autoguide
O: Options
P: Set New File Path
S: Store Image
G: Get Image
X: Export to FITS
Q: Quit

                                    08:54:42
```

Run the image acquistion software before your camera is done. When you start the program, you'll see the Main Menu. If you learn the software ahead of time, you'll be ready to go when your CCD camera is completed.

gate through the program and operate the camera. Each function has its own menu. From any menu you can do three things: you can command the software to carry out a task, you can drop to a lower-level menu, or you can ascend to a higher-level menu.

When you observe with your Cookbook camera, you will interact with its software far more than you will interact with the camera. In this chapter you'll find a command-by-command listing of the capabilities of the image acquisition software. You should also read Chapter 11 to gain a better sense of using the image acquisition software to make astronomical observations.

9.2.1 Starting AP211 and AP245

When you start AP211.EXE or AP245.EXE, you will normally see the Main Menu. This is your home base within the program; to carry out any of the camera's functions, you start from the Main Menu. However, the first time you run your camera, you will see a message telling you that no setup file exists.

Creating a setup file is covered in Section 10.2.3. You will need to determine the optimum delay loop timing for your computer and camera combination. This is set from the Options menu and it tells the program how long to wait before reading each photosite. Once you have created the setup file, you will probably never need to do so again.

9.2.2 Image and Data Files

The image acquisition software can take and save full-frame, half-frame, and quarter-frame images. Each type of image has a different function and a distinctive file name extension so that the image sizes cannot be confused. In addition, each image acquisition program maintains a setup file that tells it how to match your camera and computer.

Full-frame images contain a pixel from each photosite on the CCD chip. These are the normal image type that you will save. Half-frame images allow you to save just the lower half of the image; this is especially useful for shutterless planetary imaging. When you take a half-frame image, the camera very quickly shifts the image by half a frame, then reads out normally, acting, in effect, like a shutter.

Your camera can take two types of quarter-frame images: *find images* and *focus images*. Quarter-frame find

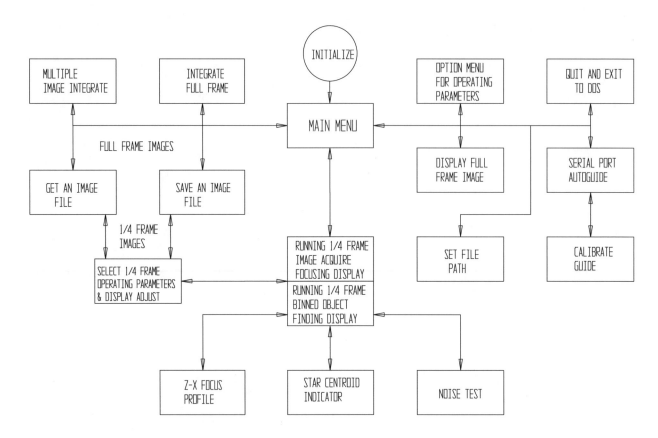

Functional Organization of the Acquistion Software

images bin the chip's photosites to give you "super-pixels." The greater effective collecting area results in much higher sensitivity but lower resolution than normal. With quarter-frame find images, you can use very short exposures—typically 1 to 2 seconds—to verify that you have found a faint target. Quarter-frame focus images hold one-fourth of the image at full resolution, and are useful for focusing the camera.

9.2.2.1 Image Formats for the Cookbook 211

Here is a summary of the image types that AP211.EXE creates with the Cookbook 211 camera:

Full-frame 211 images are saved as *.PIX files. The image contains 192×165 pixels each 13.75×16 micrometers on a side in a file of 63,367 bytes. *AstroIP*, *QuikPIX*, *BatchPIX*, and *ColorPIX*, read PIX files.

Half-frame 211 images are saved as *.PI2 files. The image contains 192×82 pixels each 13.75×16 micrometers on a side in a file of 31,495 bytes.

Quarter-frame 211 focus images are saved as *.PI4 files. The image contains 96×82 pixels each 13.75×16 micrometers in a file of 15,751 bytes.

Quarter-frame 211 find images are saved as *.PI4

files. The image contains 96×82 pixels each 27.5×32 micrometers in a file of 15,751 bytes.

Full-frame 211 images may be exported as FITS files with the .FTS extension. Each image contains 66,250 bytes. Although you cannot reload FITS images into the acquisition software, image processing application software such as *Astronomical Image Processing for Windows* can load files saved in this universal format.

AP211 setup data is stored in a file named SETAP.DAT. This file has roughly 96 bytes, though the file size may vary depending on its contents. It contains the parallel port address, timing delays for the program, and serial port configuration data for optional drive correction capabilities.

Log data is stored in a file named LOG.DAT. Each entry adds roughly 96 bytes to the size of the file. This file contains the names of image files, a date and time stamp for the exposure, the length of the exposure and an optional comment. The setup file is updated by command and the data log file is updated automatically after each image file save.

9.2.2.2 Image Formats for the Cookbook 245

The Cookbook 245 camera uses a similar scheme,

with several important variations. The most significant is that AP245 saves each full-frame image as two or three partial images.

378 × 242 full-frame 245 images are saved in three files named *.P1, *.P2, and *.P3. The full-frame image contains 378 × 242 pixels with effective dimensions of 17 × 19.7 micrometers. The P1 file contains lines 0 through 80, the P2 file contains lines 81 through 161, and the P3 file contains lines 162 through 251. Each part of the image contains 63,007 bytes. *CB24SPIX* reads these files.

252 × 242 full-frame 245 images are saved in two files named *.PA and *.PB. The full-frame image contains 252 × 242 pixels with effective dimensions of 25.5 × 19.7 micrometers. The PA file contains lines 0 through 125 and the PB file contains lines 126 through 251. Each part of the image contains 63,007 bytes. *CB24SPIX* reads these files.

Quarter-frame 245 focus images are saved as *.PC files. The image contains 126 × 121 pixels each 25.5 × 19.7 micrometers on a side in a file of 30,499 bytes.

Quarter-frame 245 find images are saved as *.PC files. The image contains 126 × 121 pixels each 51 × 39.4 micrometers on a side in a file of 30,499 bytes.

Full-frame 245 images may be exported in the FITS file format with the .FTS extension. The FITS image will contain either 378 × 242 or 252 × 242 pixels depending on the taking mode you were using when you made the image. Images 378 pixels wide contain 187,200 bytes; images 242 pixels wide contain 126,720 bytes. Although you cannot reload FITS images into the acquisition software, image processing applications such as *CB24SPIX* and *Astronomical Image Processing for Windows* can load files saved in this universal format.

AP245 setup data is stored in a file named SETAP2.DAT. This file has roughly 96 bytes, though the file size may vary depending on its contents. It contains the parallel port address, timing delays for the program, and serial port configuration data for optional drive correction capabilities.

Log data is stored in a file named LOG.DAT. Each entry adds roughly 96 bytes to the size of the file. This file contains the names of image files, a date and time stamp for the exposure, the length of the exposure and an optional comment. The setup file is updated by command and the data log file is updated automatically after each image file save.

9.3 The AP211 and AP245 Functions

The image acquisition programs control your Cookbook camera. You can select from a variety of functions with the press of a single key. What each function does is detailed in this section.

Any time the image acquisition programs are waiting for a keystroke, they are continuously flushing charge from the CCD. This prevents thermal electrons and photoelectrons from light falling on the chip between expo-

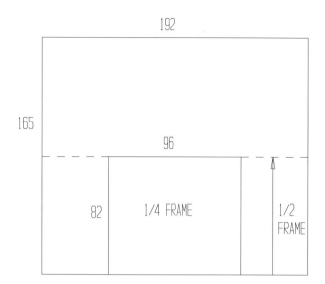

Cookbook 211 Image Areas

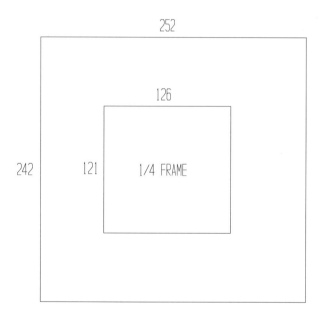

Cookbook 245 Image Areas

sures from saturating the photosites. Your CCD is thus ready to start integrating the instant you press the appropriate key.

To acquire images with your camera, connect the camera to the computer and power supplies, turn on the Peltier power supply to start cooling the CCD to operating temperature, and turn on the ±15VDC power supply. Load the acquisition program. You should see the Main Menu on the screen of your computer.

```
                  Main Menu

   I: Integrate              Ref:  0073
   M: Multiple Images        Reset:0898
   D: Display Image
   F: Focus
   C: Copy as Dark Frame
   A: Autoguide
   O: Options
   P: Set File Path
   S: Store Image
   X: Export to FITS
   G: Get Image
   Q: Quit                        10:35:21
```

9.3.1 The Main Menu

When you start AP211 or AP245, you will normally see the Main Menu. This is your home base within the program; to carry out any of the camera's functions, you start from the Main Menu. To enter any of the program functions, press the highlighted letter key.

In the upper right corner of the Main Menu screen you'll always see two important values on display. These are the reset and the internal reference ("ref") levels. Here is what they mean:

Ref is the analog-to-digital count for the CCD output when the detector node is switched to the internal reference voltage. You set it by turning the P1 potentiometer located on the preamplifier board. You should adjust this reading to a value near 75 when the camera is cooled to normal operating temperature.

Reset is the CCD voltage reference level left on the charge detection node after the reference voltage is disconnected from this node. When the switch in the CCD disconnects from the detection node, it leaves extra charge on the node. This extra charge level varies randomly so you will see a rapid fluctuation in the display. This variation is reset noise.

In the Cookbook 211, the Reset level is normally about 400 counts higher than the Ref level. In the Cookbook 245, the Reset level is usually about 800 counts above the Ref level. With the Ref value set to its nominal value of 75, the Reset level in the Cookbook 211 camera hovers near 475, and in the Cookbook 245, around 875.

Both the Reset and Ref values depend on the temperature of the CCD and on how much light is falling on it. When you turn on the Peltier cooler, the Ref and Reset values will rise. When you expose the chip to strong light, both the Reset and the Ref values will rise. If you turn the

P1 potentiometer far enough in the downward direction, you can force both values to zero, and if you turn the potentiometer in the other direction, you can force both values to 4095.

The Ref value should be between 50 and 100 with the Peltier in operation and the CCD in darkness. If it is not, turn the P1 potentiometer until Ref is close to 75.

If a moderate light level falls directly on the chip, the Reset value may rise to 4095, and if strong light falls on the chip, both values may peg at 4095. There is no harm in these values getting pegged, but you should be able to adjust them to their nominal values when the camera is cold and no light is falling on the chip.

9.3.2 The Integrate-Image Command

When you press I, you enter the Integrate Menu. From this menu you can start an integration, or exposure, for a predetermined number of seconds or minutes. Each number key stands for a preset integration time. Pressing 1 starts a 2-second integration, pressing 2 starts a 4-second integration, and so on through 6 (which startes a 1-minute integration), to 9 for a 16-minute integration.

In addition, by pressing the T key you may start an exposure for default time. Although the default integration time is displayed in the Integrate Menu, you must set the default exposure time from the Options Menu.

Because integration stops whenever any key is pressed, stay clear of the keyboard when you are making images! If you start an exposure and then kick the tripod of your telescope, you can stop the exposure by pressing any key. Even if you stop an integration, the image is read out and you can store it on disk if you want to keep it.

When you press the I key, the program ceases clearing the CCD chip so that a signal can accumulate. The program then monitors the length of the exposure. When the exposure is over, it calls a machine-code driver that sends a rapid sequence of signals to your camera, causing it to read out an image line by line and sample by sample, and send the image to your computer.

The integration time will usually lie between 15 seconds and 10 minutes. With an f/5 telescope, a 60-second exposure captures bright deep-sky objects very well. Exposures up to 10 minutes may be needed for really faint objects. Telescopes with slower focal ratios require longer integration times, just as they do for astrophotography.

9.3.3 The Multiple-Images Command

The Multiple-Image Menu allows you to take between 1 and 999 images at a specified interval using a specified integration time. The program will automatically take each image and save it with a filename that you define. Please note that this option can fill an enormous amount of hard-disk space very quickly.

The first step in taking a sequence of images is to establish a base name for the images from the Set Path Menu. In the Set Path Menu, the default pattern is ???.PI?.

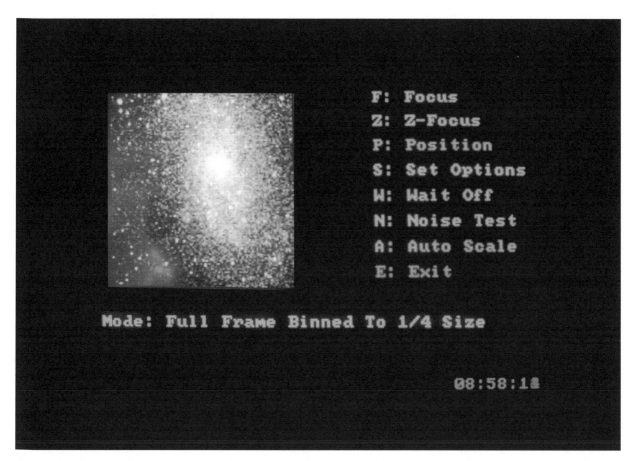

```
                                      F:  Focus
                                      Z:  Z-Focus
                                      P:  Position
                                      S:  Set Options
                                      W:  Wait Off
                                      N:  Noise Test
                                      A:  Auto Scale
                                      E:  Exit


   Mode: Full Frame Binned To 1/4 Size



                                           08:58:18
```

Object Find mode lets you locate objects—even objects like M33 that have a low surface brightness—with integrations 1.5 seconds long. Even though the *range* of pixel values is short, you can see its spiral arms.

When you trigger a series of full-frame images with the default, AP211 names your files 001.PIX, 002.PIX, and so on up to 999.PIX. (AP245 names them 001.PA and 001.PB; or 001.P1, 001.P2, or 003.P3, and so on.)

To store your files on drive C: in the 93OCT17 directory as ORION001, ORION002, and so forth, enter the new base name as C:\93OCT17\ORION. The default will become C:\93OCT17\ORION???.P?. To prevent overwriting your images, be sure to change the base name between sets of images.

Next, enter the Multiple-Image menu. Set the exposure time, interval between exposures, and the number of exposures you want. Enter each value by keying in the value and pressing the appropriate letter key. To make exposures of 43 seconds each, press 4, 3, 0, and T. Note that the values you key in are measured in tenths!

When you are ready to start the sequence, press the S key. As soon as you press this key, the first exposure begins. As soon as each exposure is done, the image is saved and the program continues to count until it's time for the next exposure. If the interval between images is less than the integration time, then a new integration will begin immediately.

You could use multiple imaging to track the progress of a variable star, follow an asteroid in its orbit, or take time-lapse pictures of a planet's satellites, to name a few examples.

9.3.4 The Display-Image Command

After you have made an integration, you can display the image by pressing the D key. Displaying an image does not affect the information in your computer's memory. In AP211, the display shows the full image. In AP245, the display mode shows a ¾-scale view of the 252×242 mode, and in 378×242 mode, shows a ½-scale view of the image.

Auto-stretching. To adjust the brightness of the display, press the A key. This automatically sets the low and high stretch levels in the display, stretching the brightness scale of the image. You will see these lo and hi values displayed to the right of the image.

Redraw. Any time you change the display parameters, you must press the R key to redraw the screen. For example, if you change the low and high levels, you must redraw the screen before you see the change.

Lo/Hi. You can also adjust the brightness of the

display by manually setting the low and high stretch levels. To set a value, type in the number using four digits. To set 325 as the pixel value that will display as black, press 0, 3, 2, 5, and L. When L is pressed, the Low setting is changed to 325. To set the High level, enter a four-digit number and then press H. To see the stretched image, press the R key to redraw the screen.

Histogram. To help judge the range of pixel values in the image, you can press the I key to generate a histogram of the image. The histogram shows, on a logarithmic scale, how many pixels have a given pixel value.

–Dark Ref. The display function allows you to see an image with a dark frame subtracted from it. To do this, press the D key, and then press the R key to redraw the screen. If the image is too dark or too light, press the A key to automatically stretch the image, or fine-tune the display by setting the high and low levels manually.

To take advantage of dark frame subtraction, you need to shoot a dark frame before you shoot your image. Cap your telescope when you shoot the dark frame, save the image to disk, and then copy the dark frame in the dark-frame buffer using the copy-to-dark function in the Main Menu. You can then shoot your image (don't forget to uncap the telescope). As soon as you have acquired the new image, save it to disk.

The display command lets you check your images as soon as you have taken them. This function is especially useful if your clock drive is erratic or if you are not sure that the object you wanted to image was in the field of view. Of course it is always a thrill to see the image you have just taken, and get instant feedback.

9.3.5 The Focus/Find Command

Use this command when you will want to locate an object in the camera field or to focus the camera on a star image. In this mode, the camera integrates for the default integration time and then displays a small image on the screen. The image is small for one of two reasons. In Find-object mode, you're seeing a full-frame image binned for extremely high sensitivity. This image is shown to you at half scale.

In Focus mode, you will see the central quarter of the frame displayed at full size. This allows you to examine the image carefully and get sharp focus on a star or planet.

You can press the A key to automatically adjust the brightness of the image. **Auto-stretching** in the Focus and Object-find modes makes the Cookbook camera extremely efficient to use when you are observing.

The F/O toggle. You can toggle between the Focus and Object-find modes with the O and F keys. Pressing the F key puts you in Focus mode; pressing the O key puts you in ''Object-find'' mode. The banner across the lower middle of the screen displays the current operating mode.

Object-find mode. Object-find mode allows you to locate faint objects. In this mode, a full-frame image is displayed as a reduced image. Because adjacent lines and pixels are binned to form "superpixels," the CCD is about four times more sensitive than normal. In Object-find mode, you can detect faint galaxies with an exposure only a few seconds long.

Focus mode. Focus mode performs a fast frame shift and then reads and displays a portion of the frame. In the Cookbook 211, the bottom center one-fourth of the CCD frame is displayed. In the Cookbook 245, the central one-fourth of the image is displayed.

Z-Focus. The Z-focus function displays an X-axis *versus* amplitude graph of the quarter-frame image. You can use this display for peaking a star amplitude during focusing or for examining the CCD noise. To obtain good data for the Z-focus mode, set the exposure time to one second or more. To exit Z-Focus mode, press any key.

Position. The position function shows the centroid of a star image within the quarter-frame image. To make the function work properly, you must set a threshold value for the star's brightness. You can use this to carry out manual guiding by keeping a star in a constant location on the CCD. Exit by pressing any key.

Set Options. When you press the S key, a menu which is similar to the Display Menu pops up. You may use this menu to set parameters for viewing images in the Find/Focus display mode. Entering the Set Options menu does not destroy the quarter-frame image buffer. When you return to the Find/Focus mode, the display functions that you have set remain active.

For example, suppose you want to locate Maffei 1, a faint galaxy in Perseus. After you make a 4-second dark frame, you press the C key to copy the dark frame to the dark buffer, and then set the low value to 0 and the high value to 30 so that very faint objects will show up clearly. You then exit the Set Options mode, remove the cap from your telescope, and make a series of 4-second exposures to locate and center your object.

The Set Options menu also enables you to save or load quarter-frame images. To save a planetary image, shoot focus frames until you obtain a particularly sharp image. Freeze it by hitting S. Enter the Set Options menu, and, after scaling and viewing the image to check its quality, save it.

When you exit the Set Options menu, you destroy the buffer frame. You can copy a dark frame to the dark reference buffer and subtract it from the image frame. Scaling an image does not affect the data stored in the buffer, but only changes the display.

Wait On/Off. With the live quarter-frame display running, you sometimes need a few seconds to evaluate each image. If you turn Wait on, the program will give you two seconds after each image to decide whether you have a good one. Suppose that you are shooting planetary images with 0.3-second exposures. With Wait turned off, the images may go by so fast that you miss good ones. With Wait turned on, you have a couple of seconds to press the S key to decide whether to save it.

Noise Test. This is a diagnostic tool for checking the operation of your camera. After you start the noise test, the program randomly selects one pixel and reads it from each successive frame then plots it on a graph. After 50 frames, you can assess the noise level of your camera.

The Focus/Find mode gives you a powerful way to locate faint celestial objects. Because it takes less than a second to display an image, you can search for and find objects that are too dim to see in your telescope. With a 4-inch f/5 telescope such as the Genesis refractor, *every* Messier object can be seen with 1.5-second find-mode exposures. If you use 5-second exposures, so that every 6 seconds you see a new image from the camera, faint objects like the Horsehead, the Leo I dwarf galaxy, and the Cocoon Nebula can be seen on your screen.

9.3.6 The Copy-as-Dark-Frame Command

When you are making long exposures of faint celestial objects, the noise in the dark frame may overwhelm your subject. To improve your assessments of the quality of the data you are taking, you must shoot a dark frame and subtract it from the raw images.

To make a dark frame, cap your telescope and integrate for the same time you do for your sky images. (The image will of course be dark and starless.) Save your dark frame to disk because you will need it to calibrate your image later. Refer to *Choosing and Using a CCD Camera* for a detailed discussion of dark frames and their use in calibrating CCD imagery.

After you save your dark frame, press the C key to place a copy in the program's dark reference buffer (note that this command actually *swaps* the image and dark buffers). The dark reference can be subtracted from each new raw image by toggling the D key in the Display function. Dark-subtracted images show more precisely the true quality of your image data.

9.3.7 The Autoguide Command

The automatic guiding command allows you to use the serial port on your computer to automatically guide your telescope. Using the serial port at 300 baud simplifies the programming and timing requirements for driving relays for the hand controller. You will find the technical details you need to put automatic guiding into operation with your Cookbook camera in Appendix E.

Although they were designed primarily with imaging in mind, the Cookbook cameras do an excellent job of guiding any telescope that has a well made, slow-motion drive system.

9.3.8 The Options Command

The Options Menu is a grab-bag of functions that allow you to modify the way your Cookbook camera and software operate. You need some of these functions to obtain top performance from your Cookbook camera. Others give you the ability to experiment with readout methods that may

reduce noise in your camera. Options for the Cookbook 211 and Cookbook 245 differ considerably.

Time. This parameter sets the integration time used for the integrate, focus, object-find, and Z-focus functions. Time is entered in tenths of a second, and may be as long as 999.9 seconds. To enter the time, fill the number buffer with the desired integration in units of 0.1 second; i.e., to make a 345.6-second integration, press the 3, 4, 5, and 6 keys. You will see 3456 in the buffer. Press the T key. When T is pressed, the value in the buffer is divided by ten. The integration time is now set for 345.6 seconds.

X-Timing *(Cookbook 245 only)*. To make full use of the image frame storage area shutter capabilities, the AP245 software has a non-poled delay loop timing function that allows exposures from 1ms to 1s in steps of 1ms. Be cautious in your expectations of high speed shutter operation. The image area is still exposed to the incoming light and it will bloom into the storage area if the object is very bright.

Interrupts On/Off. The default value for this toggle is "on." Pressing the I key toggles the program's internal real-time clock interrupt enable/disable. With I in "off" mode, your computer's real-time clock stops during a CCD read to avoid any non-uniformities caused by the clock interrupt. Each time you read out a CCD frame, the real-time clock will loose one or two seconds, but your image data will be of higher quality. With I enabled, the real-time clock will remain accurate. In practice, there is no visible loss in quality from leaving the interrupts on.

Self/Many Operators. This toggle enables a 15-second delay after you press the I key to start an integration. If you observe alone, this delay gives you time to get over to the guiding eyepiece.

Display Choice. By pressing V, C, or D, you can select a VGA display, a CGA display, or a dithered CGA display. We recommend that you use a VGA monitor if at all possible. The low-quality CGA display modes are useful, however, only if you must run your Cookbook camera from a CGA portable.

With a VGA display, you can select a normal color VGA display by pressing the V key, a screen-dimmed display by pressing the M key, and a ruddy night-vision display by pressing the N key.

Cookbook 211 framing modes. The H key switches between four operating modes of the Cookbook 211. Each time you press the H key, the mode changes. Refer to Section 3.1.3 for background information on CCD readout modes.

- **Full Frame** mode is the normal operating mode for the Cookbook camera. In this mode, the entire image is read once and digitized. The image contains the entire area of the CCD chip.

- **Half Frame** allows you to use the CCD like a shutter. The integration routine fast-shifts the lower half of the image to the top. The top of the field acts as a storage area for the half-image, which is then read out slowly. Use this toggle for short-exposure planetary photos.

• **Full Frame Low Noise** reads each pixel twice and then averages the readings in software. Averaging should reduce the amplifier noise by a factor of 1.4. You may wish to experiment with this mode.

• **Full Frame Dbl Sampl** reads the reset value for each pixel and then reads the sample value. Because the two readings are taken very close in time, the difference should be free of low-frequency noise. If you have a problem with 60Hz or other low-frequency noise in your images, this mode should cure it.

• **Future DCS Option** provides correlated double sampling in a modified Cookbook 211 camera, reducing reset noise by a factor of 2 to 3. This mode does not work with the standard Cookbook 211 design. (See the reference ''Low light level imagining . . .'')

Cookbook 245 Binning Modes. The B key switches among four different binning modes for the Cookbook 245. The chip, of course, is always read out in a binned mode; it's simply a matter of choosing which one. For more information, refer to Section 3.1.3 of this book. Note that all of the Cookbook 245's binning modes employ correlated double sampling when each charge packet is read.

• **Internal Binning** is the default mode. The image produced is 252 × 242 pixels in size. It performs three-up internal pixel binning in the 245 chip's serial register. This mode provides high sensitivity but slightly lower resolution than the 378-wide mode and less full-well capacity than the externally-binned modes.

• **External Binning** performs three-up pixel binning in the computer's memory. The image produced is 252 × 242 pixels in size. This mode gives a wider dynamic range than internal binning does because the serial register does not become saturated with electrons. To make the readout fast, the highest pixel value this mode produces is 3072, so don't get worried if the image looks a bit dark.

• **Internal/DblSamp** option is provided to reduce or remove common mode low frequency noise if it is a problem. In this mode, the computer reads the reset voltage and then reads the signal, thereby removing low-frequency common mode noise such as you might get from 60Hz power lines and ground loops. Image sampling time is doubled in this mode. The image produced is 252 × 242 pixels in size.

• **External 378Wide** produces an image 378 × 242 pixels in size. It performs two-up external pixel binning in the computer memory. This mode provides slightly higher resolution than any of the 252-wide modes with slightly reduced sensitivity.

Startup Parameters. This option allows you to set the serial communications parameters, the printer port address, and the CCD clocking delay times. After you have set these, you can save the selected parameters as a setup file. The setup data is read from the disk when the image acquisition program is started.

To select your printer port, press the P key. To set the op amp and ADC delay loops, press the Y key. To set the serial parameters, press the R key. To save this data in a setup file, press the U key.

You will need to set these parameters only once during the set up for your camera, or when installing the acquisition on a new computer. To set these parameters, see Section 10.2.

SRG Clocked/Unclocked. (Cookbook 211 only). The default value for this option is "clocked." In the Cookbook 211, have the option of clocking the SRG line during an integration or leaving it high. When you *do not* clock the SRG line, amplifier electroluminesence may saturate the left rows of pixels. However, clocking the SRG may increase the noise level in the image. You should determine which option you prefer.

Log Data. To record data, press the L key. Type in your comment about the telescope, observing conditions, or object. Each time you save an image, the file name, time, date, the integration time, and your comment are added to your LOG.DAT file. You can examine this file with a text editor such as the DOS EDIT program.

9.3.9 The Set-File-Path Command

This function allows you to operate in any directory you want to without typing the full path name for each file. From the Set-File-Path menu, press the N key to enter a new path. Type the path name *with a trailing backslash* to use a directory. To work in the 93JUN10 directory on your computer's C drive, enter C:\93JUN10\.

To save multiple images, define the root name for your files. The multiple filename default is name ???.PI?. To save multiple files with the names MARS001.PIX, MARS002.PIX, MARS003.PIX,... in the 93JUN10 directory on your C: drive, type C:\93JUN10\MARS. When you take multiple images, the number and the appropriate extension are added automatically.

9.3.10 The Store-Image Command

The Store-Image function saves files with extensions for the type of images you are taking. When you press the S key, you will see a display listing all files appropriate to the framing mode you have selected in the current path. If there are no files in this directory, the program will display an error message; press any key to continue.

To store an image, type the file name *without an extension*. The program will determine the format of the current image in memory and attach the right extension. To exit the store-image menu without saving an image, press the enter key with no name in the input buffer.

9.3.11 The Get-Image Command

To load an image from disk, press the G key to enter the get-image function. You will see a list of all files with the

09Ø7
L: 9Ø7
H:2Ø99
R:edrA
D:-REF
I: HIST
E: EXIT

Ø9:1Ø:Ø9

It's been a long evening—but the Lagoon Nebula now shines on your computer screen! Suddenly all the effort seems amply repaid. Shown is the Display function in the Cookbook 245 image acquisition software.

extension that matches the program's current imaging mode. If there are no files of the correct type in the selected path, you will see an error message; press any key to continue. To exit without a getting an image, press enter with no name.

9.3.12 The Export-to-FITS Command

If you wish to export your image data to other software, you should save it using the Export-to-FITS command. FITS is the NASA-endorsed Flexible Image Transport System used by most professional astronomers for their images. The acquisition program will store your image with a 2880-byte header that gives other programs the information they need to load your image. AP211 and AP245 store images as FITS-standard 16 bits-per-pixel integers. Exporting is a one-way street; once you have saved an image as FITS, you cannot load it back into the acquisition programs.

Do not type the extension when you export an image. The image acquisition programs automatically add the .FTS extension that is standard for FITS images.

9.3.13 The Quit Command

Press the escape key or the Q key to quit. The program will ask you to confirm your desire to quit.

Pressing the Q key again causes the program to terminate. Any images or information that you have not saved will be lost when you quit.

As you use the image acquisition programs included with this book, don't forget that they are copyrighted works, licensed to you for your use with your Cookbook camera. You are entitled to make copies of these program for your own use, but you may not lend, give, or sell copies the image acquisition software to any other person.

9.4 Practice Makes Perfect

At first acquaintance, almost any computer program can seem hard to learn. AP211 and AP245 may seem difficult at first, but their structure is clear and their operation rapidly becomes second nature. In preparation for night imaging, use the acquisition software during the daytime until you become familiar with its options and operation. Under the stars with a telescope to point and focus and a CCD camera to operate is a poor place to be learning new software. The bottom line: get familiar with the acquisition software in the daytime, and practice, practice, practice.

Chapter 10. Integrating and Testing

You have now constructed all of the subsystems of the Cookbook camera and run a functional test so that you know that your camera responds to light. In this section, you will integrate all of the parts in a working camera system and verify that all systems are "GO" before shooting some test images.

10.1 Putting the System Together

Before you take your first images, you need to get your camera ready for action. Although some of these preparations may seem unimportant, their purpose is to make the camera easier to operate at the telescope.

Tag your wires. Tag each of the jacks that go to the camera. This may sound silly, but once the camera is assembled, it's remarkably easy to forget which wire is which. Place a label or tag on each of the plugs on the ±15VDC power cable. (Without labels, how long would you remember that red is positive, green is common, and yellow is negative?) Label the ground and positive wires on the Peltier power cable and on the pump cable. Place labels on the corresponding power supply jacks.

Make a test stand. For bench testing, you'll need a simple test stand for your camera. The purpose of the test stand is to keep the camera from rolling, and to make it reasonably easy to point at test objects. Here's a simple way to build a stand: Cut a plywood square 6 inches on a side, and then nail or glue two 2-inch strips of soft wood about 1.5 inches apart at its center.

Velcro the interface box. For taking images at the telescope, apply a patch of self-adhesive loop-type Velcro to the bottom side of the interface box, and apply a corresponding piece of hook-type Velcro to your telescope close to the focuser. (Surface preparation counts even with Velcro; clean the surfaces with acetone and be sure they are warm when you apply the patches.) When you are ready to use the camera, you'll be able to attach the interface box easily and securely with the Velcro patches.

Add a lens. If your CCD is a camera, where is its lens? Although the Cookbook design is optimized for astronomy, you will almost certainly want to use it for other types of imaging. So you need a lens. Make a lens holder from a standard 1.25-inch to 2-inch eyepiece adapter and an achromatic lens of roughly 60mm focal length.

Mount the lens on the 2-inch end of the adapter, and then slip the 1.25-inch end of the adapter over the 1.25-inch tube on the camera. Add an aperture stop in front of the lens for greater depth of focus and lower sensitivity to light. F/20 is a good focal ratio.

To focus, slide the adapter on the 1.25-inch tube. Place the adapter on the camera and look through the lens at the CCD inside the camera. If you position the adapter so that the CCD appears focused to your eye, the lens will focus light from infinity. Moving the lens farther from the CCD causes the camera to focus on closer objects.

Alternatively, make an adapter so that you can put standard 35mm camera lenses on your Cookbook camera. This will make your CCD system far more versatile.

Don't forget a lens cap. Whether you add a lens or not, you will need a cap for your camera. During testing the cap will keep the CCD in total darkness. The cap can be a close-fitting cover that you slide over the eyepiece tube or over the camera lens.

Even if you painted the areas around the J2/J3 connector and the Peltier leads black, the camera may still leak a little light. Have a piece of black cloth or black plastic (preferably the conductive black plastic that is used for packaging static-sensitive devices) on hand to cover the camera to ensure total darkness.

Put it on wheels. If you will be using your Cookbook camera on a patio or driveway near your home, you may find it convenient to place the power supply, pump, water bath, computer, monitor, and a small lamp together on a cart. Look for a cart with large wheels to reduce vibration when you roll it out for a night's observing. If you need to transport the camera system by automobile, you may instead wish to make foam-lined containers for the camera and electronics, and several sturdy boxes for carrying the computer, monitor, pump, and water bath.

Relax. As you become familiar with operating the camera, you'll find it's not much different than any other type of astrophotography. To make images, you'll need to have a large number of components ready to run on short

All checked out and raring to go, this Cookbook 211 has passed its tests and is ready for astronomical imaging. The lens mounted on the focus tube gives an image good enough to verify the CCD's performance.

notice. Think through how you can best store these when you aren't using them, and how you can assemble the system speedily and efficiently for a clear night.

10.2 Critical Camera Check-Out

Running a complete "physical" on your Cookbook camera requires that you check three things: setting the correct timing parameters in the image acquisition program, verifying proper performance of the cooling system, and checking for radio-frequency interference. In addition, it's a good idea to run the components in the camera system with a four-hour "burn-in" test. And, of course, you will want to prove to yourself that the camera really can take pictures!

Camera check-out consists of six test steps:

- Prepare yourself.
- Set the Ref value.
- Set the delay timing.
- Verify proper cooling.
- Check for interference.
- Run the camera four hours.

As a side benefit of performing the check-out, you will become more familiar with the image acquisition software. Later, when you're running the camera in the dark or near-dark at the telescope and cannot read up on the details, you'll be familiar with the software.

To perform the check-out, set up the camera components in your work area. Place your computer, monitor, and power supply on a workbench and put the cooling system on the floor beside it. Stretch the coolant tube harness to its full length, and on a sturdy table or bench place the interface box and camera head.

Because your CCD camera is very sensitive, arrange for dim room lighting. Although one 7-watt lamp provides more light than you need for making test images, you *will* need to see your equipment to run the camera, so obtain a small lamp with a shaded 7-watt bulb. Set up two targets for imaging: a finding target and an imaging target. The finding target should be a white cross of tape on a sheet of black cardboard. The imaging target should be a small, recognizable object such as a wristwatch mounted on a sheet of crumpled aluminum foil. Crumpled foil provides points of light that you can easily focus on.

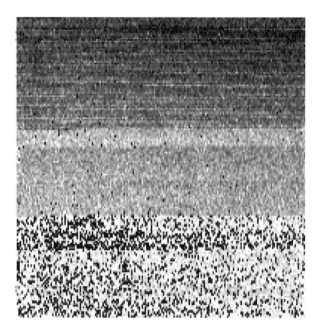

These broad streaks show that the delay is too short. Here the op-amp and ADC loop values are set to 1.

There's still too little delay with both loop values set to 3. The computer used is a 25MHz 386 PC-clone.

Turn on your computer and create a test directory with a name you can easily remember, such as C:\CCDTEST. Copy AP211.EXE or AP245.EXE to the imaging directory, and then switch to that directory. Connect the power cable to the ±15VDC supply jack; connect the pump cable to the pump power jacks, and connect the Peltier cable to the Peltier jacks. Connect the parallel cable from the camera to your computer's printer port.

Turn on the ±15VDC supply. At the DOS prompt, type AP211 or AP245, and press enter. The program will immediately encounter an error because it will not find the SETAP.DAT file. You will see an error message at the bottom of the screen. Not to worry: you will soon create the missing SETAP.DAT file. Press any key to continue.

The image acquisition program starts in the Main Menu. The first thing you'll need to do is make sure that the software is talking to your computer. By default, AP211 and AP245 use the LPT1 printer port. If you are using LPT2 for the camera, enter the Options Menu by pressing O, and then enter the printer port selection menu by pressing P. Select LPT2 by pressing 2, then return to the Option Menu by pressing E. (If LPT2 is not available, the software will not switch to LPT2 even if you select it.)

10.2.1 Test Step 1: Ready Yourself!

Check-out may prove frustrating and upsetting if you've never run a CCD camera before. Because you may not be sure that your camera is functioning properly, you may have a tendency to overreact to small problems—and you will surely encounter some small problems. Here are some things to keep in mind as you test the camera.

You start out not knowing the software. You need to know the software to test the camera, and you can't learn the software without a camera: it's a classic Catch 22 situation. Once you have gotten to know it fairly well, the image acquisition program is easy to use. But it won't seem that way at first. Take your time and don't fret when you hit wrong keys. You can't break the camera with the software. Period.

The coolant pump sounds like it's dying. Windshield-washer pumps are not designed for continuous duty, but they're inexpensive and experience has shown that many of them take a licking and keep on ticking. In fact, they usually get better with age. Don't worry about the pump unless it becomes too hot to touch or stops entirely. If the pump dies, replace it.

The CCD's field of view is microscopic. With a 50mm focal-length lens on the Cookbook 211, you'll have a 3-degree field of view. From 6 feet away, a baseball card will fill the frame. Think of a 50mm lens as a 500mm lens. Your white-tape-on-black-cardboard target should be recognizable even if it is far out of focus.

The depth of focus is microscopic. The first time you try to focus you'll be sorely tempted to heave the whole camera out a window and take up scuba diving as a hobby. You may not be able to distinguish *anything* if the lens is more than a millimeter or two out of focus. The first challenge is to *find* your target; but the second challenge is to *focus* on it.

Your camera does not have a shutter. Even as the computer clocks out a picture, more light falls on the CCD. If the light level in your work area is fairly high and

At last the delay loops are right! With the default values set to 10, you see a smoothly tapered screen.

your exposure times are short, more light will fall on the CCD as it clocks out than fell on it during the exposure. As a result your images will be smeared and blurry. To get good results, you need to darken the room and make longer exposures.

Your camera is very sensitive to light. The Cookbook cameras are designed for astronomy. That means that they work best under light conditions similar to those found in astronomy, that is, where it's dark. It's easy to overwhelm the camera with light. Take your test pictures under dim, dim, dim conditions.

You have been warned. You should be prepared. Expect the worst. Chances are that your tests will go smoothly and you will prove reasonably adept at coaxing great results out of your camera the first time you use it. Great results lie at the end of a steep learning curve that you must climb.

10.2.2 Test Step 2: Set the Ref Level

Cover the lens of the camera. In the Main Menu you will see the *Ref* reading. It should read between 50 and 100 counts. With the Cookbook 211, the Reset count usually reads about 400 counts above the Ref value; with the Cookbook 245, it usually reads about 800 counts above the Ref value. If the Ref level is less than 50 or higher than 100, adjust potentiometer P1 on the preamp card until the count is correct.

If you cannot bring the Ref level into the 50-to-100 range, first check that the ±15VDC supply is turned on and then check your cable connections. (If the camera is off, for example, both the Ref and Reset values will be fixed at some arbitrary value.) Next, with your voltmeter, check that the ±15VDC power supply is generating the proper voltages. Finally check that you have selected the correct printer port address.

When light falls on the CCD, it raises the Ref and Reset levels. In strong light, the Ref level will rise to 1500 or so. Whenever you set the Ref level, be sure that your CCD is in total darkness.

The Ref and Reset values drift with temperature. When you turn on the coolant system, for example, the Ref and Reset values will rise. You will have to find a setting where they will reach their nominal values after the camera cools down..

Under typical operating conditions with the Cookbook 211, if you set the Ref level to 20 when you first turn on the camera, the Ref level will rise to around 75—the middle of the desirable range—when the camera has fully cooled. With the Cookbook 245, if the Ref level is set to 75 when the CCD is warm, it will rise to around 300 when the CCD is cold. The bottom line is this: You will need to readjust the Ref level so that it reads 75 after the camera has fully cooled.

10.2.3 Test Step 3: Set Delay Timing

Because most computers are faster than they need to be for CCD imaging, the image acquisition software requires that you determine two critical delays. One delay allows the CCD amplifier about 5 microseconds to slew and settle. The other delay allows the analog-to-digital converter about 10 microseconds to digitize the signal from the CCD. You must adjust these timing parameters from within the image acquisition program. Once the timing is set, the delay parameters are stored in the SETAP.DAT file.

To set these delays, you must take a series of test images, evaluate them, and set the delays by trial and error. Timing delay parameters are different for each computer. Proper operation is possible on virtually any PC-compatible computer, AT-compatible computer, and newer 386 and 486 machines. Your computer's speed, wait states, and bus speed all affect the timing delays.

To take a test image, enter the Focus/Find menu from the Main menu by pressing F. Change to Focus mode by pressing F again; this gives you continuous quarter-frame readouts for critical focusing. Enter the Option Setup submenu by pressing S.

Set the integration time to 0.5 seconds by pressing the following key sequence: 0 0 0 5 T. Set the low-level black display level to 0 by pressing: 0 0 0 0 L. Set the high-level white display value to 4095 by pressing: 4 0 9 5 H. Exit the Set Options submenu by pressing E.

Place your lens cap over the camera window or lens so that no light falls on the CCD and observe the quarter frame display. Press the A key to auto-stretch the display. Since you have not yet turned on the cooler, you

First light for one of the Cookbook 211 prototype cameras was the drain pipe under a darkroom sink!

Try some portraits. Kara Kanto sat patiently for this image, taken by one of her dad's first CCD cameras.

should see a noisy but uniformly tapered brightness from the top of the screen to the bottom. If you see subtle steps in the brightness gradient, these are normal. However, if you see broad white and black streaks, the ADC delay timing is too short.

Later, when you test the cooler, the image will be uniform from the top to bottom. Horizontal white and black streaks still indicate that the ADC delay loop value is too low. You must lengthen the delay so that the op amp and the ADC have enough time to function.

To increase the delay timing, exit to the main menu by pressing E and then press O to enter the Option Menu. Enter the "delaY" menu by pressing the Y key. The default delay loops are 10 for the op amp delay and 10 for the ADC delay. To set the timing, press two digits and then press the O and A keys. Set timing delays of 30 for both the op amp and the ADC delays by pressing: 3 0 A O. (In this keystroke sequence, the 3 and 0 enter a timing value of 30 and the "A" and "O" apply that value to the op amp and analog-to-digital converter delays.)

Return to the Focus/Find menu and look at the image again. Unless you have a *very* fast computer, the delay should now be long enough. If you still see stripes, return to the Options Menu and make the delay still longer. If the streaks are gone, decrease the delays until you see streaks. Once you have determined the shortest delay that gives no streaks, increase it by 25% and use that value as your delay. If the streaks first appear at 7, you should use a value of 10 for the delay.

A basic 8088 PC running at speeds up to 8MHz should use values of 1 for each delay. Press 0 1 A O to set

the timing for an 8088 PC. For faster systems, increase the op amp and ADC delays until the streaks disappear. For example, to set the delay to 15, press: 1 5 A O. After setting these values, exit and return to the Find/Focus menu by pressing E E F.

Once you have eliminated timing streaks, save the parameters. To do this, exit to the Main Menu and then enter the Option Menu by pressing O. To save the parameters, press the U key.

If you run your Cookbook camera from three different computers, you will probably need to create a new SETAP.DAT file for each computer. You can change the parameters at any time, and you can create a new SETAP.DAT file at any time.

10.2.4 Test Step 4: Check Cooling

When you turn on the Peltier cooler in your Cookbook camera, the thermal signal from the CCD will drop by a factor of 100. To test the operation of the cooling system, therefore, you can shoot a series of thermal frames and measure the level of the thermal signal.

To measure the level of thermal signal, however, you must separate the thermal signal from the zero-point offset of the amplifier and electronics. At each successively lower temperature, make two images: a dark frame with an exposure long enough to show the thermal signal, and a bias frame, a very short exposure which will show only the zero-point offset. To measure the effect of cooling, subtract the bias frame from the dark frame. The resulting image should contain only the thermal signal.

Finally, you need to calculate the rate at which the thermal signal grows by dividing the average pixel value

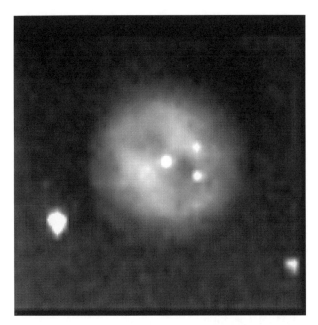

Veikko and John tried their CCD on the Owl Nebula. This is a 10-minute integration with a 10" f/10 SCT.

Start your deep-sky explorations with bright objects like Messier 82 and work your way down to dim ones.

of the thermal frame by the length of the exposure. At room temperature, that is, at temperatures near 20°C, you should measure a thermal signal close to 1,600 in your 8-second exposure, for a rate of increase of 200 pixel values per second. With the Peltier cooler on, the thermal signal will drop below 2 pixel values per second.

If you have done every step in order, you'll begin the cooling test with your camera operating but with the Peltier and pump turned off. Cover the camera so that no light can reach the CCD. Make an integration 8 seconds long and store it with the file name DKRT8S, for dark frame, room temperature, eight seconds. Make another integration, this time 0.1 seconds long, and store it as BIASRT for bias frame at room temperature.

Next, enter the Find/Focus menu and then enter the Z-focus mode by pressing the Z key. In this display, you see a cross section of each new image as it comes from the CCD. You can watch the dark current level and easily see changes in it when it drops.

Place the cooling coil in a water bath that is room-temperature. Do not use a water bath that is at or below the dew point—if you do your camera will soon be dripping with condensation!

Turn on the Peltier cooling system. The pump should immediately start. Set the Peltier voltage to about 2VDC and watch for a decrease in the dark frame level and noise. Cooling occurs quite rapidly: within 30 seconds you should see a marked decline. (If the noise increases, the Peltier may be plugged in with the wrong polarity.) If you see no change in the signal, check the power supply for a correct voltage at the output jacks and check for a correctly wired system.

When the signal level stabilizes, exit to the Main Menu and take an 8-second dark frame integration and a 0.1-second bias frame. Save them as 2-volt-cooled frames, naming them DK2V8S (dark frame, 2 volts, 8 seconds) and BIAS2V.

Repeat the process of taking a dark frame and a bias frame with 3 volts, 4 volts, 5 volts, 6 volts, and full voltage applied to the Peltier cooler. As the temperature drops, you will need to make longer exposures to get a strong thermal signal. At 6 volts, for example, you may be able to shoot a dark frame for 4 minutes integration.

In the Cookbook 211, even if there are no light leaks, the dark frame will be bright in the upper left corner because of electroluminescence of the output amplifier. The remainder of the image area should be below the half saturation level.

When you have completed taking test data, slowly turn down the Peltier voltage then shut down the system after the test is completed.

For the Cookbook 211, use a program such as *AIP* (included with *Introduction to Astronomical Image Processing* or *QwikPIX* (included with *Choosing and Using a CCD Camera*) to measure the level of the thermal signal at each temperature. For Cookbook 245 images, use a program such as *CB245PIX* or *Astronomical Image Processing for Windows*.

Load the dark frame and the bias frame, then subtract the bias frame from the dark frame. The resulting image will be pure thermal signal. Measure the average pixel value of the frame, and then divide this by the length of the exposure to get the rate at which thermal signal builds up in your CCD.

If the cooling in your camera is working properly, you will see a dramatic decrease in the thermal signal: at room temperature the thermal signal typically grows by 200 pixel values per second, but just 2 volts on the Peltier causes the thermal signal to drop to 20. With 6 volts on the Peltier cooler, the rate at which the thermal signal grows should drop to less than 2 pixel values per second. This means that your camera can make exposures of at least 10 minutes, reaching very faint objects.

The thermal signal should drop by a factor of 100 or more when the Peltier is running at full power. If the thermal signal drops less than 100-fold, check that the CCD is properly seated on the cold finger, that the cold finger is snug against the Peltier module, and that coolant is circulating through the heat exchanger.

The cooling system is so simple that poor cooling should be extremely rare. In the prototype cameras, the thermal signal usually fell by a factor of 250 from room temperature, and on dry, cold nights, the thermal signal fell to 0.2 pixel values per second.

10.2.5 Test Step 5: Check for RF Noise

During the cooling test you took a series of bias frames that are ideal for checking for radio-frequency interference. Load your bias frames and stretch them so that the narrow range of pixel values spans the range from black to white. (The auto-stretch function in the Display menu does this type of stretch very well.) Ideally, you should see a random salt-and-pepper scatter.

Strong banding, herringbone patterns, or stripes in the bias image could be the result of ground loop noise or external radio-frequency (RF) interference noise. Your computer is the best candidate for radio-frequency interference; plugging its 120VAC power plug into a different outlet may eliminate the path for the interference.

If changing where the computer and power supply are plugged in doesn't help, check the ±15VDC supply voltages. They should be greater than 15V and the AC ripple should measure less than 200mV. Excessive ripple could mean that your power supply has a bad filter capacitor or a filter capacitor with the wrong value. Low voltage can occur if you have low line voltage in your area. Low voltage may also result from excessive current draw from your camera, which happens if one of the tantalum capacitors is in backwards.

If the power supply appears to function correctly, the power cable may serve as an antenna for radio-frequency noise. You can probably reduce or eliminate the banding by installing two filter capacitors in the interface box. Solder a 1000μF 35-volt electrolytic capacitor across each side of the ±15VDC power where it enters the board.

If the problem persists, go to the Options Menu and select the double sampling mode. If the interference is low-frequency noise, double sampling should remove it or reduce it significantly. In the Cookbook cameras, low-level banding with an amplitude of 1 to 2 pixel values results from random variations called "popcorn noise" in the 2.5VDC reference circuit on the preamplifier board; double sampling almost entirely removes this noise.

10.2.6 Test Step 6: Camera Burn-In

In electronics, component failures are most likely to occur within a few hours; this effect is called "infant mortality." Although you would prefer that nothing fail, it's probably better to encounter problems in the testing stages than later on, when you're out observing.

To conduct a burn-in test, turn on your camera and cooling system and run the system for at least 4 hours. Monitor the following every 30 minutes for a minimum of 4 hours:

- Ref level.
- Reset level.
- Pump operation.
- Peltier voltage.
- Frost on the CCD.

Keep the CCD in total darkness except when you check for frost. Record each datum in your CCD observing logbook.

Performance is satisfactory if the Ref and Reset levels remain stable or drift slowly. You should see no frost on the cold finger or CCD. The Peltier voltage should remain constant within 0.05 volts, and the pump should run steadily throughout the test.

After the system has stabilized, if the Ref level drifts more than 25 counts in a 30-minute period, try to figure out why. A changing Ref level means that the temperature of the CCD is changing. If the Peltier voltage drifts more than 0.05 volts, check the circuit in the power supply for incorrect wiring or failed components.

The formation of frost signals a major problem, probably an air leak in the CCD housing. Inspect the entire system carefully for poor seals, and when you locate the leak, remove the tube cap, dry the interior with warm air, seal the leak, and close the camera.

The pump tends to speed up and slow down from time to time, but this is normal. Indeed, you will find that the pump runs better after a few hours of operation than it did when it was new.

10.3 Shoot Your First CCD Image

If you cannot wait to take an image, adjust the Ref level and set the delays—then proceed. Set up the camera on its test stand, and place the test stand on a table. Slide the lens holder over the eyepiece tube. Remember to stop the lens down to f/20 and work in a dim room. Cap the lens so that no light can reach the CCD.

Starting from the Main Menu, press the O key to enter the Options Menu. Set the exposure time to 1 second

The easiest way to start shooting astronomical images is to use a 35mm camera lens on your Cookbook camera. This 15-second wide-angle shot was made with a 50mm f/1.5 lens on a Cookbook 245 CCD camera.

by pressing 0 0 1 0 T, then press the E key to return to the Main Menu. Now go to the Find/Focus Menu by pressing the F key. The camera will start taking finder pictures; you will see a new image every few seconds. Let a few scans go by, then go to the Set Options menu by pressing S. Press C to copy a dark reference frame to the dark reference buffer. Press D to toggle on the dark reference subtraction option. Set the high stretch level to 4095 by pressing 4 0 9 5 H and set the low level to 0 by pressing 0 0 0 0 L. Exit to the Find/Focus display menu by pressing E. Every few seconds a new image will appear on the screen, but because the camera is capped, the image should be dark.

Uncap the lens. The screen should get lighter. Place a white object in front of the camera and move it around. The screen should brighten and change. If the screen stays dark when you put your target in front of it, turn up the lights. If the target is too bright and saturates the CCD, turn down the lights. Adjust the light level until you see blobs that change when you move the target around

slowly in front of the camera.

Place the target on a support about 4 feet away from the camera. Slowly slide the lens forward and back until you think the image is getting brighter and sharper. If you don't know where the focus is, you may see nothing but blobs for quite a while. If you cannot move the lens close enough to the CCD, move the target closer. Eventually you will see your target swim fuzzily into view.

Continue to slide the lens until the image you see is sharp and crisp. Success at last!

After you have gotten the focus and exposure times set once, taking images becomes much easier. The first image is the most difficult. Take lots of indoor images. Get your spouse and your kids to pose. Take pictures of watches and dollar bills (if you have any left) and whatever else you can find. Get lots of practice using the camera and the program so that when you have a telescope to operate and a star to find, the camera and the software will be familiar.

And congratulations. Your CCD camera works!

Chapter 11. Enjoying Your CCD Camera

When you complete your Cookbook camera, you need to change your thinking. The camera, which has been a "cloudy-night construction project" for several months, has suddenly transformed itself into powerful astronomical tool. This chapter deals with using your Cookbook camera for astronomy. We hope the tips you'll find here will help you to get started in CCD imaging.

11.1 How to Use a CCD for Imaging

CCD observing closely resembles astrophotography but with a new twist. You'll need to do everything you would do for astrophotography, plus operate a computer and CCD equipment.

Prepare your telescope. To take good CCD images, your telescope must find, focus, and follow to rather tight specs. Add the accessories you'll need to carry out these operations with precision. You will need a high-power finder to locate celestial objects, you need a tight, responsive focuser to get sharp images, and you need a good clock drive and/or guide telescope to eliminate trailing.

Work out mechanical arrangements. Figuring out where to place the equipment is the first important step in CCD observing. How you accomplish this depends on whether you plan to observe patio-style, indoor-style, or observatory style.

If you carry everything outside and set it up on the patio, that's *patio-style observing*. We recommend building or buying a portable computer stand because it will save you a lot of disconnecting and reconnecting cables. Although card tables will serve, if you have to connect and disconnect everything each time you set up, you'll soon weary of the routine. Patio-style observing includes front-yard observing, driveway observing, barbeque-pit observing, backyard observing, and gazebo observing.

If you don't want to put your computer outside, then you're a candidate for *indoor-style observing*; that is, you keep your computer indoors and put your telescope outdoors. We have found that Cookbook cameras work with ribbon cables up to 35 feet long. (But please, make a cable and test it because the camera may not operate properly with over 15 feet of cable.) Place your computer near a convenient door or window, and be prepared to spend a lot of time running back and forth.

If you have a backyard observatory, you can leave everything ready to go from one night to the next. Ideally, you can even leave your computer in the observatory. Nothing beats *observatory-style observing* for set-up speed and freedom from hassles. If you have an observatory, running the Cookbook camera can be a one-person operation.

If you need to set up your telescope and computer each time you observe, it's a big help to find an observing assistant or a partner. There are enough switches, key strokes, cable hook-ups, telescope-pointing operations, and important things to check on and remember to keep two people fully occupied. Whatever style of observing you decide to try, get the setup down to a system that is fast and efficient so you can concentrate on observing.

Work out the electrical arrangements. For safety's sake—as well as to reduce electrical noise—use a three-prong grounded power cord to bring power to your observing site. If possible, the outlet you use should be equipped with ground-fault protection. Plug your computer and monitor into the 120VAC outlet on the power supply; this insures that the electronics share a common electrical ground.

Set up the cooling system. In addition to the electronics, you'll need a place for the cooling system. Put the water bucket where you will not accidentally step in it or kick it. Put the pump on the ground beside the bucket. For indoor-style observing, remember that the cooling system can be outdoors even if the computer is indoors. If you have an observatory, place the cooling system in a convenient but out-of-the-way location.

Set up your telescope. Get good polar alignment, and align the finder scope with the main scope. For patio-style observing, set up the table to hold the computer, monitor, and power supply box near the telescope, but be sure to leave enough space that you can point the telescope to any place in the sky without moving the table.

Set up the camera. Attach the Cookbook camera to the focuser of the telescope. Because the Cookbook

Your first forays into CCD imaging will be patio-style observing. Here Tucson amateur Phil Bright has placed his computer and telescope close together so that he can easily operate both without running back and forth.

camera weighs about what a 35mm camera body does, its weight should not be a problem. Attach the interface box to the telescope near the camera head with adhesive-backed Velcro strips. However, *do not let tubes and cables hanging from the interface box pull on the telescope.* Clamp them to a stationary part of the mounting and arrange them so that they are free to flex without dragging on the telescope.

Take time for a safety check. When the entire system is lashed together, check for voltage between major units. Verify that you have zero volts AC between the metal parts of the telescope, camera, and computer. It is possible that some piece of equipment is not properly isolated from the hot side of the AC line, posing a threat to you, your computer, and your Cookbook camera.

Power up the system. Turn on the computer, load the image acquisition software, turn on the ±15VDC and check that Ref and Reset read what they normally do when you first power up the camera.

Verify that the Peltier supply is turned to minimum output. (This should always be the case because you should always turn it down slowly before you shut down.) Turn on the Peltier power and water pump supplies.

Increase the voltage on the Peltier a volt or so at a time, pausing a few minutes after each increase to let the chip stabilize.

As the Peltier cools the CCD, you should see the Ref and Reset levels start to rise. If you enter Focus/Find mode, you should observe a steadily dropping thermal signal. When the Ref value stabilizies, touch up the reading by adjusting the P1 potentiometer. About 15 minutes after turning on the power and the Peltier, you'll be ready to make CCD images.

11.1.1 Finding

Because CCD detectors are physically small, they cover small angular fields of view on the sky. As a result, it may be difficult to find *anything* the first few times you use your Cookbook camera. If at first you don't succeed—relax—you'll eventually get the hang of it.

Equip your telescope with a finder telescope having *at least 20× magnification* and illuminated cross hairs. You will need to align the high-power finder to match your CCD camera, and you will probably need to tweak the alignment each time you observe. (Because the CCD chip in your camera may not be in the precise center of

This 4-minute integration of M51 is the first astronomical image taken with the first Cookbook 245. It was made with a patio-style observing setup using a 10-inch f/10 SCT. Image by Veikko Kanto and John Munger.

the camera body, the CCD alignment may not match the alignment for eyepieces.)

To find objects with the Cookbook camera, go to the Focus/Find menu. If you use the default integration time of 1.5 seconds, then every 2.5 seconds you will see a new screen update. Press the A key to autoscale the display. (Here's where learning the software in advance in a warm, dry room in your house comes in very handy.)

With the camera in Find mode, point the telescope at some bright and obvious celestial object (like the moon) and align the finder telescope approximately. Using that alignment, locate a bright star. Even if a bright star is way out of focus, you can usually tell when it's in the field. (Indeed, when a bright star comes into the field of view, the computer monitor may suddenly light up the entire area.)

Once you have fairly good focus, find a star of about seventh magnitude. Align the finder as precisely as you can. Proceed to fainter and fainter stars until you can put any object you can see through your finder telescope dead center on the monitor.

If your telescope has mechanical or electronic setting circles, use them. Although you might not land on every object every time, they'll get you close enough that a little scanning using the Focus/Find mode will always pick up the object.

Your ace-in-the-hole for finding objects with the Cookbook is its high sensitivity and rapid image display. The Cookbook 211 and the Cookbook 245 cameras are so sensitive that deep-sky objects are visible with very short integrations. For example, with a 6-inch f/5 reflector you can see the spiral arms of M51 using 1.5-second integrations. At magnitude 14.5, Pluto is readily visible on the monitor using 1-second integrations. By using 5-second integrations, you can see and precisely center faint deep-sky objects like Cygnus Loop and the Cocoon Nebula. With the Cookbook cameras, you'll be doing real-time electronic deep-sky observing!

11.1.2 Focusing

Focusing and finding are inextricably related because you cannot find faint objects until your camera is focused, and you cannot focus precisely until you can find things. The trick is to focus roughly as you align the finder, so that by the time your finder is aligned, the camera is also focused. Find the approximate focus with bright objects that you cannot miss, and do your final, precise focus with much fainter objects.

Initially it helps to locate the position of your telescope's focal plane by catching an image on a slip of paper or on ground glass. With Newtonians and refractors, the position of the focus is fixed, so once you've located it, it will always be there. Mark the focus position with a piece of tape or a scratch on the tube of the focuser; this will save you time later.

Although you can bring the telescope to a rough focus using the Find mode, for critical focus, press the F key to get the enlarged view of the Focus mode. As you approach best focus, it may become difficult to tell whether the image is focused or not. Atmospheric seeing and telescope shake conspire to change the image unpredictably from one frame to the next.

Critical focusing requires patience: watch five or six images of a faint star and mentally average them. Shift focus by a small amount and watch another five or six images. Decide whether the image got better or worse. If it became better, continue to shift focus in the same direction; if it became worse, reverse the direction. When you can no longer decide whether the image gets better or worse, you've got it as good as you ever will.

If you find this method frustrating, try a commercial or homemade caustic mask. Place a mask with two small holes over the telescope. If you have an 8-inch telescope, for example, cut two 2-inch holes 6 inches apart in a sheet of cardboard. When a star is out of focus, you'll see two separate star images or a little oval, but when the image is focused, you'll see a small, round dot.

Alternatively, find a fairly bright star and focus for maximum blooming. Blooming occurs when too much light strikes the CCD. The more blooming you see, the better the focus. One advantage of focusing by the length of the blooming trail is that you can watch the blooming trail even when you are some distance from the monitor.

If you have an observatory or use your telescope primarily for CCD imaging, it's very handy to leave the camera on the telescope at the end of an observing session. That way, the system will be close to focus and ready to go the next time you start to observe. If you cannot avoid removing the camera from the telescope, place scribemarks or pieces of tape to help you recover the focus.

11.1.3 Following

CCD imaging demands good tracking. To obtain good CCD images, you need a clock drive that is accurate enough to keep images within a fraction of a pixel for the duration of your integration. You'll probably get your best deep-sky images using integrations between 1 and 10 minutes long. It would be sad indeed if errors in your telescope's drive system were to limit your integrations to 30 seconds.

Even with an excellent drive, you will discover tracking flaws that you had not previously known about. Do not despair—you may be able to improve the drive. Often something as simple as adding a dab of lubricant will help a reluctant drive run more uniformly. (Engine Assembly Grease, with graphite and molybdenum disulfide in an all-temperature base, can work wonders.)

With worm drives, you may have excellent gears sloppily assembled. Examine the worm as it turns and then adjust it to remove backlash and eliminate small angular misalignments. After a careful tune-up, you should be able to run integrations up to 5 minutes long without needing to guide. With an f/5 telescope, this may be all you ever need.

You may also wish to take advantage of the autoguide/background PEC function built into the image acquisition software and described in Appendix E. This feature allows you to calibrate your drive and perform background periodic-error correction while you make integrations.

For guiding CCD images, we recommend a guide telescope. Although off-axis guiders are superior for long-exposure astrophotography, guide telescopes are more practical for the relatively short integration times of CCDs. An 80mm f/15 refractor with an illuminated crosshair eyepiece works quite well. Locate the object using the Cookbook camera's Focus/Find, lock the clamps on the main scope, and offset the guide scope to a star suitable for guiding. It is usually best to begin guiding about 15 seconds before you start the integration. Trigger the integration by pressing the I key and a time key, for example, pressing the 9 key for a 16-minute integration.

As your neck gets stiff while you guide your "long" CCD integrations, console yourself by remembering how much *shorter* CCD integrations are than comparable exposures with photographic film.

11.2 Making Astronomical Images

There are as many approaches to CCD imaging as there are astronomers, but everyone works to the same set of basic ideas. For an in-depth discussion of the fundamentals of CCD imaging, consult *Choosing and Using a CCD Camera*. The descriptions that follow should serve as guidelines to help you get started.

11.2.1 Choosing the Integration Time

As a rule of thumb, the integration times for individual images should be as long as you can make them before tracking, blooming, sky background, and the growth of the thermal signal force you to stop. Longer integrations mean a larger signal and a better signal-to-noise ratio. Integrations typically last from a few seconds to around 10 minutes depending on the relative importance of these limiting factors.

This 4-minute integration shows the faint outer loop of the Orion Nebula. The image was made using a 6-inch f/5 reflector from a small observatory near Cedar Grove, Wisconsin. Cookbook 245 image by Richard Berry.

Tracking. Tracking is likely to be the most flexible limiting factor that you encounter because there are lots of ways to get around poor tracking. When tracking errors limit integration times less than a minute, you can still obtain excellent images with a short-focus telescope or a telephoto lens piggybacked on your main telescope. Future releases of the Cookbook image acquistion software may support a track-and-accumulate mode to automatically register and sum a series of short exposures.

Blooming. Bright stars "bloom" in the Cookbook cameras, that is, long tails of leaking photoelectrons extend from the images of bright stars. If you cannot stand blooming in your images, you must make your integrations short enough that the CCD does not bloom. With an object like the Orion Nebula, the brilliant Trapezium stars may bloom with integrations longer than a few seconds, meaning that you must tolerate blooming or underexpose the nebula itself. However, by shooting a few dozen short-integration images and summing them, you can avoid blooming and still obtain a good signal-to-noise ratio in the nebulosity.

Sky Background. Although CCDs cut through city lights, a bright sky background nonetheless reduces the longest integrations you can make. The point of diminishing returns occurs when the sky background reaches roughly one-third of the dynamic range of the camera, or about 1,000 pixel-value units. Under reasonably dark skies, reaching this level takes about 60 seconds with an f/1.5 lens, about 10 minutes with an f/5 telescope, and around 40 minutes with an f/10 telescope. Under city skies, sky light will probably limit you to shorter integrations.

Thermal Signal. Under summertime conditions, the thermal signal in your Cookbook CCD grows by about 2 pixel-value units per second. Thus it takes about 500 seconds, or 8 minutes, to reach 1,000 pixel-value units. Under winter conditions, thermal noise may not limit your integrations until they reach 20 to 30 minutes.

The bottom line for deep-sky imaging is that most of your integration times will lie between 1 and 10 minutes. You will have to determine for yourself the trade off between the number of images you can shoot in a night (which favors many short integrations) and the quality of each image as measured by its signal-to-noise ratio (which favors fewer long integrations).

To reach extremely faint objects, you can sum multiple images. For example, if you shoot sixteen 5-minute integrations, you can reach the same limiting magnitude you can by shooting a single 80-minute integration. Be aware, however, that you must also obtain sixteen 5-minute dark frames. With CCDs, equivalent integration times of many hours are possible.

11.2.2 Making Dark Frames

In the total absence of light, an ideal detector would make an image consisting entirely of zeros. Real CCDs generate an image that contains a zero-point bias and a thermal signal that accumulates during the integration. If you shoot an image of the sky and then shoot a dark frame, you can remove the unwanted thermal and bias signals by subtracting the dark frame from the image. When an image is corrected in this way, it is called a dark-corrected or dark-subtracted frame.

Because the thermal signal that accumulates depends on both the integration time and the temperature of the CCD, the dark frame must be made with the same integration time with the CCD at the same temperature it was when you made the image integration. The Cookbook cameras maintain their temperature very well; dark frames taken 45 to 60 minutes apart are nearly identical.

An easy way to improve the signal-to-noise ratio in your dark-corrected images is to average several dark frames. By averaging, you obtain a composite dark frame that has a better signal-to-noise ratio than any single dark frame because random variations between the individual dark frames are averaged out.

A good strategy for making high-quality dark frames is to make two dark frames for each 30 minutes of observing. In the intervals between these dark frames, you make as many integrations as you can. Later, to calibrate the images, for each observing interval you prepare an averaged dark frame made from the two dark frames you took before and the two dark frames you took after the interval. In calibrating, you subtract the averaged dark frame from each of the images taken in the interval.

11.2.3 Flat-Field Frames

Flat-field frames map photosite-by-photosite sensitivity variations of a CCD chip. By flat-fielding, you can eliminate the effects that these sensitivity variations in the CCD might otherwise have on your images.

To make a flat-field frame, you take an image of a uniform source of light such as the twilight sky or an illuminated section of your observatory's dome. You then subtract a dark frame made with the same exposure time from the raw flat-field integration to obtain a dark-corrected flat-field frame. The flat-field represents the sensi-

Here is how a 4-minute integration of the Orion Nebula (see page opposite) looked when first taken.

Above is the dark frame used to correct the Orion image. Thermal noise gives the image a grainy look.

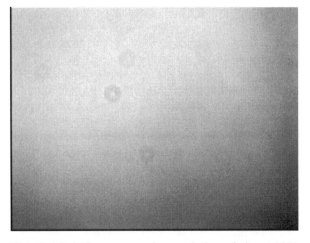

This flat-field frame reveals a variation of about 10% across the CCD. Dust specks made the dark circles.

tivity of each photosite on the CCD.

When you divide a dark-corrected image by a dark-corrected flat-field frame, you produce a calibrated image. In a calibrated image, the signal from the CCD is proportional to the amount of light that fell on the chip. By taking multiple dark frames and flat-field frames, you can produce calibrated images with signal-to-noise ratios as high as 1,000.

If you keep the optical configuration of your telescope the same all night long, you need only make one master flat-field frame per night. To make a master flat-field frame, place a diffusing screen (frosted Mylar drafting film answers well for this purpose) over your telescope and shoot at least eight integrations of a uniformly illuminated screen. The integration times will be short. Shoot the same number of dark frames.

Using image-processing software, average the flats and darks, then subtract to produce a single dark-corrected master flat-field frame. You can use this to flat-field correct all of the images you took that night.

11.2.4 Making Multiple Images

The Cookbook image acquisition software allows you to shoot up to 999 images with any integration time and any interval between integrations. This makes the Cookbook camera ideal for monitoring celestial objects such as asteroids and variable stars. You could, for example, follow an eclipsing binary star through minimum by taking a 1-minute integration every 2 minutes for 3 hours. You would not need to supervise taking this data; the image acquisition program would do it for you. Although this would generate 10.9 megabytes worth of images, you can erase them after you have extracted an accurate light curve for the variable star.

11.3 Image Processing

Image processing is to CCD imaging what darkroom work is to astrophotography—only more so. Through image processing, you can extract everything there is to see in an image. Basic to all image processing is calibration to produce an accurate linear record of the light that fell on the CCD. Only after an image has been calibrated is it ready for analysis or processing.

Image analysis includes photometry to measure the total light of stars or extended objects, and astrometry to derive the precise positions of star images. Image processing includes scaling to derive the optimum scale of gray tones to show the range of values in the image, and filtering to restore detail lost in the atmosphere and optics.

11.3.1 Image Calibration

Calibration is essential before you can analyze or process image data. To carry out calibrations, you need raw images, dark frames, and flat-field frames. In calibrating each image, you should use dark frames taken with the same integration time and CCD temperature, preferably within 30 minutes of the image. If you have made

more than one dark frame, you can average them. The flat-field frames should have been made with the same optical configuration as you used for your raw images. Averaging multiple dark frames and flat-field frames can significantly boost the quality of your images.

To calibrate an image, subtract the dark frame from the raw image frame, and then apply a flat-field algorithm to divide out the pixel-to-pixel sensitivity variations to produce a calibrated image that precisely reflects the amount of light that fell on the CCD.

11.3.2 Image Analysis

Image analysis is fundamental to quantitative uses of CCD imagery; in astronomy, these include photometry and astrometry. Photometry depends on measuring the total light in stellar images, and astrometry depends on determining the precise center of light in stellar images.

The basic job of a photometric routine is to determine, from the array of pixel values around a stellar image, how much light is in the region containing the star and how much light would have come from the sky if the star were not there. The difference is the star's brightness, that under favorable conditions should be accurate to roughly 0.01 magnitude.

For astrometry, the goal is to figure out, again from an array of pixel values, the location of the center of the star image. Because the starlight has spread over several pixels, the routine must estimate how much light came from the star, and find a weighted average position of the illuminated pixels. This is the star's position, accurate to a small fraction of a pixel, a few μm in the focal plane, or depending on the telescope, better than a second of arc.

11.3.3 Scaling Image Data

Scaling alters the brightness scale of an image to make a wide range of features visible in the image. Scaling can be as simple as a linear scaling in which a narrow range of pixel values are "stretched" to fill the entire brightness range of the display, or as complex as histogram shaping, in which pixel values in the original image are force-fit into a predetermined optimum distribution of brightness values.

Depending on what you want to display in your images, scaling can pop barely-visible low-contrast nebulae out of a bright sky, reveal image features over an enormously wide range of brightness, or enhance the visibility of subtle planetary cloud features.

Scaling changes brightness values. If you plan to do photometry, astrometry, or any other quantitative measurement, work with calibrated but unscaled images.

11.3.4 Filtering and Image Restoration

The image that reaches the CCD has been perturbed by the atmosphere and the telescope optics, softening and blurring its fine details. Filtering can often restore lost detail, giving CCDs the ability to capture diffraction-limited detail on nights with imperfect seeing through tele-

When an object like NGC2024, the Flame Nebula, first appears on the monitor, you'll hardly be able to believe your eyes. After you center the object and check the focus, here's what you'll get in a 4-minute integration.

scopes with imperfect optics.

The key to successful image restoration is estimating how the original image was degraded. For this estimate, image restoration software attempts to determine what the image would have looked like had it been captured by a perfect telescope in space. Image restoration requires enormous amounts of number-crunching, and therefore tends to be slow.

Filtering techniques can enhance the visibility of the low-contrast features without changing the overall contrast of the image. For example, a technique called unsharp masking can be used to reveal subtle structural details in nebulae and galaxies that, because of the low contrast of the features, may be difficult for the eye to see. After filtering, the features stand out clearly.

11.4 Basic CCD Troubleshooting

Your Cookbook camera may operate for years with no problems, and suddenly begin to act up. If this happens, you'll need to do some troubleshooting. In troubleshooting, the goal is isolate the problem. Once you have figured out which of the subsystems has caused your camera to act strangely, you can find the fault and fix it.

Because you have built your Cookbook camera, you know a lot about it. And as you use it, you will come to know its strengths, weaknesses, and its odd little quirks. We recommend that you keep a logbook of your camera's performance so that you can spot long-term changes, and have a record of its normal operating voltages, Ref and Reset levels, and other potential diagnostics.

11.4.1 What Can Go Wrong?

Vibration, wetness, and static electricity are the principle enemies of your Cookbook camera. Vibration can break cold solder joints, unseat DIPs, and cause plugs to work free. Dampness causes corrosion, makes short circuits, and weakens plug connections. Electrostatic discharge can damage or destroy ICs and CCDs. Prevention is the best cure for all of these dangers: always treat your Cookbook CCD camera gently, keep it dry, and never, ever zap it with static electricity.

11.4.2 Regular Maintenance

Time takes its toll on people, machines, and CCD cameras. But regular maintenance can forestall problems. Here are some suggestions to keep your Cookbook camera in good operating order:

Clean the window. Over a period of time, the camera window may accumulate dust, grease, and bug footprints. Check the window, and when it's dirty, clean it with a swab and isopropyl alcohol.

Check the coolant. The coolant consists of deionized water and isopropyl alcohol. If the coolant leaks, becomes cloudy with micro-organisms, or discolors from chemical reactions, your camera might not function properly. Drain the coolant if you know that will not use the camera for a month or more, and refill it when you next use it.

Check the cooling system. From time to time, it's a good idea to check that the Peltier is still doing its job as well as it did when you built the camera. Section 10.2.4. describes a simple bench test to assess how well the cooling works, a test that you could run on a cloudy night. If the CCD is not cooling as well as it should, check that it has stayed seated on the cold finger.

Check for frost. Every time you fire up the Cookbook camera, the pressure in the camera body drops as the air inside cools. If a little moist air leaks in each time, water vapor will build up in the camera because it cannot escape. If you see odd streaks and swirls in your images, check the CCD for frost. To cure frost, open the camera, bake it dry it at a temperature not over 40°C for a few hours, and reseal it.

Check the power supply. Test the voltages on the ±15VDC, the Peltier, and the pump power supplies both unloaded and running the camera. Record the results in your logbook. This could prove helpful if you suspect a problem in the power supply.

Check plugs, DIPs, and connectors. After the camera has been exposed to vibration, inspect anything you think could come loose. Check the power supply for failed solder joints after an automobile or plane trip.

Use ESD procedures around your camera. A big "zap" can damage your camera, just as it would damage any kind of electronic gear. To be on the safe side, employ standard ESD procedures when you perform any kind of work on your camera, especially indoors or in dry weather. Refer to Appendix A for more detail. It takes only seconds to put on a grounded wrist strap.

11.4.3 If Your CCD Fails...

What should you do if your Cookbook camera suddenly stops working? Your first response to any failure of the Cookbook camera is to **shut off the power**. Turn off the ±15VDC and the Peltier power. Next, unhook the Cookbook camera from the power supply. These actions prevent compounding the difficulty and are the first steps in troubleshooting the problem.

Did anything get hot? Carefully sniff around the power supply and camera. Do you smell the smoky scent of burned insulation or the acrid odor of hot thermoplastic resin? These may indicate a blown fuse, a short circuit, or a failed component.

Did the camera act erratically? Did you notice anything unusual in the camera's performance before it failed? For example, if the pump suddenly change speed and died a minute later, start by checking the pump power supply and its fuses. If you saw erratic or fluctuating Ref and Reset values when you touched the case body, the preamp card may have come out of the J2/J3 socket.

Check the fuses. If there is a short or component failure, the fuses should be the first thing to go. A blown fuse tells you something about where the problem lies. Replace the fuse with another fuse *of the same rating*. Do not hook up the camera, but turn on the power. If the new fuse blows, the problem lies in the power supply and not in the camera.

Check the ±15VDC supply. With your meter, test the voltages on the ±15VDC supply, both AC and DC. You should see between 15 and 18 volts DC with the proper polarities, and less than 200mV of AC ripple.

Hook up the camera. Reattach the camera to the power supply. Make sure that you have made all the connections properly, then double-check yourself. Getting the cables hooked up wrong may not harm the camera, but it certainly won't work unless the cables are right.

Check all cabling. Cables can come unseated. Check that they are all plugged in and properly seated. Tug on them gently to see if the internal wiring is loose or broken. If you store the camera in observatory environment, inspect the plugs for corrosion.

Turn on the computer. Boot the computer and run some software. Does the computer behave normally? Can it access the drives? Load the image acquisition program. You should see Ref and Reset readings that are normal for your camera with power off.

Check the parallel port assignment. Go to the Options menu and reset the parallel port. The camera won't respond if the program is trying to communicate through the wrong parallel port.

Turn on the ±15VDC supply. Apply power to the camera. You should immediately see normal Ref and Reset readings. Measure the voltages and the current draw from the ±15VDC supply with the camera attached. Are the readings normal? If the voltages are low, shut off the power supply. Something in the camera is drawing too much current.

Check for a loose chip. If one of the ICs is not fully seated, the camera will behave strangely. It may produce weird-looking images, it may be very noisy, or it may sit and do nothing. The chips can work loose if you subject the camera to vibration from automobile or airplane

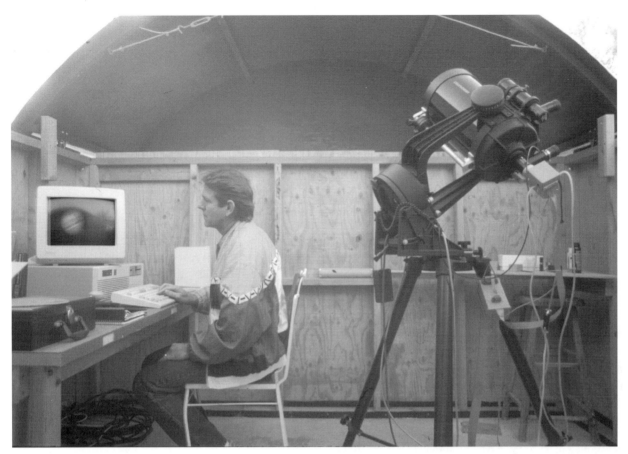

Observatory-style imaging, from a stressed plywood rolloff observatory, is the best way for Phil Bright to use his CCD camera. Everything he needs is close at hand—and he can turn on the camera and be taking images in 15 minutes.

travel, or if you drop or bump the camera. Taking ESD precautions, open the camera and inspect the boards. If an IC is loose, reseat the IC.

Check for a loose card. If the preamp card has come loose from the J2/J3 socket, you may see wildly fluctuating Ref and Reset values. Touching the camera may cause these values to hop erratically from 0 to 4095 and back. Shut off the power, and with ESD precautions, remove the preamp cover and reseat the card.

After building a dozen prototype cameras, we have never seen a camera die and stay dead. The problem has usually turned out to be something simple like a failed solder joint or a loose plug.

All in all, we believe that the Cookbook camera is a tough design. We have mistreated the prototype cameras and they have survived. One of the prototype Cookbook 245 cameras has logged thousands of air miles as checked baggage, fallen off a telescope and hit the ground, and been shipped across the U.S. via UPS ground service— and it still works.

However, it is important to treat your Cookbook camera with care. Mechanical bangs and bumps unseat

chips, loosen connections, break solder joints, and unseat circuit boards. Plugging in the ±15VDC power backwards *should* blow a fuse. And ESD can damage an assembled camera in ways that are hard to troubleshoot.

To avoid problems, we offer these suggestions:

• Every six months, refurbish your camera. Inspect it, clean it, change the coolant, and then bench test it. Keep a record of its performance as baseline data.

• If you plan not to use your camera for several months, drain the coolant and pour out the water bath. This should prevent leaks and corrosion.

• If you set up and break down the camera each time you use it, store and transport it in a cardboard box lined with newspapers or an unpainted wooden box lined with conductive foam.

• If you use your camera in an observatory, leave it set up all the time. This minimizes handling. Inspect it regularly for insects and dirt, and protect it and the power supply from moisture.

If you treat your Cookbook camera well, there is every reason to believe that it will give you many years of dependable service.

Chapter 12. CCDs in Amateur Astronomy

Twenty years from now, we may look back on the 1990s as the "daguerreotype era" of CCD imaging. No matter how primitive our current CCDs seem in that future era, there is no denying their abilities today. Because of CCDs, small telescopes under bright skies have become capable of showing off the familiar deep-sky wonders in their full glory, and large telescopes under dark skies can probe the limits of the universe.

12.1 The CCD: A Cheap Linear Detector

With CCDs, amateur astronomers at last have a cheap linear detector. Linearity is crucial because it means that you can build a camera using a detector that has thermal noise, a bias offset, and variations from one sensing element to the next, and through simple calibration procedures, correct the faults of the detector to produce images that are faithful representations of the light from the night sky.

Linearity lets you acquire reliable data. It is far more difficult to carry out "real science" with non-linear detectors such as photographic films and plates. Linearity means that you can add, subtract, multiply, and divide pixel values as substitutes for light from the sky.

Linearity means that an amateur astronomer can take an image with a small telescope, compute the sum of the pixel values in a star image, subtract a modeled sky background, and obtain a quantity that is directly proportional to the brightness of the star.

Linearity also means that the brightness of the night sky now matters far less than it ever has before. Moonlight and light pollution become flat background levels that you can subtract from your image. Although you pay a penalty in higher noise levels, you can now observe faint galaxies on nights when the full moon rides high in the sky.

12.2 The CCD for Making Pretty Pictures

Amateur astronomers sometimes look down on astrophotography, gently demeaning this most enjoyable craft as "making pretty pictures." Yet the magazines that serve amateur astronomy squeeze as many pretty pictures as they can into their pages. Clearly such images play an important role in amateur astronomy. As imaging technol-

ogy matures, we can be sure that CCD images will take their place beside silver-halide images in books and magazines about astronomy.

Astronomical "pretty pictures" are not necessarily pretty in the conventional sense. Often they are coarse and grainy. As amateur astronomers, we learn from "pretty pictures" what the universe really looks like. Because we have seen pictures, we visualize and enjoy objects that would otherwise be little more than fuzzy glows in the telescope; although we see the universe with our eyes, those "pretty pictures" tell us what to look for.

Because their quantum efficiencies exceed 50% over a large part of the visible and near-infrared spectrum, and they integrate a faint signal, CCDs easily reach three to four magnitudes fainter in a 1-minute integration than the eye can see through the same telescope. This means that all of the Messier objects and nearly every object in the New General Catalogue and Index Catalog are "easy" objects for small telescopes. CCDs will thus become a potent force in shaping the amateur astronomer's vision of the universe.

The current generation of CCDs are small, making them ideal for taking striking close-up images of celestial objects. When they are used with small telescopes, the Cookbook cameras provide fields of view that we generally associate with much larger telescopes. This means that as the 1990's progress, celestial objects that have always been considered too small and too faint for amateur astronomers will become familiar to us from our own observations.

In the meantime, skilled astrophotographers will press their CCDs into hard service on larger telescopes. It is likely that by the end of the decade we will see amateur-made catalogs showing every NGC and IC object, as well as hundreds of still fainter galaxies and dozens of galaxy clusters and quasars.

Even though CCDs will show amateur astronomers deeper views of the universe than ever before, it is vital to understand that CCDs will not replace "eyeball observing." Nothing will ever replace the impact of a direct view through the eyepiece. Rather, the views that come from CCD cameras supplement visual observing, just as pho-

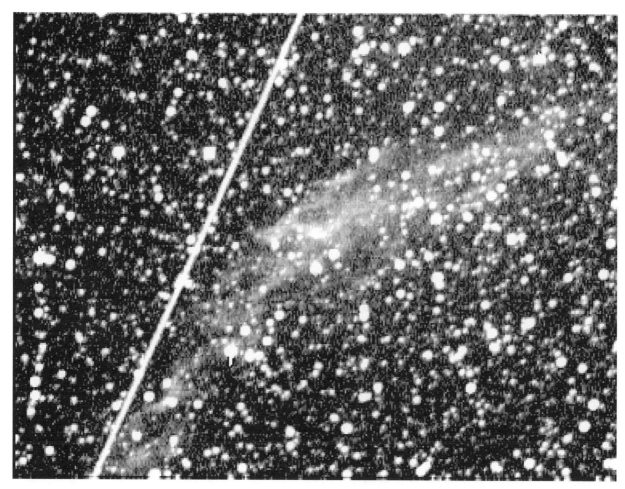

A satellite left its trail across this 4-minute integration of NGC6992, the northeastern arc of the Cygnus Loop, made with a prototype Cookbook 245 camera and a 4-inch f/5 Genesis refractor. Image by Richard Berry.

tography has in the last 100 years, by supplying these observers with a growing list of interesting and exotic subjects to search out and see with their own eyes.

12.3 The CCD for Obtaining "Real" Data

CCD imaging also opens significant areas of "real astronomy" to amateur astronomers. CCDs have already proven their value in planetary imaging; amateur-made images of Jupiter, Mars, and Saturn have caught the attention of professional astronomers. CCDs have likewise proven suitable for astrometry, with amateurs reporting precise asteroid positions to the IAU, and the AAVSO is actively investigating photometry with CCD images. Here are a few ideas for observational work that can be done with CCD imagery.

Stellar photometry. The key to good photometry is making your images through filters that define standard photometric colors. When calibrated, such a CCD image contains a record of the brightness of every reasonably bright star in the field to a precision of a few hundredths of a magnitude.

You can apply the CCD to any type of stellar photometry, from the once-a-month and once-a-week schedules of the long-period variables to once-a-minute observations of eclipsing binaries or flare stars. CCDs are further attractive because even on small telescopes, they can reach very faint stars.

Photometry of planetary nebulae. For many planetary nebulae, the only magnitudes available are photographic and visual observations that are decades old. Amateur astronomers with relatively large telescopes, working under the guidance of a professional astronomer, could, for example, survey all of the known planetary nebulae and measure their diameters and brightnesses on a uniform scale.

Photometry of galaxies. Amateur astronomers who observe galaxies visually are often frustrated by multiple and inconsistent published magnitudes for galaxies. However, what matters for visual observation is the surface brightness of the galaxy, and this quantity can be measured directly from CCD images!

Brian Manning of Worchestershire, England, has put this early version of the Cookbook 211 camera to work tracking comets and asteriods. Manning uses a fan-cooled Peltier, and built the electronics on a DIP board.

This 4-minute integration shows Comet Mueller 1993a with Manning's 20cm f/6.5 Wright telescope.

Shoemaker-Levy 9's distinctive chain of nuclei show clearly in this 8-minute integration by Brian Manning.

From CCD images, Manning measured the position of the asteroid he discovered and named for his wife.

Thirty-six minutes later, (4751) Alicemanning has moved 6.5" east. These are 10-minute integrations.

It would be an interesting project, perhaps for a club or network of deep-sky observers, to measure the surface brightnesses and sizes of the several thousand brightest galaxies. It would be necessary to make these observations through filters so that the spectral sensitivity of the CCD matches the sensitivity curve of the human eye.

Monitoring prestellar systems. Objects such as Hubble's Variable Nebula fluctuate in brightness and shape, yet professional astronomers have not observed them regularly. If several such objects were imaged roughly once a month, in collaboration with a professional astronomer interested in analyzing the resulting data, much might be learned about these stars in the making. The CCD camera offers the linearity and sensitivity required to make such observations valuable.

Astrometry (and photometry) of asteroids. So many asteroids and so few astronomers! It is easy to measure precise positions of starlike objects from CCD images and, once you have established sufficient credibility, carry out observations for and report positions to the IAU. Brian Manning, whose picture appears in this chapter, has done this using a home-built CCD camera on his 20 cm Wright telescope. Manning's positions are accurate to a few tenths of an arcsecond!

Comet positions. During the apparition of a comet, astronomers need as many accurate positions as possible. CCDs enable an amateur astronomer to record a comet against the background of stars, then to measure the position of the center of light of the comet with respect to the background stars. The Hubble Guide Star Catalog now provides a wealth of background stars that can be used with some degree of confidence. As with many projects, doing it right means that a network of amateurs must work with one or more professional astronomers.

Binary star observations. Measuring the position angles and separations of binary stars from CCD images should be both easy and accurate. The key to making successful observations is the cooperation of a few professional astronomers willing to help interested amateurs set up rigorous observing protocols that will lead to accurate and valuable data. In *CCD Astronomy*, Christian Buil has demonstrated the power of autocorrelation techniques to extract good position angles and separations.

Monitoring planetary features. For years, members of the Association of Lunar and Planetary Observers have observed the planets and established a rich collection of data. With the advent of CCD cameras, however, the best amateur images rival the images that professional planetary astronomers take. High quality planetary images taken on a regular basis have been used for studies of the Jovian clouds, the advance and retreat of the Martian polar caps, and tracking the position of cloud formations on Saturn.

These suggestions, biased toward quantitative studies, represent just the tip of the iceberg. Equally exciting is a wide range of qualitative programs, from recovering periodic comets to searching for supernovae. With CCDs, amateur astronomers have a new tool—and a very powerful tool—to aid their exploration of the heavens.

Appendix A. Personal and ESD Safety

In constructing your own CCD camera, you will come into contact with materials and carry out tasks that can potentially harm you. If you use the proper techniques, however, there is no reason for you to be injured. The purpose of this Appendix is to alert you to areas of potential hazard and suggest some of the safety precautions necessary. If at any time you become concerned that you are not sufficiently familiar with proper procedures, we advise you to seek the help of a person who can advise you of the safest and most proper procedures. At all times, place your safety at the top of your list of priorities.

As you handle the electronic components of your CCD camera, you should also pay attention to proper electrostatic discharge (ESD) procedures. Electrostatic discharge is commonly called "static electricity." In a fraction of a second, ESD can destroy CCDs and finished circuit boards. Not to worry, though—you can protect your camera against ESD. Follow the procedures outlined in section A.2. and ESD will not bother you.

A.1 Danger! House Current

Anything that plugs into the wall is dangerous. The reason is that 120-volt AC power is potentially lethal. When you work with house current, the primary rule is: Never work on a circuit while it is plugged in. Always check that the power plug is unplugged before you work on any 120-volt circuit.

In the Cookbook camera, the AC circuit in the power supply is the only 120VAC circuit. Building it is basically like wiring house outlets. If you really don't feel comfortable about doing it, consider buying a commercial supply or having an "electro-nomical" friend help with the power supply.

In working with line voltage, the idea is to prevent current from flowing through your body. Isolate yourself from ground by wearing rubber-soled shoes. When you make measurements on powered-up circuits, keep one hand in your pocket. This insures that current cannot flow from one arm to the other arm through your heart.

For proper ESD protection, you should ground yourself while working, but for working on 120-volt circuits, you should isolate yourself so that a harmful current cannot flow through your body to ground. Although it sounds odd, you can be safely grounded for ESD and still be isolated from ground for 120-volt AC providing you wear a wrist strap with a $1M\Omega$ resistor to ground.

If you accidentally contact a live 120VAC wire while wearing a wrist strap, the maximum current that would flow through your body to ground is $170\mu A$. Although the wrist strap would protect your life, the sensation is decidedly unpleasant, so don't try it. Remember that you can also hurt yourself if you suddenly pull away from an unexpected electric shock.

Common sense should prevail. Don't solder powered up circuits. Don't measure ohms with power on. Double-check your 120VAC wiring before plugging it in. The filter capacitors in your power supply can store a considerable charge for some time after the unit is unplugged. Before you touch anything, check it with the voltmeter. Even with the power off, always check both AC and DC volts with respect to ground.

Lest you become *too* wary, remember that touching powered or charged-up circuits with 24 volts and less is unlikely to harm you. However, between the leads of the ±15 VDC is a 30-volt potential, so be careful. Even a small "tingle" can make you jump and break things! Place low-voltage electronics in a box or enclosure not only because it prevents anyone from touching the components and getting shocked or burned, but also because it protects the electronics and shields them from electrical noise.

Don't be nervous, have fun. Take reasonable precautions. With attention to safety and good work habits, you can build electronic circuits safely.

A.2 Electrostatic Discharge

Everyone is familiar with the hot, blue sparks that jump from your finger to the doorknob when you walk across a carpet on a dry day. Sparks like that often have 6,000 volts or more. Yet voltages as low as 70 volts—too low to feel—could zap your CCD. The secret of preventing destructive "zaps" is to prevent static charges from building up. There are two ways to do this: avoid materials that accumulate static electricity and bleed away static

Electrostatic Discharge Procedures

Prevent Static Build-Up

Work at an unfinished wooden workbench.

Sit on a wood or metal chair or stool.

Seek low-static wood, concrete, or asphalt-tile floors.

Wear low-static cotton clothing.

Place components on conductive foam.

Store circuit cards in anti-static bags.

Leave components wrapped until you need them.

Prefer humid work areas to dry work areas.

Wear a Grounded Wrist Strap

The strap should have a 1MΩ series resistor to ground.

Attach the ground lead to a good electrical ground.

Watch that the ground lead doesn't knock things over.

Always wear your wrisp strap!

---

electricity with a grounded wrist strap.

ESD damages integrated circuits because the components in the ICs are so small. The electrical energy of a static discharge is concentrated into such a small area that it melts the device. For example, metal-oxide semiconductor (MOS) gates are glass dielectrics only a few hundred Angstroms thick. Designed to operate at a few tens of volts, this insulation breaks down when higher voltages are applied—and with static electricity you can barely even *feel* 5,000 volts.

Whenever you handle or touch any electronic component of your Cookbook camera, whether a single component, the assembled cards, or wires attached to circuit cards, follow ESD procedures. ESD procedures fall into two key areas: prevent the accumulation of static charges, and discharge the static charges that do occur.

Prevent ESD Build-Up. Static charges accumulate on insulating surfaces such as plastics, rubber, Formica, man-made fibers, and glass. To prevent ESD, avoid bringing these materials to your work area.

Your workbench should be unpainted, unvarnished, and unwaxed wood, and your work chair either metal or unpainted wood. (Particle board is an excellent bench-top material for electronic work.) The floor in your work area should be concrete, wood, or asphalt tiles. Wear cotton clothing that has been washed in an anti-static detergent.

Because humidity makes surfaces conductive and dry air makes them better insulators, static electricity thrives in dry climates. If you have a choice, choose a humid part of the house as your work area. Although a muggy basement may feel terrible to you, it's a comfortable static-free place for electronics.

Your soldering iron should also be the grounded, three-prong type, because an ungrounded soldering tip can couple voltage from the power line or your body to the card or device that you're working on.

Store ICs with the leads stuck into conductive foam. Store partially assembled cards in astatic bags; these bags are available at computer and electronics supply stores. (Most computer boards come in astatic bags.) Astatic pads on the bench top provide a safe work surface. These can also be obtained at computer supply stores.

Leave ICs in the shipping packages until you need them. There is a powerful temptation to pull your newly arrived prizes from their bags to see what they look like. If you *must* do it, make sure you're grounded or strapped up. Parts are sometimes shipped with little regard for static precautions. If the shipping bag appears to be ordinary plastic or seems charged (you feel hairs raising as your hand approaches the bag), breathe into the bag. This introduces enough humidity to dissipate the charge. After you're grounded, stick the parts into conductive foam.

Discharge Static Charges. Despite your care, you will inevitably generate static charges. To bleed away this static charge, always wear a 1MΩ grounded wrist strap. The wrist strap is a band of conductive plastic or metal that contacts the skin. A wire with the series resistor of 1MΩ connects the strap to ground. The resistor allows charge to bleed off but protects you from serious shock if you touch powered-up circuitry.

Attach the wire from your wrist strap to a good electrical ground. The metal screw on a ground power strip or the plate mounting screw on a three-prong grounded outlet is a good ground. When you are working on your Cookbook camera, the ground terminals on your power supply are good grounds when the power supply is plugged in.

The wrist strap is a doubly good idea because you're always grounded when you're wearing it. Just remember to put on the strap when you sit down to work on your camera. The wrist strap also reminds you to "engage brain before starting work," a good rule in any event.

The most important thing to remember about your wrist strap is this: Always wear it! When you slide around on the seat of your chair, you can generate charge. The wrist strap will bleed away the accumulated charge.

As a practical side note, don't let the wire on the wrist strap cause problems. Remember Murphy's Law, and place your cup of coffee where the wrist strap won't knock it over. (And with Murphy's Law in operation, if the cup weren't full, you wouldn't spill it.) Park cans, cups, and tools safely aside when you're building or using the equipment.

Don't let ESD procedures make you paranoid: Just do them. If you simply follow anti-ESD procedures, ESD won't harm your electronics.

A.3 Always Check for Correct Wiring

Miswiring is the easiest way to damage a device or card. Suppose that you wire a circuit quickly and, in your excitement to see things happen, hook it up to 15 volts and flip the power switch. In your haste, though, you wired the 15-volt lead straight to the input pin of an integrated circuit. Something happens all right: the metallized traces on the chip melt and short the input to ground. You won't see any damage, but the chip is now dead.

The remedy: always check wiring. You can double check the wiring and have a friend check it, too.

Make sure plugs and connectors are mated correctly. Murphy's Law still applies: If you can plug it in backwards, you will. On one of the prototype cameras, we plugged the camera preamp card in one pin over and burned up two resistors. Luckily, nothing else was damaged. We also put a power supply capacitor in backwards. When the output voltage was wrong, we saw the capacitor bulging ominously at one end. A new capacitor was installed and no harm was done.

Even when the camera is finished, check your wiring. During camera testing, we fried a ±15VDC power supply because we hooked up the leads wrong and had not yet selected the right fuses to protect the power supply. The camera didn't work! After some tense troubleshooting, we replaced a burned-out 26VAC transformer.

"Beep-out" or "ohm-out" every circuit before putting ICs into the sockets. Pin-by-pin check that the circuit *as wired* matches the schematics. Apply power to the circuit before plugging in the ICs and check that the supply voltages are on the correct pins.

When you build the power supply, check that the polarity of the electrolytic filter capacitors is correct before applying power. These large-capacitance-value parts can explode if they are installed backwards. You may want to wear safety glasses during initial check out. Newer caps are vented with rubber gaskets that pop less dramatically than the older types which can go off like a firecracker. When the supplies are finished, check the output voltages independently first before connecting them to the camera circuitry.

If any of the small-value tantalum capacitors are installed backwards, they are likely to die quietly while you are testing the circuit. If a fuse blows, take it as a warning. Check the installation of the diodes and capacitors. Small tantalum capacitors may operate from several minutes to several hours if they are installed backwards. When they fail, they become hot. Because delayed failure can cause confusion during later tests, touch the parts but be careful not to get burned. The electrical symptom of a failed capacitor is a voltage drop on the line that supplies the failed capacitor.

When it's time to put the ICs in the sockets, make sure you don't put them in backwards. You can mark pin one on the board. Use the notch in the package to identify pin one. (On separate occasions, we plugged an ADC and an LF357 op amp in backwards. Luckily no harm was done in either case.) If an IC is not fully plugged into its socket, it may not work or it may work partially.

One popular way to damage circuits is to slip with a test lead when you make measurements. Suddenly, you have two problems: the old one you were trying to troubleshoot and the new one you just made by shorting those two adjacent pins.

Nothing should go seriously wrong if you do the wiring right and install the components with the correct orientation. The CARD.EXE and PREAMP.EXE software supplied with this book will help you test, set up, and check out your wiring and even catch most problems with an IC that you've plugged in backwards. Even if you're an old hand with electronics, resist the temptation to build the cards and apply power. Use the software. Check every step and you won't go wrong.

A.4 Never Forget Safety!

As we put more and more electronic devices on our telescopes, electrical safety must become part of amateur astronomy. Your computer, power strips, extension cords and telescope wires should all be three-prong grounded and connected to a properly wired AC three-prong outlet. When you work outdoors, the outlet should have a ground-fault interrupt circuit.

Although most new homes have ground-fault protection on the outside outlets, older homes do not. Check whether the outlet has ground-fault protection. Ground-fault protection is usually connected to a bathroom outlet; you can test to see whether the outside outlet is ground-fault protected by disabling the bathroom outlet with the test button. If it is protected, this will also disable the outside power plug.

When the entire system is assembled, it is likely that you'll have equipment from many makers in use together. Check the major units before you connect them to each other. With your meter, check for chassis-to-chassis volt-ages. Check every telescope, camera, and computer combination. It is always possible that a piece of equipment is not isolated from the hot side of the AC line.

To check for AC voltage, connect a 100kΩ ½-Watt resistor across the voltmeter terminals to prevent false readings caused by capacitative AC coupling, set the meter on AC volts, and measure between the metal parts of the chassis. Keep your fingers off the exposed resistor and probe leads. It won't hurt to repeat the measurements checking DC volts just in case.

While low-voltage circuits are harmless to touch, watch out for high-current hazards. At one star party, we saw a telescope-builder's 12-volt battery cable short out. The cable became white hot and showered flaming pieces into knee-high, bone-dry grass. (Smoking and barbecuing weren't allowed at this function for fire safety reasons!) Inspect cords and fix worn insulation. Make sure everything is properly fused.

Watch for little things. For example, when you cut off leads with diagonal cutters, little wire pieces shoot from the jaws of the cutters with something approaching the velocity of a good Daisy BB gun. Wear safety glasses to protect your eyes. Don't let these little pieces lodge somewhere in the stuff you're building because they could cause a short later.

Solvent safety is another area where is little care can prevent a big problem. Read the warning labels on solvents, paints, and adhesives that you use. Don't smoke around flammable materials, and if you are interested in preserving your health, don't smoke. Use solvents, paints, adhesives in a well-ventilated area. Just because something doesn't smell bad doesn't mean it won't harm you.

Take care around the obvious dangers, too. Power tools like a milling machine, drill press, lathe, and table saw pose clear dangers. Follow the manufacturer's instructions for these and any other tools you use. Loose clothing can be caught and so can neckties. Avoid watches, rings, bracelets, gold chains, and other dangling adornments. Metal increases the possibility of being seriously shocked when you work around 120VAC power. Wear safety glasses. Finally, alcohol and drugs can dull the senses and should never be used when working with machinery or electronic equipment.

Appendix B. Building Electronic Circuits

We've compiled this appendix to help electronics novices through their first experiences with assembling electronic circuits, and to serve as a brief refresher for those who have built Heathkits or had a fling with amateur radio in their younger days.

If you're totally new to electronics, we recommend finding someone who has worked with electronics before, to help you through the doubts and uncertainties that attend starting out fresh in any new field.

Also for the novice, we recommend an inexpensive and handy guide called *Getting Started in Electronics* by Forrest Mims, III which is sold through Radio Shack stores (#276-5003a). This unpretentious 128-page booklet contains background information that you'll appreciate as you build the circuits for your Cookbook camera.

B.1 Identifying Electronic Components

This section contains a few basic hints so you won't be delayed looking for reference books when you'd like to be stuffing the correct components in the circuit cards.

Resistors. Resistors are usually marked with color coded bands. The bands are always closer to one end of the resistor than the other; read them in order from the end they are closer to. Here are the codes:

Resistor Color-Band Codes	
Black	0
Brown	1
Red	2
Orange	3
Yellow	4
Green	5
Blue	6
Violet	7
Gray	8
White	9
Gold	±5%
Silver	±10%

A resistor with orange-orange-orange gold banding has a resistance of 3 3 plus 3 zeros, or 33,000Ω, and the gold tolerance means that the actual resistance lies between 31,350Ω and 34,650Ω.

Sometimes there is a fifth band indicating the stability of the resistor expressed as a percentage change in value per 1000 hours, brown for 1%, red for 0.1%, orange for 0.01%, and yellow for 0.001%. So a resistor marked brown-black-green-gold-yellow has a value of 1 0 plus 5 zeros, or 1MΩ ±5% with a very stable value (yellow = 0.001% change per 1000 hours). A yellow-violet-red-gold-yellow resistor is 4 7 plus 2 zeros, or 4.7kΩ ±5% with high stability.

Sometimes flat-sided resistors such as trimmer potentiometers are marked using the same scheme used for capacitors (see below). A trimmer pot marked 102K should have a maximum resistance of 1kΩ. If you have any doubt, you can always measure the value of a resistor with your volt-ohm meter.

It does not matter which way you place a resistor on a circuit board. Resistors can point in either direction.

Capacitors. Capacitors that have three numbers followed by a letter are rated in picofarads (pF) as follows. The first and second numbers are the first and second digits of the capacitance and the third number is the multiplier. The letter indicates the tolerance, either M for ±20% or K for 10%. The value of a capacitor with 102M printed on the side is 1 0 multiplied by 100 picofarads, or .001μF with a tolerance of ±20%. One labelled 121K is 1 2 multiplied by 10 picofarads, or 120pF ±10%.

Small ceramic capacitors can be installed facing either direction; they are non-polarized. However, it is important to know which end is which in electrolytic capacitors. In addition to printed plus signs on the package, the positive end of the capacitor has a band, ring, dimple, or other distinctive marking.

Diodes. Diode part numbers (for example, 1N3600) are printed on the body of the diode but, because many diodes are quite small, may be difficult to read. The cathode end of the diode is marked by a painted band; this band corresponds to the straight-line end of the diode symbol in circuit diagrams.

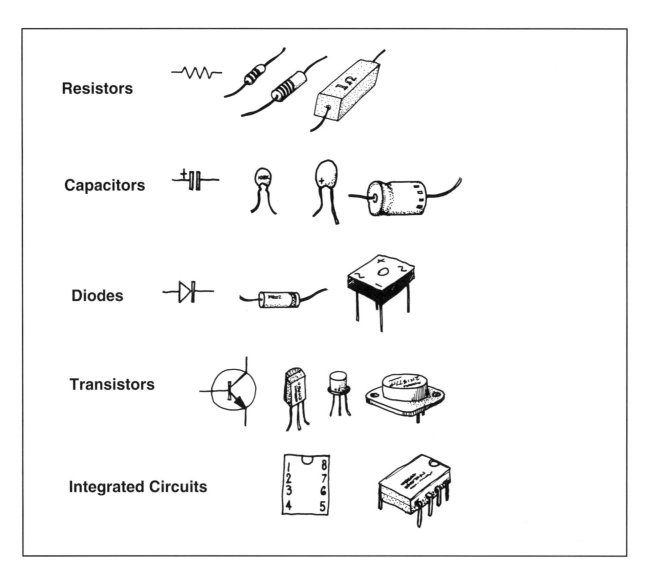

Resistors

Capacitors

Diodes

Transistors

Integrated Circuits

Transistors. Transistors have a letter and number designation such as 2N2987 stamped on the top of the case or package. Three wires come from a transistor case, the emitter, base, and collector. Depending on the transistor, these may be labelled E, B, and C or their identification may depend on their position.

To aid in placing them correctly in circuits, transistors are always asymmetric in some fashion. Often the case has a flat side, and the orientation of the flat side will be shown in the circuit board. By orienting the transistor so that it corresponds to the outline on the circuit board you can place the transistor correctly.

Integrated Circuits. Integrated circuits such as amplifiers, regulators, and logic circuits all have a letter and number designation stamped on the top of the case or package. You can usually recognize this from context, that is, if you are looking for the 74LS157 chip and the package has three lines of printing on it, one line will read 74LS157 and the others will be the manufacturer's name and perhaps a coded date and place of manufacture.

Three-pin voltage regular packages might have pin markings printed on the package near the leads. If you do not see *in*, *out*, and *adj* designations printed or embossed on the device itself, check the sales package the IC came in for a diagram showing which lead is which. Alternatively, the package may be asymmetrical so that you can orient it as you would orient a transistor.

All of the schematic diagrams in this book are drawn to show regulators correctly from the the top, that is, on metal-tabbed regulators with the plastic side up, and on plastic regulators, with the flat side up.

Although DIP packages appear symmetrical, a notch at one end of the package tells you how to insert the chip in its socket and where to start numbering the pins. With the notch at the top and the pins pointing away from you, pins are numbered counterclockwise from the top. In addition, a little dimple in the package marks pin 1.

The American Radio Relay League Handbook has an excellent section on interpreting the markings on electronic components, and many other technical reference

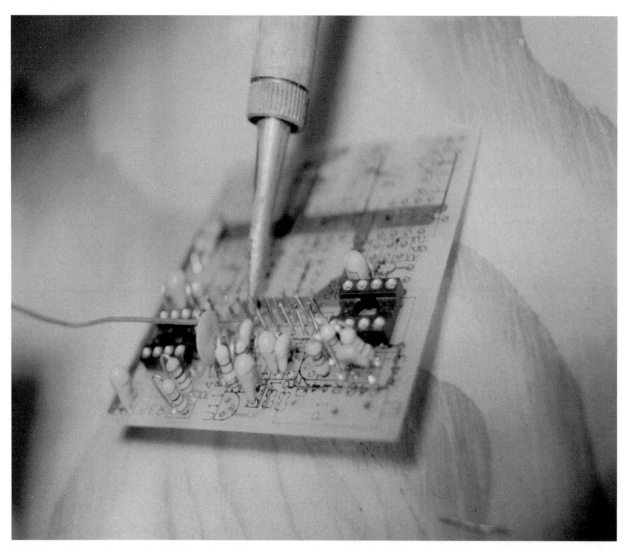

With the right solder and soldering iron, it's easy to make a good solder joint. At each joint, you touch the tip of the iron to the joint, heat for a few seconds, apply the solder, and then raise the solder and soldering iron.

books are available from your local electronics store.

B.2 A Lesson on Soldering

Soldering is easy with the right tools. If you're new to the field, purchase good tools and don't try to save a few dollars on second-rate equipment.

Start by purchasing a 15-watt grounded soldering iron with a small chisel tip, or a 25- to 40-watt grounded soldering iron with a temperature-controlled tip. Buy or make a soldering iron holder so that you cannot accidentally touch the hot tip. The holder should prevent the soldering iron from rolling or being pulled off the bench onto your lap. (Need we say more? Get a holder.)

Also purchase a roll of 0.030-inch rosin core solder, either 63/37 or 60/40 composition (i.e., 63% tin and 37% lead). For the Cookbook camera circuit boards, a 25-foot roll should be plenty. (By the way never, ever use acid-

core solder for electrical work. It's for pipes and the acid in it corrodes wires and circuit cards.)

Also buy a small scraping tool made for circuit board work. This tool comes in handy for scraping away little flecks of solder and rosin, bending leads, and checking the integrity of solder joints.

Keep a damp rag or sponge at hand when you solder to wipe away burned rosin and oxidized solder which accumulates and smuts the tip of the soldering iron.

If your soldering iron has a temperature-controlled tip, set it for 100° to 200° Fahrenheit above the melting point of the solder. For 63/37 solder which melts at 361°F, this would be about 500°F. Although a 15-watt iron may not have a temperature controlled tip, the tip should be close to the correct temperature.

A good solder joint forms alloys of the materials

being connected. The idea is to make a low resistance electrical contact. Although solder imparts some physical strength to a joint, solder has little mechanical strength. Circuit board holes and pads can support light components, but heavy parts must be supported with a good mechanical connection.

The wires, component leads, and card pads that you solder should be clean and solder-plated or tinned. (Component leads are ready to be soldered.) To solder a wire to a circuit board, lightly tin the tip of the soldering iron and press the wire against it for a second or two. Touch the solder lightly to the wire: the solder should melt and flow onto the wire.

To solder a component to a circuit board, insert the leads into the holes in the board. Lightly tin the soldering iron. Press the tip between the lead and the pad so that it touches both, and then add a small amount of solder. Use just enough solder and heat to get a shiny, wet, fillet on the joint. Pull the tip away from the joint. The whole operation takes a few seconds.

The resulting solder joint should be smooth, uniformly shiny, and lustrous. The solder should blend smoothly with the work. If the pieces move while the solder solidifies, the solder may look gray and granular meaning that you have made a "cold" joint that will not provide a good connection. Even if a cold joint holds at first, it may fail later from handling stress or vibration.

It normally takes just two or three seconds to make a good solder joint. If it takes longer than five seconds, let the joint cool between tries. Too much heat can damage the circuit board and cause pads to lift. Components can also be damaged if the leads are overheated during soldering. If you can make the joints in two to five seconds (and you easily can with practice), none of the camera components of your Cookbook will be damaged.

If you are new to soldering, practice making joints with some wires and an old PC board. Once you get the hang of it, you'll find there's a jazzy little tempo to soldering: tip down, beat, beat, solder on, beat, beat, tip up, beat, beat, perfect joint! (You can even say this to yourself as you solder.)

From time to time as you solder, wipe the tip of your soldering iron free of burned rosin and oxidized solder. All it takes is a quick wipe on the damp cloth or sponge. You may be able to make six or eight joints between cleaning, or just one or two, depending. After you wipe the tip, it should be shiny with solder. If it looks dull, add solder until the tip is tinned, or shiny and wet with solder. Wipe off excess solder before resuming work.

Component leads are pushed through the component side card holes then soldered on the solder side. After you insert them into the card, bend the component leads over at about 45 degree angles to hold the part in place. You can hold sockets with short pins with masking tape on the component side or back them with a small wooden block on your work bench.

After you have soldered them, cut off protruding leads just above the solder which has wet to the leads at the bottom of the plated through holes. When you cut them, beware of flying ends. Short stout leads really zip and may ricochet around the room. Wear safety glasses and point the lead into a waste basket or in a safe direction. Make sure the leads don't land in your electronics: they can cause shorts.

When you finish a board, inspect your work. Look for loose connections, cold joints, solder splashes, shorts, and IC pins that might be shorting. Check that none of the leads you cut off got caught on the circuit board. For critical areas in the camera body, clean off the residual flux with isopropyl alcohol (i.e., rubbing alcohol). Residual flux is okay on cards but can contaminate the inside of the camera body.

If you get too much solder on a joint, press desoldering braid against the joint and heat it. The braid will soak up the excess solder leaving a clean joint.

For more information on soldering, see Chapter 24 of the 1993 Amateur Radio Relay League Handbook. This book also suggests sources for inexpensive soldering irons and describes a variety of soldering stations.

B.3 Get a Good Meter

We recommend a three-and-a-half-digit digital multimeter to measure the camera circuits. If you don't have one, borrow one. You should probably buy one, however, since it will help you fix your car, the dryer, and a whole bunch of telescope gear which is more and more electronic.

Two classes of digital multimeters are available: low cost and high cost. The low-cost economy models are pocket-sized with volt, ohm, diode, and continuity test capabilities. The more expensive hand held models offer more functions, but you really don't need them for testing the camera. Expect to pay around $25 for a meter that will do the job and about $100 for a fancy one.

Old-style multimeters have an electromechanical analog meter movement with scales graduated for volts, amps, and ohms. They are still available and sell for less than $20. However, we do not recommend them because the input impedance is usually too low. For the cheapest ones, the input impedance is typically $1,000\Omega$/volt. According to Ohm's Law, to the one volt circuit that you want to measure, the meter looks like a $1,000\Omega$ resistor.

These meters load the circuit that is being measured. To measure 1 volt accurately, the circuit must be able to supply 1mA of current. The voltage can't be measured accurately unless a significant current is flowing through the meter. The lower the input impedance or sensitivity, the less accurate the readings.

For good results, you need a meter sensitivity of about $20k\Omega$/volt. Some of the better old-style analog meters are very good. A vacuum-tube voltmeter (VTVM)

The secret of successfully building the electronic circuit boards for the Cookbook camera is testing at every step. Here a simple voltage divider circuit applies a test voltage to camera CCD input plug on the finished interface board.

usually has an input impedance of 10MΩ or more and this is just fine. Meters with field effect transistor inputs (FET inputs) have an input impedance from 2MΩ to 11MΩ.

To measure resistance in digital circuits, you must know your meter. To measure resistance, the meter forces a current to flow between the test leads. The voltages necessary can damage digital ICs. Consult the manual for the meter or measure the test voltages and currents on the test leads with another meter. Check the ohm ranges from R×1 to R×1MΩ. The R×1 range is by far the most dangerous. For example, our 20-year-old RCA VoltOhmyst puts out 1.5 volts on this range and can force 100mA through a component. So we wouldn't recommend using this scale to test semiconductors. We've got a newer one we use these days.

Digital volt-ohm meters are really the way to go. These are widely available with input impedances of 10MΩ. On the ohms measurements, they apply low voltages and currents which do not damage integrated circuits. There is usually a continuity or "beep" mode for low-resistance measurements. For checking diodes, you can display the voltage drop across the circuit being measured. When the test voltage from the meter is applied in the forward bias direction (that is, with plus to the anode and minus to the cathode), the meter typically beeps once and displays the forward voltage drop across the diode (0.5 to 0.7 V for silicon diodes). When the leads and measuring voltage polarity are reversed, the meter reads open and there is no tone.

The inexpensive meters generally have only auto range selection and a range hold function. Some of the test programs supplied on the disk request a given range on the meter. For auto ranging meters without manual range selection, it is best not to set the range hold. Leave the meter in the auto mode.

Read the instruction manual for your meter. They're usually clear and well illustrated. The meter makers want you to make good measurements (and so do we).

B.4 Troubleshooting with a Multimeter

This section offers a few tips on using a meter to test the circuits and components of your Cookbook CCD camera. Above all else, when you use a test meter, remember to keep your fingers off the metal probe tips. After all, you want to measure the electrical properties of the circuit and not your fingertips, and when you're measuring high voltage you don't want a nasty shock.

All voltage measurements are made with respect to two points or nodes. The nodes are conductor points which are either component leads, circuit traces, solder connections, component leads, the metal inserts in the sockets, etc. Measurements cannot be made across insulators such as the epoxy circuit card, the plastic insulation on the wiring, or the dipped epoxy coating over the component leads on the capacitors.

To measure AC or DC volts, set the meter to AC or DC volts. To measure resistance, set the meter to ohms. Use the right range setting if the meter has them.

For most DC voltage measurements in the camera, the black (or common) test lead goes to ground and the red (positive) lead connects to the voltage you want to measure. If you measure the voltage across a component, a transistor emitter-to-base voltage for example, the polarity of the reading is always with respect to the lead which is plugged into the common or ground terminal on the meter. The polarity of the leads has no significance for AC voltage.

Resistance measurements are made across two nodes in the circuit. You might measure the resistance between two pins on an IC socket or across the leads of a resistor. Residual flux from soldering can interfere with measurements to component leads or to pads/traces on the cards. Poke through any flux or clean it off with a little isopropyl alcohol and a cotton swab.

Don't measure ohms with the power on. Unplug supplies before "ohming" and remember that filter capacitors can hold a significant charge even after the power has been shut off. This won't damage most meters but if voltage is present, you're likely to get a negative resistance reading or an inaccurate positive one. If power has recently been applied to a circuit, it's a good idea before you measure ohms to check for volts AC and DC. If you get AC volts, you forgot to unplug it. "Holy Marconi—I unplugged the soldering iron, not the supply!"

The disk included with this book contains a computer-aided resistance and voltage test check for the circuit cards. The program gives on-line suggestions should you come across an incorrect reading. Because it is impossible to predict every possible problem, you may have to do a little detective work on your own. Trace through the circuit using the block diagram and schematics. Use the last good reading and first bad reading to isolate the fault in a certain part of the circuit.

Most problems are simple: the meter is set to read AC volts instead of ohms, there is no solder on the component to board connection, or there is too much solder and the circuit is shorting to adjacent traces, the component was installed in the wrong orientation, or the component is the wrong one.

Watch for parallel circuits that could affect the reading. Parallel circuits are not always obvious even in the simplest situations. The safest comparisons are made when the suspect component has been isolated from the circuit. To isolate it, lift (that is, unsolder from the card) one end of the suspect part.

Further hints on measuring follow.

B.4.1 Measuring Diodes

A good diode usually reads about 5 to 10 times higher resistance than it does when you swap the test leads. Forward bias, the low resistance reading, occurs with the positive voltage (red test lead) on the anode and the negative (black test lead) on the cathode. Exactly how much higher reverse bias and lower forward bias depends on the diode. If you have a spare or an identical diode somewhere in the circuit, use that one for comparison to the suspect one. That way, no matter what meter you're using you find which one is bad.

As mentioned, if your meter has a diode check range, you're in Fat City. The meter will read 0.5 to 0.7 volts in forward bias and probably open when the leads are reversed. Compare another good diode. For example, all the diodes in the same rectifier bridges in the power supply will have virtually identical forward voltage readings. They should be the same in the other polarity also.

With the analog meter, use a high resistance range for testing diodes. The resistance readings will be low in the forward bias direction and higher in the reverse bias direction. Usually a bad diode measures either shorted or open for both directions.

B.4.2 Measuring Transistors

The diode-check feature on your meter can be used to check transistors. Emitter-to-base should read 0.5 to 0.7V in the forward direction and open in the other. The base corresponds to the cathode of a diode for the PNP 2N2907 transistors and to the anode for the NPN 2N3904 transistor. The base-to-collector can also be measured as a diode. Emitter-to-collector usually reads open in both polarities. If you are in doubt, compare the suspect device with good device.

With the analog meter it's the same except the readings will be 5 to 10 times higher for the reverse diode direction than the forward bias direction. The emitter to collector should read open or high resistance.

With in-circuit power applied, a transistor will be in one of two states: off or conducting. The 2N3904 circuit is designed to operate in a conducting linear mode. However, when the CCD is not connected to its base, the transistor will be in the off state and you will see no voltage drop between the base and emitter.

To test the 2N3904 in the conducting mode, apply a positive voltage greater than 2VDC to the base though a 10kΩ resistor. The transistor will conduct in a linear mode and it can be tested. The emitter voltage should measure 0.5 to 0.7 volts (i.e., the drop across a diode) lower than the base voltage.

The 2N2907 transistors function as PNP current switches. They can be either off or conducting in a linear mode. The base is tied to ground and the emitter turns on the transistor. With a voltage greater than 0.6V on the 150Ω input to the transistor, the transistor will turn on and the emitter-to-base voltage will show a diode voltage drop. With no voltage applied to the 150Ω emitter resistor, the emitter-to-base voltage will be zero. The transistor will be in the off state, that is, there will be no current flowing from the collector lead.

You can determine whether current is flowing in a 2N2907 under test by measuring the collector voltage with respect to –9.5 volts. The collector will measure 9.5V in cutoff and around 7.5V when the voltage on the emitter resistor input is 2.5V.

B.4.3 Measuring Capacitors

The large, electrolytic polarized and tantalum capacitors can be checked out of circuit by measuring their resistance—but check for residual charge first. If you get a negative reading, a charge is present.

A good capacitor acts as follows: the resistance reading starts at a fairly high value—kilohms or megohms—and increases as the capacitor charges from the meter battery. When the capacitor has charged, it reads open. If you reverse the leads, which can be done without harm since the voltage is low on the test probes, you will see a high negative value. This value will slowly decrease and then increase positive again as the capacitor discharges and charges up to the other polarity. The speed of charging depends on the value of the capacitor and the properties of the meter.

A defective capacitor will generally have a constant low-ohm reading. Check a suspect capacitor against a comparison capacitor of the same or similar value.

Good small-value capacitors will either read open or show a momentary jump on the bar graph feature of a digital meter, or they will twitch from low to open on an analog meter. If the leads are reversed, the effect is more pronounced, and you will see another momentary indication as the capacitor first discharges and then charges up the opposite polarity.

Degraded capacitors usually have low to midrange and constant resistance readings. It is rare for small ceramic capacitors to fail. When they do, you can usually see that they are mechanically damaged, such as cracks in the package. In a circuit, it is usually necessary to lift one end of a suspect capacitor and electrically compare it to a spare part of the same value.

B.4.4 Measuring Resistors

Well, obviously use ohms. Beware of the parallel paths if you are measuring a resistor in a circuit. Resistors don't fail very often but you can degrade the internal connection between the lead and the resistance element when you solder them into a circuit. With resistors, however, it's more likely you've put in the wrong part than it is that the resistor is damaged.

B.4.5 Measuring Integrated Circuits

If you have an oscilloscope for signal tracing, that's fine. You can skip this section. If you don't, then logic probes are an inexpensive substitute for a scope. A logic probe requires a 5VDC power source to operate and it is only useful for measuring logic levels from the digital circuitry on the printer interface card in your printer. (The logic levels are defined in the printer interface theory section in Chapter 6.) An LED on the logic probe indicates if the pins are high, low, or pulsing. This gives you a lot of information for troubleshooting and it might be all you need if you also have a good meter.

The advantage that a logic probe has over a DMM for measuring logic levels is that the probe can detect short pulses. The convert command signal to the analog-to-digital converter chip is too fast to measure with a meter. If the ADC is not functioning properly, use a logic probe to check for the presence of the convert pulse.

If, for some reason, an IC is suspect, always check the power and ground pins particularly if some other pin looks wrong. It is fairly common for one or more pins in an IC to miss the terminal and bend under the IC. Visually check that the IC is seated properly in its socket. Put the circuit in a static, unclocked mode with the CARD or PREAMP test program so that you can examine the input voltages and check the circuit function so you know what the outputs should be.

Use the diode check range of a digital meter to evaluate ICs out of circuit. With the red lead connected to ground, the supply pin, output pins, and input pins will generally act like diodes with respect to the ground pin. Blown open or shorted inputs can be detected this way. The forward voltage drop will be about the same for all pins with the same function, for example, the address inputs. The chip enable pin may look a little different. There are many identical chips in the circuits that can be compared pin for pin with respect to ground and the supply pins. Check these in both polarities.

B.4.6 Measuring Regulators

Integrated circuit regulators generally do not fail from circuit faults but they can be destroyed if they are installed backwards.

Visual checks are the first choice on these devices. The fixed regulators should be within ±10% of their rated output voltage if they are working properly. The adjustable regulators depend on the two resistors which connect between the output, adjust, and ground for the correct output voltage. Incorrect resistor values will affect their voltage outputs.

If the input voltage to the regulator is low, then something is probably loading the regulator output and it will be low also. Feel the regulators in circuit. The +5V and –9.5 volt regulators run hot (it is a good idea to temporarily install heat sinks on these regulators during testing) but the others should be touchable. (This goes for all other devices as well.) If a regulator is hot it may have shut down from its internal protection circuit. Let it cool off and try again. If it does not come back up, it is probably current limiting. Take the load off the circuit by removing components from the sockets one at time (be sure you turn the power off to remove each IC). If one of the ICs were plugged in backwards or defective, the voltage should come back up as soon as you remove it.

The tantalum capacitors which connect to the outputs are also good candidates for failure if one were installed with the wrong polarity. Check that each is installed in the card with the plus sign on the correct side.

B.4.7 Substituting Parts

When you cannot find the exact part called for, what can you put in its place? Your options depend on what part you want to substitute. Here are a few suggestions:

Resistors. Most of the resistors used in the camera are carbon film types rated at $\frac{1}{4}$W. It is okay to use metal film types of the same power rating. If you cannot find the right value, solder two resistors in series; the resistance of the series combination is R1+R2. If you need a 1.5kΩ resistor, you can use a 1kΩ resistor plus a 470Ω resistor and come within 2% of the desired value.

Never substitute a power resistor with one of lower rated wattage. It is okay to use a higher rated wattage.

Capacitors. The small-value ceramic capacitors can be replaced with silver-mica types, and, with the exception of the capacitor on the Cookbook 211's SRG, a slightly higher value will probably work. If you increase the value of one capacitor, however, the others should match. If you substitute a 120pF capacitor for a 100pF, make all the 100pF capacitors 120pF.

Decoupling capacitors such as the 0.1µF ceramics and tantalums can be replaced with parts having up to 2.5 times the specified capacitance. Do not use lower voltage ratings; higher voltage ratings are okay. This also holds for the electrolytic capacitors in the power supply.

Diodes. It is okay to use diodes with a higher current or peak inverse voltage (PIV) rating.

Integrated circuits and transistors: You want to use the device type specified, but changing the package type or using a better grade of device is okay. The 74LSxx DIP packages come in plastic, but you can use 54LSxx types that are ceramic. The AD1674J converter is a monotonic 12-bit converter, but it is only linear to 11 bits. Better grade converter chips such as the AD1674K are available, but they are more expensive.

In the Cookbook cameras, we have replaced the hard-to-find LM137—a mil-spec component with the readily available LM336.

If possible, use transistors packaged in plastic for the 2N2907 and 2N3904 devices. Metal-cased parts will work, but the case is connected to the collector so you must keep it from shorting to nearby conductors.

Fuses. Do not substitute fuses—ever—with higher current ratings. Lower ratings are okay, but they may blow open in normal use.

CCDs. The Cookbook 245 design specifies a TC245-40 CCD, which is the lowest grade of TC245. Two higher grades of the same device, the TC245-30 and the TC245-10, are available from Texas Instruments, but they cost considerably more. The higher grades offer better uniformity, fewer light and dark pixels, and a slightly lower thermal signal. In building the Cookbook camera prototypes, we have seen no loss of performance because of nonuniformities or abnormal pixels, and therefore do not necessarily recommend the higher grade TC245s.

Appendix C. Improving Your CCD Camera

Here are some suggestions for customizing the Cookbook camera to perform its best for you, your local environment, and your particular needs. Feel free to try these and other modifications you may dream up yourself.

C.1 Add One-Plug Convenience

If you often set up your camera enough times in near darkness, sooner or later Murphy's Law will get you. You'll manage to swap the leads on the Peltier or plug in the ±15VDC supply backwards and suffer a hot CCD or an apparently dead camera.

To eliminate the possibility, install an 8-lead spade-lug jack and plug ("Jones plug") between your power supply and camera. Wire the ±15VDC, the pump, and the Peltier supply into the plug, and use the remaining two lugs to complete the circuit for the red indicator LED.

If you're a real fanatic, you can also put fluid quick-connects in the cooling water circuit. Murphy isn't going to get you if you plug them in backward, but the camera will be easier to move around and service.

C.2 Extend Your Cables

Although we recommend a printer adapter-to-camera cable 15 feet long, considerably longer cables *do* work. We have driven the cameras with cables up to 35 feet long, and still longer cables may be possible. Problems with cross-talk and ground noise ultimately limit the length of a signal cable. However, unless you plan to install complete remote control on your telescope, it is best to stay within easy reach of the telescope and computer.

If you want a long cable primarily because the idea of having your $2,000 computer outdoors bothers you, it is probably most practical to resurrect an old PC-XT or 286, equip it with a VGA card and monochrome VGA monitor, and use this *el cheapo* computer solely for imaging. Using a commercial communications package, you can transmit data from your observatory computer to your expensive indoor computer over a serial cable, or you can save the images to disk and carry them in for evaluation.

With differential line drivers connected to twisted-pair lines and line receivers, cables longer than 100 feet are possible. Since a line driver, twisted pair, and a line receiver are required for each bit, 13 sets would be needed for the Cookbook 245.

Another approach, suitable for a telescope under full remote control, is to use a commercial keyboard and monitor extender package such as Cybex's PC Companion Plus that allows you to work up to 250 feet away from your computer.

C.3 Improve Noise Immunity

To take advantage of the full dynamic range of the camera, you cannot let electrical or electronic interference degrade its image. Your first line of defense against noise is to use your camera in double-sampled mode (see Section 9.3.8). This should eliminate noise in which the noise varies more slowly than the sampling interval.

Some Cookbook cameras may display a low-frequency "popcorn noise" fluctuation that comes from a combination of the internal voltage reference on the CCD and the voltage reference on the preamp board. This shows up as broad horizontal bands in the image, with an amplitude of less than 1 pixel value. Double-sampling mode eliminates this fluctuation.

However, if you see patterns in your images— stripes, herringbones, tweed-like weaves, or wavering bands—then your camera may be picking up external noise. The camera circuit is especially sensitive to electromagnetic interference in the 4 to 5 MHz range. If you live close to a high-power AM-radio station, you may pick up noise from the transmitter.

Test for noise by running the noise test routine in the AP211 or AP245 image acquisition program. Study the plot for periodicity. If there is no noise, the plot will appear completely random, but in the presence of noise the test may show a periodic rise and fall of the signal.

One of the simplest ways to improve the camera's immunity to external noise is by adding two 1,000μF 25WVDC electrolytic capacitors to the interface card. Connect the capacitors between the +15V input and ground and between ground and the −15V input. Check the polarity on the capacitors when installing them, and secure the capacitors so their leads won't fatigue. The capacitors reduce RF coupling into the circuit and they

These images of Jupiter, Saturn, and Mars were made with prototype Cookbook cameras. Kanto and Munger captured Mars with a 10" SCT, and their friend Phil Bright recorded Jupiter and Saturn with an 8" f/10 SCT.

also reduce 60Hz noise caused by ground loops.

The Peltier device is fed by a long wire which can act as an antenna for RF interference. Because the Peltier device is not grounded at the camera head (you can't ground it because the voltage drop in the wire will force a voltage on the interface-to-computer ground), RF might feed into the camera cavity. Place Ferrite beads over the Peltier wires where they exit the camera body and connect a 0.1μF 100VDC film capacitor between the negative Peltier wire and the camera body.

The slow-motion motors on some telescopes are another possible source of high-frequency noise. Install a decoupling capacitor across the terminals of these motors to eliminate noise, or don't use the motor when the camera is reading out the frame after the integration.

Ground loop noise may also appear as a problem. Try changing where the AC power plugs are connected. It is a good idea to put a transient and noise suppressor on your power supply plug (available at Radio Shack) even if you don't have a noise problem. The suppressor keeps spikes from electric motors in your house from feeding into the power supply.

If none of these suggestions correct RF interference, you may have to shield the external wires. Test the need for shielding made by wrapping aluminum foil around the camera cable in a spiral pattern and connecting the foil shield to ground. If the foil eliminates the noise, replace the foil with a braided wire shield.

C.4 Optimize Charge Transfer

The Cookbook cameras use a fixed voltage reference to bias the antiblooming gate. Although the cameras operate quite well with the fixed bias of our circuit, data sheets from Texas Instruments suggest that this voltage can be adjusted for optimum transfer efficiency. To measure the charge transfer efficiency, consult section 2.4.6 of *CCD Astronomy* by Christian Buil.

The voltage on the antiblooming gate can be set by adding fixed resistors between J2 pin 4 and ground or −9.5V. The voltage in J2 pin 4 should lie between −2.0V and −3.0V.

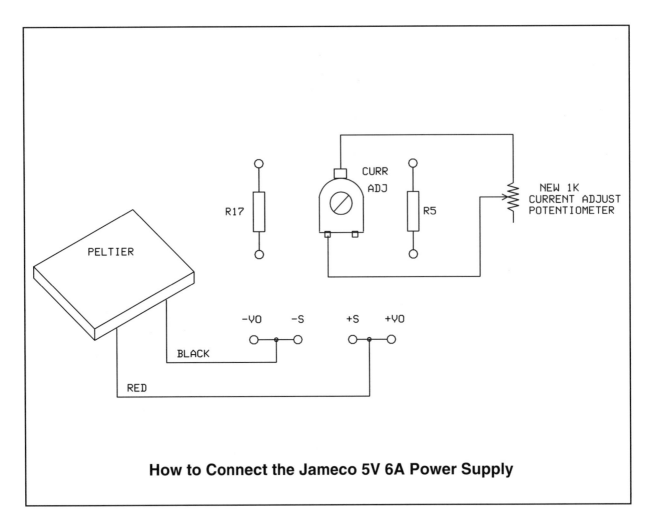

How to Connect the Jameco 5V 6A Power Supply

To pull the voltage toward −2.0V, connect a 4.7KΩ or greater resistor from ground to J2 pin 4. To pull the voltage toward −3.0V, connect a resistor from −9.5V to J2 pin 4. Select a resistor that is 10kΩ or greater.

Use a potentiometer to pull the voltage while you measure the charge transfer efficiency. Once you know the optimum voltage, measure the resistance of the potentiometer and solder in a fixed resistor of the same value.

C.5 Beef Up the Cooling System

The cooling system was designed to operate within the environmental limits specified for the TC211 and TC245 CCD chips, that is, for −30°C minimum. However, Texas Instruments has reported applications that involve cooling their CCD chips to −60°C, even if they do not officially sanction this degree of cooling.

A gain of about 5°C is possible by using a larger single-stage Peltier cooler. A Melcor CP 1.4-71-045L device is a slightly higher capacity device than the cooler used in the Cookbook design. The device requires a power supply that can deliver 8 amps of current at 9VDC to run full-out, but for anyone who runs the Peltier from a standard 5VDC power supply, there will be some gain.

For a much lower chip temperature, you can build a two-stage Peltier cooler. Refer to Chapter 3 of *CCD Astronomy* by Christian Buil for some excellent comments on the design of two-stage Peltier coolers and problems with low-temperature CCD operation. In addition, Melcor offers several cascaded Peltier devices that might allow you to reach lower temperatures.

C.6 Run on Battery Power

For operation in the field, it's possible to run the camera from batteries—but you'll need a large storage battery to power the Peltier, the pump, your telescope drive, and a computer for any reasonable length of time.

For the electronics, wire two 9-volt batteries in series for each side of the ±15VDC supply. It is a good idea to fuse the batteries. (Do not mix battery types, especially alkaline batteries. Alkaline batteries can explode if they are used with other battery types.) Four batteries thus wired should run the camera all night.

The most obvious simple solution for the pump and Peltier is to use a 6V lead/acid storage battery. Be sure you fuse the battery at 6A.

Alternatively, you can run the pump from a 12-volt

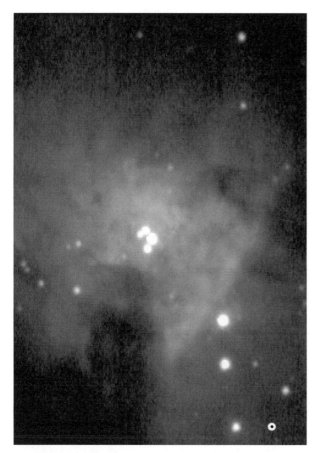

By adding short integrations, you avoid blooming on bright stars. Above are seven 2-second integrations.

Tucson amateur astronomer Phil Bright uses a surplus 5V 6A supply (available for $15 from Jameco Electronics as part #28935) for powering his Peltier module. You can save quite a few dollars on the cost of the supplies by using Phil's method. Set it up as follows:

• Connect the AC plug and fuse the supply per the instruction sheet which is shipped with the supply.

• Connect the force and sense terminals on the supply, as shown in the accompanying schematic.

• Apply AC power to the supply and adjust the knob marked VOL ADJ until the voltage between the $+V_0$ and $-V_0$ terminals is between 5.5 and 6.0 VDC.

• Unplug the supply and wait for the output voltage to bleed off of the capacitors.

• Find the potentiometer marked CURR ADJ and leave it at the factory setting of 6 amperes. Connect a 1kΩ potentiometer between the CURR ADJ leads as shown in the schematic. The potentiometer adjusts the current output of the supply.

The current limit of the supply is used to slowly bring up the voltage to the Peltier device. Measure the output voltage and mark the position on the 1kΩ potentiometer for reference.

It is possible to use an inexpensive 9-volt or 12-volt 1-ampere power pack in series with a 5Ω 10-watt power resistor to run the pump. Power packs are available for around $6. By using a power pack, the surplus 5VDC supply from Jameco, and the ±15VDC supply described in Chapter 5, you can run the camera for less than $40.

battery by using a dropping resistor to reduce the voltage (as described below). Fuse the pump with a 1A fuse.

It is also possible to use a 12-volt storage battery to run the Peltier regulator shown in Chapter 5. Connect the negative terminal of the battery to ground, and wire the positive terminal through a 6A fuse. To avoid overcharging the battery, connect the fuse output to the anode of a 10A diode, and connect the cathode to the positive side of capacitor C1.

Because lead/acid storage batteries generally do not tolerate deep discharge cycles, never drain the battery beyond half its capacity. For example, you would not want to use a battery rated at 25 ampere-hours to run the camera for more than 3 hours.

C.7 Use a Commercial Power Supply

If you do not want to wire circuits that connect directly to household power, purchase one or more commercial power supplies for the camera. The supply should be a linear supply. Because supplies with adjustable voltages and currents generally cost more, try to find fixed supplies except for possibly the Peltier supply. You will need supplies that can provide the following:

C.8 Open-Collector Parallel Ports

The printer interface cards on some computers may have an open-collector output or an insufficient high-level drive to work properly with the Cookbook cameras. If this is the case, the data output lines will not go to a high level when the computer toggles them. You will discover this when you use the CARD test program.

On the interface card, the 4.7kΩ resistors R11 through R18, connect to ground through eight small traces. By cutting these traces, you can isolate the connecting trace. Connect the isolated ground trace to +5V so that R11 through R18 function as pull-up resistors.

Alternatively, solder a pull-up resistor with a resistance of 2.7kΩ from the ungrounded end of each 4.7kΩ resistor to the +5V trace. The printer card will then be able to drive the interface card properly, and the CARD program will confirm proper function.

Appendix D. Converting the 211 to a 245

The Cookbook 211 and Cookbook 245 differ from one another in detail only; they are basically the same system. It is therefore possible to convert a completed Cookbook 211 to a Cookbook 245 with changes that are minor compared to the effort of building a Cookbook 245 from scratch.

The key changes are: (1) on the preamplifier card, adding new electronic components; (2) on the interface card, adding new electronic components, and (3) in the camera body, replacing the TC211 and its cold finger with a TC245 chip and its cold finger.

In preparation for these changes, drain the coolant system. Remove the preamplifier cover and any stress-relief clips that interfere with opening the camera body. Take off the body cap, and then remove the TC211 and store it in conductive foam. Remove the preamplifier card and the printer interface card and unplug the preamplifier card from the interface card. Unsolder the six wires from J2/J3 to the CCD socket.

D.1 Changes to the Interface Card

If you are using the standard Cookbook camera circuit board remove the bridge wire that you installed when you constructed the Cookbook 211 board. Add the jumpers specified by CARD.EXE for the Cookbook 245 and solder in the jumper wire specified.

Solder in these additional parts:
☐ 14-pin DIP socket: U1.
☐ Resistors: R1, R2, R3, R10, R11, R12.
☐ Capacitors: C1, C2, C3.

Perform the following CARD.EXE test routines. Use the hook-up and meter settings called for in the test sequences, but carry out *only* the test sequences listed below. These test sequences were selected to test the parts of your card that you have modified.

Printer Port Interface Card Resistance Test.
☐ Test-1, steps [2] and [22].
☐ Test-2, steps [2] and [3].
☐ Test-3, steps [8], [9], [10], [16], [17], and [18]*
*Note that the reading in step [18] will be less than specified because of other components in the circuit, but it should not read as shorted.

Printer Port Card Supply Regulator Test.
☐ Test-1, steps [5], [6] and [7].
Computer to Interface Card Logic Level Test.
☐ Test-2 [15], [16], [17], [18], [19] and [20].
Card Functional Test #1, Inverters and MUXs.
☐ Install component U1, a 74LS14
☐ Test-1, perform all test steps.
☐ Test-2, perform steps [1]–[15], [22] and [23].
Card Functional Test #2, Converter.
☐ Perform all test steps.

D.2 Changes to the Preamplifier Card

From the preamplifier card, remove R31, R32, R49, R43 and C38. To do this, heat the solder pads with the iron to reflow the solder and gently pull on the component lead with needle-nosed pliers. If the hole in the solder pad fills in with solder, place a piece of stranded wire over the pad and heat it with a soldering iron. The solder should wet the wire and flow away from the soldering pad. A commercial product called Solder Wick is extremely effective.

Solder in the following replacement parts:
☐ R31 becomes 100Ω.
☐ R32 becomes 100Ω.
☐ R49 becomes a jumper wire.
☐ R43 becomes 39kΩ.
Solder in these additional parts:
☐ 8-pin DIP sockets: U7, U9, U10.
☐ 2N2907 PNP transistors: Q3, Q4, Q5, Q6.
☐ Resistors: R25, R26, R27, R28, R33, R34, R35, R36, R37, R38, R39, R40, R41, R42.
☐ Capacitors: C27, C28, C34, C36, C37, C39.

Perform the following PREAMP.EXE test routines. Use the hook-up and meter settings called for in the test sequences, but carry out *only* the test sequences listed below. These test sequences were selected to test the parts of your card that you have modified.

Preamp/Driver Card Resistance Test.
☐ Test-1, steps [9], [11], [12], [13] and [16].
☐ Test-3, steps [2]*, [9], [10], [11], [12], [13], [14], [17], [18], [19] and [20].
*Note that the reading in step [2] will be less than

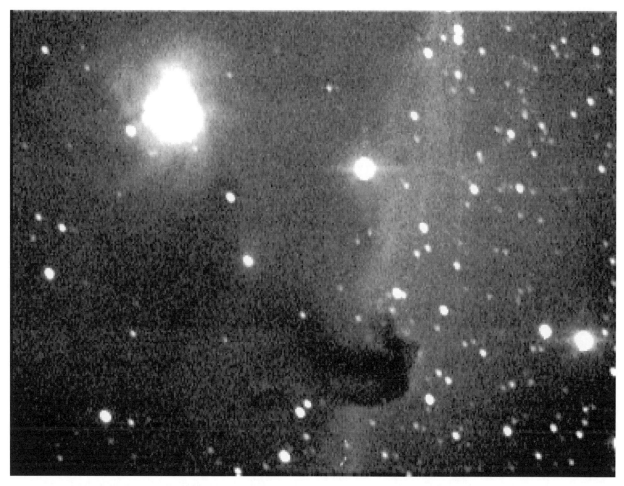

The Cookbook 245, with a 4.8-by-6.4-mm sensing area, large pixels, and on-chip correlated double sampling, is extremely sensitive. Richard Berry made this 4-minute integration of the Horsehead with a 6-inch f/5 Newtonian.

$41k\Omega$ because of other components in the circuit, but it should not read as shorted.

Preamp/Driver Voltage and Logic Input Test.

☐ Test-2, steps [5], [9], [10], [15], [16], [17], [18], [19], [20], [21] and [22].

Preamp/Driver Clock Driver Functional Test.

☐ Install DS0026 chips U7, U9 and U10.

☐ Perform all tests.

Preamp/Driver Op Amp Functional Test.

☐ Perform all tests.

D.3 Install the TC245

Machine a cold finger for the TC245 (you will find directions for making component parts for the Cookbook 245 in the main text of this book). With needle-nosed pliers, remove the TC211 cold finger and install the TC245 cold finger in its place. Wire the TC245 as described in the main text of this book, and carefully check

your wiring. (Because the TC245 is installed without a socket, it is better to check carefully than to risk damaging the CCD with too much testing.)

Assembly from this point forward should be carried out just as you would bring a new camera up to operating status, bearing in mind, of course, that these steps have been largely completed.

The changeover should go smoothly because you have already completed a working Cookbook 211 camera and know what to expect. What comes as a big (and very pleasant) surprise is how much more resolution, field of view, and sensitivity the Cookbook 245 delivers. Not only will you have twice as many pixels in the 252×242 mode and three times as many pixels in the 378×242 mode, but with on-chip double-correlated sampling and larger effective photosites, your upgraded camera will be about four times as sensitive to light.

Appendix E. Constructing an Autoguider

With the addition of an interface between your computer and your telescope, the Cookbook cameras will function as an automatic guider for your telescope. This function is fully supported by the image acquisition software. However, you must add an interface box to pass control signals to your telescope's drive system.

Because there are so many different ways to control the telescope electronics, do not consider building an autoguider unless you feel confident about digging into the electronic controls of your telescope, or have knowledgeable friends whom you trust to modify your telescope's drive controls.

E.1 Building the Serial Port Interface

The AP211 and AP245 use the serial port interface on your computer to send data to your telescope's drive corrector. The interface circuit that receives serial data and converts it to control the telescope drive corrector is shown in the accompanying circuit diagram. In addition, if your telescope uses a synchronous-motor worm-gear drive, the software supports periodic-error correction.

The guider uses four data bits from the serial receiver chip to actuate the push buttons on your hand controller. The simplest method of translating the control data bits to a button action is by using a relay to operate as the control button switch. You may have to disassemble your hand controller to wire the relay controls to your button switches. In the accompanying diagrams, we show several switch combinations and suggest methods of connecting a relay for control both by computer and by hand.

To take advantage of the periodic-error correction, your telescope's drive circuit must be able to supply a TTL-compatible clock signal that is fed directly to a divider circuit input. Some drive circuits have a high-level clock signal that varies from 0 to 12 volts. This signal must be reduced with a voltage divider network before it can be fed into the 74LS163 divider circuit input.

If you don't have access to or can't find the clock signal, the 120VAC input to the drive's synchronous motor can be transformer-coupled to the divider circuit input. Be careful because there is high voltage on the synchronous motor.

E.2 Operating the Autoguider

With the guider interface box attached to the telescope drive controller via your computer's serial port, you can use the Autoguide function in the AP211 and AP245 Cookbook camera software supplied with this book.

Begin by entering the Options menu. Press the R key to reach the "seRial" menu. Press the X key to reset the serial interface, then exit the serial port setup menu. Exit from the Options menu.

Locate and center a suitable guide star using the Find function. The star should be bright enough to give a strong signal with a 1-second exposure. Enter the Select options menu and set the Lo value to clip the background level to pure black. The guider routine uses the Lo value as its detection threshold. Exit to the Main menu.

Enter the Autoguide from the Main menu.

Calibrate the system by pressing the C key. The calibration routine moves the star image a short distance east and west in right ascension, and north and south in declination, so that the software knows how rapidly the telescope drive motors move the star image.

Lock the guider on the star by pressing the I key. The guide software should lock onto the star and keep it centered accurately on the cross hair displayed on the computer screen.

As it operates, the program shows the guide error in pixels times ten. Thus, a guide error of 1.5 pixels is displayed as 15 on the left side of the screen. On the right, the software displays the total brightness of the star image. If this number becomes zero, it means that the star has been lost. This can happen if clouds cover the star or if the telescope's drive motors cannot center the star.

Under reasonable operating conditions, that is, with a telescope whose drive motors have little or no backlash and a star that is bright enough to give a good signal, the Cookbook cameras can guide with an accuracy of approximately 1 second of arc. If your telescope mounting has appreciable backlash, it is unreasonable to expect any guider, human or electronic, to guide well.

Obtaining the best possible operation in guide mode takes some experimenting to find the best parameters. The

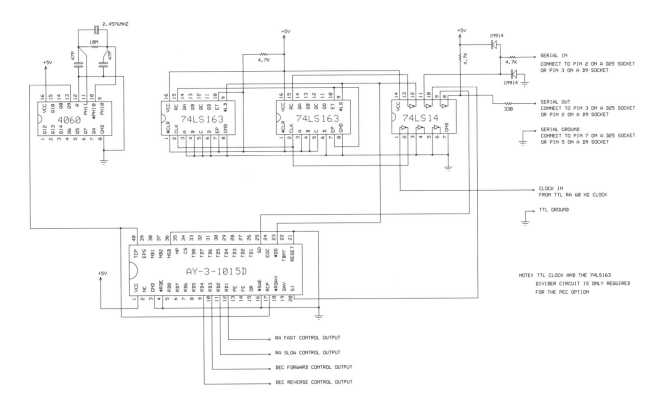

Serial Port Autoguider Circuit

following parameters can be set in the software:

T This is the integration time for the CCD, but it may not be the "loop time" for the guider. The loop time equals the integration time plus about 0.5 seconds. The guide calculations are performed during integration, and if the calculation time is greater than the integration, the program clears the CCD and then restarts the integration. Thus there is an optimum integration time that yields the shortest sample interval, or "loop time."

R This is the right ascension calibration time. The RA control is turned on for this period during calibration. The time must be long enough that the star is driven across at least one-tenth of the field, but short enough that the star does not leave the field of view.

D This is the declination calibration time. This function operates exactly like the right ascension calibration time, but it is used to set the declination calibration time. The RA and declination times depend on the relative speeds of the motors on your telescope mounting.

L This is the clipping level for the star image. Pixel values greater than this level are used to calculate the star's centroid. This value must be greater than the background sky value, but safely below the lowest level that

the star could have due to seeing and image motion.

B Use this command to control moderate backlash in the declination drive. The default value is zero pixels. For example, if you set the backlash value to 12 (that is, 1.2 pixels), then whenever the software changes the direction of the declination drive, it will add an additional 1.2 pixels to the error correction command to cancel backlash.

C This command invokes the calibration routine. The new coordinate angle of the telescope with respect to the CCD is displayed in degrees. When the calibration routine has finished, the program displays the RA and declination calibration constants and movement in pixels expected from a one-second motion command.

I This key toggles the guide-star lock.

Z Toggles the drift correction of the electrical offset of the CCD. When this function is toggled on, the offset value changes as the CCD drifts. This correction should be toggled on if you are guiding on a faint star.

H Sets the size of the control dead band. If H is set to 7, then the controller will not issue a command to correct errors that are smaller than 0.7 pixels.

M Tells the system when the number of reflections in the optical system of the telescope is odd. Pressing M

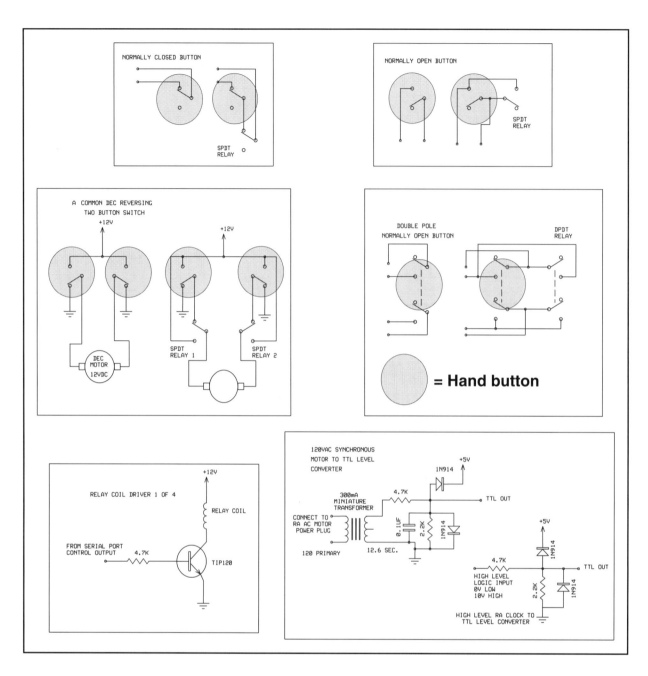

reverses the direction of the declination motion commands. Use this command only when you are entering calibration parameters manually.

A Sets the angle for the coordinate system transposition. The user can select a new angle rather than use the calibration system. To set the proper angle, use the hand controller to move the telescope and watch the error display. For best results, no declination motion should be visible when you press the right ascension control. If the autoguider drives the right ascension in the wrong direction, add 180° to the angle.

RAS This value is the right ascension slow calibration constant in 0.1-pixel units. This value times the right

ascension error in corrected pixels is used to generate the drive command. For example, suppose that the RA controller drives the system at 2.5 pixels per second, or 25 units. The calibration constant is the number of $^{1}/_{30}$-of-a-second-long corrections needed to move the telescope by 1 unit. In this example, it is $^{30}/_{25}$, or 1.2. Given a right ascension error of 0.6 pixels, the software will send 6 × 1.2, or 7 RA-slow commands through the serial port. The resulting motion is the same as it would have been if you had pressed the RA-slow button for $^{7}/_{30}$ of a second.

RAF, DECX, DECY These values are the right ascension fast calibration constant and the declination calibration constants. The calibration routine calculates

To get good performance from the drive of his 10-inch f/10 SCT, Veikko Kanto used the background PEC mode in the AP245 image acquistion software. This image of the Crab is made from four 2-minute integrations.

them when you calibrate the system, or you may enter them by hand. If you write the calibration constants the system derives with each use, you can keep tabs on the performance of the telescope and its drive.

PEC The periodic error correction system is a data recorder that remembers the autoguider commands for both RA and declination for one cycle of the worm, and replays these corrections later while you are making images with your Cookbook camera.

The period for your gear is set with the "@" key which toggles to a recorder count of 100 for 359- and 360-tooth gears and 200 for 180-tooth gears.

To actuate the autoguider's "learn mode," press the lower case p key. When you put the system in learn mode, the status indication at the lower right corner of the screen changes from 1 to 2. After one period of the worm, the status changes to 3, indicating that the system is replaying stored guiding commands. With PEC running

in the background, you can then exit from the Autoguide menu and make your integrations.

Periodic error correction assumes that the errors in the drive repeat with each rotation of the telescope's drive gear. This may hold true only for a limited section of the gear, giving you 30 to 60 minutes worth of excellent tracking. For best results, go back to the autoguider's "learn mode" as it becomes necessary.

Background PEC continues until one of three events occurs.

1. If you enter the Autoguide menu and press the shift and P keys simultaneously, that is, type an upper-case P, background PEC stops or,

2. It stops if you enter the Options menu, then press the R key and the X key to reset the serial port and finally,

3. If a disk-write error occurs, the error handler in the program shuts down the serial port, and background PEC ceases.

References and Resources

Newsletters

The Cookbook Camera Newsletter will keep you up-to-date on the latest improvements and upgrades, as well as answering your questions. $28 domestic ($38 Foreign) for six issues. Order from Richard Berry, 22614 N. Santiam Hwy, Lyons, OR 97358

Books

ARRL Handbook for Radio Amateurs, by the American Radio Relay League, published annually. In-depth background information for anyone who wants to learn more about electronics. The American Radio Relay League, Newington CT, 06111.

Astronomical CCD Observing and Reduction Techniques, edited by Steve B. Howell. Astronomical Socity of the Pacific, 1992. Professional-level introduction to CCD observing with an aim to producing scientifically valid results. An excellent sourcebook. A.S.P., 390 Ashton Avenue, San Francisco, CA 94112.

CCD Astronomy, by Christian Buil. Willmann-Bell, 1991. About the construction and use of CCD cameras. Willmann-Bell, Inc., P.O. Box 35025, Richmond, VA 23235. (804) 320-7016.

Choosing and Using a CCD Camera, by Richard Berry. Willmann-Bell, 1992. Detailed instructions on how to take and calibrate CCD images with any CCD camera. Includes QwikPIX software to demonstrate the principles of image calibration. Willmann-Bell, Inc., P.O. Box 35025, Richmond, VA 23235. (804) 320-7016.

Electronic and Computer-Aided Astronomy: From Eyes to Electronic Sensors, by Ian S, Mclean. Graduate-level introduction to CCDs and CCD observing; very thorough. John Ellis Horwood/Wiley & Sons, 1989. Ellis Horwood Ltd, Market Cross House, Cooper Street, Chichester, West Sussex, PO19 1EB, England.

Introduction to Astronomical Image Processing, by Richard Berry. Willmann-Bell, 1991. Book plus software with sample images; runs on any PC-compatible computer. Works with Cookbook 211, Lynxx, ST4, and Electrim images. Willmann-Bell, Inc., P.O. Box 35025, Richmond, VA 23235. (804) 320-7016.

Cookbook Camera Kits

Cookbook camera body. Aluminum castings machined to Cookbook camera specifications. Available as unfinished castings or machined and finished parts. Call for pricing. University Optics, Inc., P.O. Box 1205, Ann Arbor, MI 48016. (800) 521-2828.

Cookbook PC boards. Quality epoxy/fiberglass circuit boards with plated-through holes, silk-screened. $19.95 + $1.00 handling per set. Willmann-Bell, Inc., P.O. Box 35025, Richmond, VA 23235. (804) 320-7016.

Cookbook Electronic Parts. Various electronic parts sets will be offered for sale by University Optics. Call for specific details. University Optics, Inc., P.O. Box 1205, Ann Arbor, MI 48016. (800) 521-2828.

Parts Suppliers

Arrow Electronics. Sells CCD chips. Call for current availability and pricing. Also carries a full line of general electronics parts. (602) 437-0705 or (800) 932-7769.

Auto-parts stores. Look for a generic windshield-washer pump kit in your local auto-parts store.

B.G. Micro. Wide selection of new and suprplus parts. P.O. Box 280298, Dallas, TX 75228. (214) 271-5545.

Digi-Key Corporation. Huge selection of electronic components. 701 Brooks Ave. South, P.O. Box 677, Thief River Falls, MN 56701-0677. (800) 344-4539.

Edmund Scientific. Sells optical windows that would work for the camera. 101 East Gloucester Pike, Barrington, NJ 08007-1380. (609) 547-8880.

Hall-Mark Electronics. Sells TC211, TC245, ADC1674J. Minimum order is $250; can be reached with purchase of the other components. (602) 742-0515.

Herbach and Rademan. The *primo* electromechnical/electroptical supplier, their stock includes mechanical and electrically-operated shutters, power supplies of all types, geared synchronous and stepper motors; just what the telescope maker wants! 18 Canal St., P.O. Box 122, Bristol, PA 19007-0122. (215) 788-5583.

Jameco. Sells the DS0026, capacitors, sockets, cables, transistors, regulators, etc.; source for a surplus power supply that can be adapted to power the Cookbook

Don't have a machine shop in your basement? University Optics offers the machined parts of the camera body in the kit form shown here. Note that the tube cap has T-threads so you attach camera lenses directly.

camera. See Appendix C. Jameco, 1355 Shoreway Road, Belmont, CA 94002, (800) 831-4242.

JDR Micro Devices. Sells capacitors, components, and ribbon cables. Also sell PC parts; get their electronics catalog. 2233 Samaritan Drive, San Jose, CA 95124. (408) 559-1200.

Marshall Electronics. Sells CCD chips and general electronics parts. (602) 496-0290.

Melcor Material Electronics Products Corp. Sells Peltier modules in a wide variety of sizes and shapes. The Cookbook camera uses their CP 1.4-71-06L for $18 (1993). $10 handling on orders iunder $100. Melcor, 1040 Spruce Street, Trenton, NJ 08648. (609) 393-4178.

Mouser Electronics. In-depth selection of general parts, including ICs, heat sinks, etc. Four stores. 12 Emery Ave., Randolph, NJ 07869-1362. (800) 346-6873.

Newark Electronics. Sells CCD chips and general parts. Based in Chicago. (312) 784-5100.

Parts listings. The part suppliers list in the *American Radio Relay League Handbook* is very good. Listings are by type of part. If a supplier does not have what you want, be sure to ask, "Well, if you don't have it, can you please tell me where I can get one?" The *ARRL Handbook* is widely available in public libraries.

Radio Shack. Sells reasonably priced transformers for the power supply as well as a rather limited range of general electronics parts.

Surplus electronics stores. These are excellent places to buy filter capacitors, transformers, meters, resistors, and other non-critical components for the camera and power supply, as well as surplus power supplies and project boxes. However, it's best to buy all critical parts from regular electronics supply houses.

Focus Aids

P & S Skyproducts, RR #1 20095 Con. 7, Mt. Albert, Ontario, Canada L0G 1MO. Kwik Focus focus aids. (905) 473-1627.

Cookbook-Compatible Software

BatchPIX by Richard Berry. Designed for TC211 images. Script language permits automatic calibration and processing of up to 255 images. Built-in functions include five scaling laws plus histogram shaping, five types of unsharp mask, center, zoom, rotate, translate, flip, flop, save in camera formats and FITS, export to TIFF. With manual, $29.95. Richard Berry, 22614 N. Santiam Hwy, Lyons, OR 97358.

CB245PIX by Richard Berry. For processing TC245 images. Script language permits automatic processing of multiple images. Built-in functions include five scaling laws, five types of unsharp mask, histogram shap-

After you have captured an image, image-processing software brings out all the image has to offer. Images in this book were prepared using Richard Berry's BatchPIX, CB245PIX software, and AIP for Windows.

ing, save in FITS, export to TIFF format. With manual, $49.95. Richard Berry, 6388 Sauk Trail Rd., RR1 Box 58A, Cedar Grove, WI 53013. (414) 285-3305.

ColorPIX by Richard Berry. Designed to create 24-bit color TIFF output from color-filtered TC211 images. This is the software that Don Parker uses to create his outstanding planetary images. Subpixel registration, works with any VGA graphics card. Use with BatchPIX. $29.95. Richard Berry,22614 N. Santiam Hwy, Lyons, OR 97358.

Imagine-32, by CompuScope. Software package for PCs with 80386 and higher CPUs, math coprocessor, 2+MB of RAM, and SVGA graphics card. Mouse-oriented image viewing and image-processing software. Cookbook camera compatible; loads FITS files. CompuScope, 3463 State St., Suite 431, Santa Barbara, CA 93105. (805) 687-1914.

MIRA (Microcomputer Image Reduction and Analysis), by Axiom Research, Inc. Software for 80386 and higher CPUs, 2+MB, 3-button mouse. Requires specified graphic card. Highly integrated image process-

ing environment for PCs. Cookbook camera compatible; loads FITS files. Axiom Research, Inc., Box 44162, Tucson, AZ 85733. (602) 791-3277.

PhotoShop by Adobe. For graphic artists; Macintosh or Windows. Wide range of filters and special effects for monochrome and color images. Handles monochrome images in the TIFF and 8-bit raw formats, but cannot read 12-bit or 16-bit camera files. Adobe Systems Inc., 1585 Charleston Rd., Mountain View, CA 94039-7900.

PhotoStyler by Aldus. Graphic arts softwares; runs under MS Windows. Powerful features for retouching and manipulating monochrome and color images. Handles monochrome images in the TIFF and 8-bit raw formats, but cannot read 12-bit or 16-bit camera files. Aldus, 411 First Avenue South, Seattle, WA 98104-2871. (206) 622-5500.

Windows version, Astronomical Image Processing by Richard Berry and Jack Hudler. Powerhouse software for calibrating, processing, and analyzing 8-, 16-, and 32-bit CCD images. Reads all standard CCD camera files, FITS, TIFF, and popular formats. Functions include image sharpening through deconvolution, automatic scaling, false color, and 24-bit true color. Scheduled for release late-1997 through Willmann-Bell, Inc.

Technical Literature

—, **Applications Note for Cambion Thermoelectric Devices**, Cambridge Thermionic Corp., 1980.

—, **Area Array Image Sensor Products: Data Manual**, Texas Instruments, 1992. Describes the complete line of Texas Instruments CCD sensors, associated chip sets, and cameras. Texas Instruments, P.O. Box 655303, Dallas, TX 75265.

—, **CRC Handbook of Laboratory Safety**, Second Edition, Editor Norman V. Steere, P.E., CRC Press Inc., Boca Raton, Florida, 1985.

—, **Fairchild TTL Databook**, Fairchild Semiconductor, 1978. See section 2 on TTL characteristics.

—, **Handbook of Surface Preparation**, Snogren, Richard C., Palmerton, 1974, For preparing surfaces for adhesives, see pages 127 and 423. Palmerton Publishing Co. Inc., New York, NY.

—, **Machinery's Handbook**, 22nd Edition, Oberg and Jones, Holbrook L. Horton Industrial Press Inc., NY, 1984.

—, **MELCOR: Solid State Cooling With Thermoelectrics**, Melcor product catalog, 1993. A rich source of design information about Peltier-effect devices. Melcor Thermoelectrics, 1040 Spruce Street, Trenton, NJ 08648.

—, **Optoelectronics and Image Sensor Data Book**, Texas Instruments, 1987. Specifications for TI CCDs on pages 2-29 through 2-107, 1987. Texas Instruments, P.O. Box 655303, Dallas, TX 75265.

—, "Reliability Evaluation of Imaging CCDs," Young, V. F. and Wilson, D. D., Martin Marietta Corporation, in **Proceedings ATFA-78, Advanced Techniques in Failure Analysis**, IEEE catalog no. 78CH1407-6, Reg 6, 1978.

—, SN28835 1/2-Inch NTSC Timer, *Texas Instruments Data Sheet*, 1991

—, TC245 786x488-Pixel CCD Image Sensor," *Texas Instruments Data Sheet*, 1992.

Hsieh, S. M., Hosack, H. H., "Low Light Level Imaging With Commercial Charge-Coupled Devices," *Optical Engineering*, Vol. 26, No. 9, September 1987.

Hynecek, Jaroslav, "High-Resolution 8mm CCD Image Sensor with Correlated Clamp Sample and Hold Charge Detection Circuit," *IEEE Transactions on Electron Devices*, Vol. ED-33, No. 6, June, 1986.

Hynecek, Jaroslav, "Theoretical Analysis and Optimization of CDS Signal Processing Method for CCD Image Sensors," *IEEE Transactions on Electron Devices*, Vol. 39 No. 11, November 1992.

Jourdain, R., **Programmer's Problem Solver for the IBM PC, XT and AT**, Brady Books, 1986.

Scott, M., Siegel, B. **Applying Modern Clock Drivers to MOS Memories**, National Semiconductor AN-76, 1975.

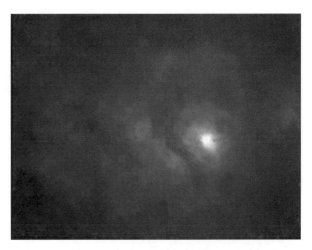

In this picture, special image processing routines have removed stars, leaving only the nebulosity.

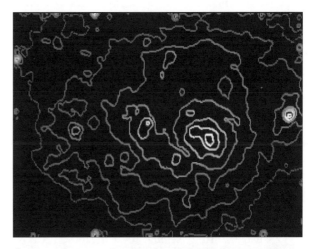

Contour lines enclose regions of equal brightness so that you can see the distribution of light in an object.

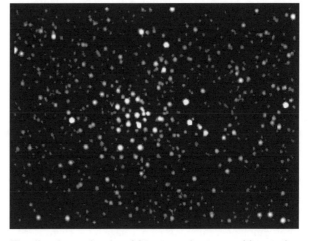

Finally, here is the M8 star cluster—without the nebula. Image processing using AIP for Windows.

Technical Notes on the CCD Images

The images in *The CCD Camera Cookbook* were taken with Cookbook 211 or Cookbook 245 CCD cameras. To prepare them for publication, Cookbook 211 images were processsed using BatchPIX software and exported as TIFF files. Cookbook 245 images were processsed using CB245PIX software and exported as TIFF files. Blooming from stars was removed using PhotoStyler graphics arts software. The images were imported into Ventura Publisher software and are reproduced in this book using a halftone screen with 120 dots per inch and a 45-degree screen angle.

Preface: **Orion Nebula.** 6-inch f/5 Newtonian, Cookbook 245 in 378×242 mode, 60-second integration. Gammalog scaling plus unsharp masking to enhance nebular structure. Image by Richard Berry.

Chapter 1: **Lagoon Nebula.** 4-inch f/5 Genesis refractor, Cookbook 245 in 252×242 mode, 60-second integration. Gammalog scaling. Image by Richard Berry.

Chapter 2: **Ring Nebula.** 10-inch f/10 SCT, Cookbook 245 in 252×242 mode, 4-minute integration. Linear scaling plus zoom. Image by Phil Bright.

Chapter 2: **M81 Supernova.** 8-inch f/10 SCT, Cookbook 245 in 252×242 mode, 60-second integration. Linear scaling. Image by Phil Bright.

Chapter 4: **Omega Nebula.** 20-inch f/4.5 reflector, Cookbook 245 in 378×242 mode, 30-second integration. Gammalog scaling. Image by Dave Otto, Dan Joyce, and Richard Berry, taken at 1993 AstroFest.

Chapter 6: **Coccoon Nebula.** 4-inch f/5 Genesis refractor, Cookbook 245 in 252×242 mode, 60-second integration. Gammalog scaling. Image by Richard Berry.

Chapter 9: **M33 Galaxy.** 6-inch f/5 reflector, Cookbook 245 in Find mode, 1.5-second integration. Photograph of computer screen. Image by Richard Berry.

Chapter 9: **Lagoon Nebula.** 6-inch f/5 reflector, Cookbook 245 in 252×242 mode, 60-second integration. Photograph of computer screen. Image by Richard Berry.

Chapter 10: **Delay loop tests.** No telescope, Cookbook 211, 0.5-second integrations. Linear scaling. Images by Richard Berry.

Chapter 10: **Drain pipe.** 3-inch focus f/20 lens, Cookbook 211, 1.5-second integration. Unsharp masking plus gammalog scaling. Image by Richard Berry.

Chapter 10: **Kara Kanto.** 3-inch focus f/20 lens, Cookbook 211, 0.5-second integration. Unsharp mask plus linear scaling. Image by Veikko Kanto.

Chapter 10: **Owl Nebula.** 10-inch f/10 SCT, Cookbook 211, 10-minute integration. Gamma scaling. Image by Veikko Kanto and John Munger.

Chapter 10: **M82 Galaxy.** 10-inch f/10 SCT, Cookbook 211, 10-minute integration. Gamma scaling. Image by Veikko Kanto and John Munger.

Chapter 10: **Milky Way in Sagittarius.** 50mm focus f/1.5 Wollensak lens, Cookbook 245 in 378×242 mode, 15-second integration. Gammalog scaling. Image by Richard Berry, taken at 1993 Stellafane Convention.

Chapter 11: **M51 Galaxy.** 10-inch f/10 SCT, Cookbook 245 in 252×242 mode, 4-minute integration. First astronomical image made with a TC245. Log scaling. Image by Veikko Kanto and John Munger.

Chapter 11: **M42 Loop.** 6-inch f/5 reflector, Cookbook 245 in 378×242 mode, 4-minute integration. Gammalog scaling. Image by Richard Berry.

Chapter 11: **Raw frames for M42 Loop.** 6-inch f/5 reflector, Cookbook 245 in 378×242 mode, image and dark frame are 4-minute integrations; flat-field is 2.5-second integration of observatory wall minus 2.5-second dark frame. Linear scaling. Images by Richard Berry.

Chapter 11: **Flame Nebula, N2024.** 6-inch f/5 reflector, Cookbook 245 in 378×242 mode, 4-minute integration. Gammalog scaling. Image by Richard Berry.

Chapter 12: **Cygnus Loop.** 6-inch f/5 reflector, Cookbook 245 in 378×242 mode, 4-minute integration. Gammalog scaling. Image by Richard Berry.

Chapter 12: **Comet Mueller** on Oct 4, 1993. 20cm f/6.5 Wright reflector, Cookbook 211 equivalent, 4-minute integration. Gammalog scaling. Image by Brian Manning.

Chapter 12: **Comet Shoemaker-Levy 9** on May 7, 1993. 20cm f/6.5 Wright reflector, Cookbook 211 equiva-

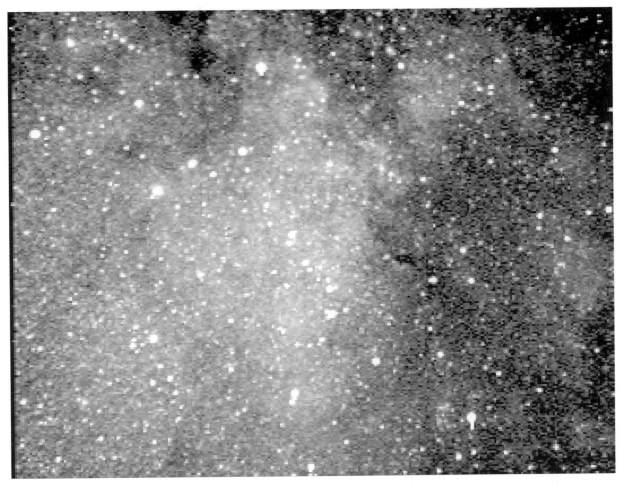

If it's a camera, how come you can't put a *lens* on it? No reason you can't! A 50mm-focus lens on your Cookbook 245 gives a 10-degree field of view, about what a 250- to 300mm lens would give on 35mm film.

lent, 8-minute integration. Linear scaling. Image by Brian Manning.

Chapter 12: **Asteroid (4751) Alicemanning** on Oct 15, 1993. 20cm f/6.5 Wright reflector, Cookbook 211 equivalent, 8-minute integrations 36 minutes apart. These images used for astrometry of asteroid positions. Linear scaling. Images by Brian Manning.

Appendix C: **Planets.** 8-inch f/10 and 10-inch f/10 SCTs with Barlow projection, Cookbook 211 and 245 cameras used in pseudo-shuttering mode. Gamma scaling. Images by Phil Bright, Veikko Kanto, and John Munger.

Appendix C: **Orion Nebula.** 10-inch f/10 SCT, Cookbook 245 in 252×242 mode, average of seven 2-second integrations. Gammalog scaling. Image by Veikko Kanto and John Munger.

Appendix D: **Horsehead Nebula.** 6-inch f/5 reflector, Cookbook 245 in 378×242 mode, 4-minute integration. Gammalog scaling. Image by Richard Berry.

Appendix E: **Crab Nebula.** 10-inch f/10 SCT, Cookbook 245 in 252×242 mode, four 2-minute integra-

tions. Gammalog scaling. Image by Veikko Kanto and John Munger.

References and Resources: **Lagoon Nebula.** 6-inch f/5 reflector. Cookbook 245 in 378×242 mode, 60-second integration. Gammalog scaling. Image by Richard Berry.

References and Resources: **Variations on the Lagoon Nebula.** Image processing by AIP for Windows to remove stars, generate contour lines, and the eliminate nebulosity. Image processing by Richard Berry.

This page: **Scutum Star Cloud.** 50mm focus f/1.5 Wollensak lens stopped down to f/2.8, Cookbook 245 in 378×242 mode, 60-second integration. Gammalog scaling. Image by Richard Berry, taken at the 1993 Stellafane Convention.

Back cover: **Author portraits.** 3-inch focus f/20 lens, Cookbook 245 in 252×242 mode, 1-second integrations. Gamma scaling plus unsharp masking. Images by Veikko Kanto and John Munger.

Index